BRL998/088

W6

E H
M10

J Henning 1803   Robt C. Bell

JAMES WATT.

MEMORIALS

OF

THE LINEAGE, EARLY LIFE, EDUCATION, AND DEVELOPMENT OF THE GENIUS

OF

JAMES WATT.

BY

GEORGE WILLIAMSON, ESQ.,
LATE PERPETUAL PRESIDENT OF THE WATT CLUB OF GREENOCK.

Printed for the Watt Club
BY THOMAS CONSTABLE, PRINTER TO HER MAJESTY.
MDCCCLVI.

TO THE MEMBERS OF THE WATT CLUB.

GENTLEMEN,

I am at length enabled to place in your hands the WATT MEMORIALS, collected during many years by my Father, your late President.

When, a few months ago, your Deputation waited upon the family with a Minute of the Club, expressive of your desire that these Memorials might be placed at its disposal for the purpose of publication,—being aware that it had been my Father's own intention to have had something of the nature of the present collection printed for private circulation amongst his friends, as, several years ago, he had done with a small portion of the same,[1]—I was under the impression that the materials had been left by my Father in a more complete state of preparation for the press than a reference to his repositories afterwards proved to be the case. Beyond the portions embraced in the earlier half of the collection, the Manuscript was found to be still in a rough and unfinished state. The time, in consequence, that was necessary in order to become familiar with the entire subject, with a

---

[1] "Letters respecting the Watt Family, by George Williamson. Printed for the Author. Greenock 1840. Pp. 69."

view to its completion, will account to you, in great measure, for the unexpected delay which has taken place in giving effect to your wishes in the matter.

In the revision of the first portion of the Manuscript I was induced to avail myself of several additional documents, to which the careful examination of my Father's repositories introduced me, from the consideration of their being likely to afford to the subject greater interest and fulness ; while in completing the last portion, I readily took advantage of much valuable information in the shape of papers, very ample notes, and memoranda under my Father's hand, to which the same repositories gave me access. This is particularly applicable to the full, and, it is to be hoped, not altogether uninteresting chapter, on the Rise of Steam Navigation in the Clyde,—a subject, in connexion with the authentic details of which the author had bestowed much pains during a long series of years.

With regard to the editorial labour involved in such preparation of the work for your acceptance, although the modifications alluded to have been those of the form merely, and not of the substance of the original collection, there will be found occasion for the exercise of much indulgence on the part of the Club, with respect to the execution of a task entered upon under circumstances peculiarly unfavourable to any intellectual exertion, and while reluctantly laid aside from the exercise of far more congenial and sacred functions. But for this, the Editor might have felt himself under some stronger obligation than he has done, to hazard the implementing of a hope expressed by the author himself, in the Preface to his former short publication,—that some other than he might, from his collected materials, at a future time, extract such reflections as might the better aid in throwing light on the personal history and genius of the great man, to the illustration of whose life these unpretending pages are meant to form a contribution.[1]

Trusting, therefore, to your favourable reception of the following pages, and to your indulgence towards their many defects,

I have the honour to be,

GENTLEMEN,

Your very obedient servant,

JAMES WILLIAMSON.

GREENOCK, 9th July 1855.

POSTSCRIPT NOTE.—For much of the trouble, and the entire responsibility, connected with the *Publishing Arrangements*, the Club is indebted to two of its Members, WILLIAM DAVIE, Esq., LL.D., and its Secretary, JOHN GRAY, Esq., who, in the outset, kindly charged themselves with this office,—a task, in the event, by no means trivial, owing to the nature of the numerous illustrations accompanying the

---

[1] It is perhaps not unnecessary here to observe, that the collection of the following details, as well as the first publication of portions of them, were, by many years, anterior to the appearance of the interesting sketch of the life of Watt, by his Son, in the *Encyclopædia Britannica*, and, consequently, also, of the *Eloge* by M. Arago.

volume, and for which it is indebted in a great degree to the perseverance and the zeal with which these Gentlemen prosecuted the duty
they had undertaken.

On the other hand, the thanks of the Club are due to those several
Gentlemen who so cordially seconded the objects of the Work, and
added some of the most valuable contributions to its illustration : to
DAVID CRAWFORD, Esq., for facilities afforded in consulting the Char-
tulary of the Barony of Cartsburn, with other documents ; to Mr.
GRAY, for the original sketch of Watt, by Henning, now for the first
time engraved ; to J. T. CAIRD, Esq., for the lines of the splendid
modern steam-ship, *Atrato;* to ROBERT NAPIER, Esq., among other
interesting contributions, for the portrait of Watt, after Sir W.
Beechey's, the original of which forms part of his valuable Collection
at West Shandon ; to PETER M'KENZIE, Esq., for the original advertisement relating to the sale of John Watt's Map ; to PROFESSOR
RAMSAY of Glasgow College, for the courtesy with which he secured
every facility to the Artist of the Club, who was kindly permitted to
copy the famous Newcomen's Engine, in the possession of the University ; and to Mr. SCHENCK of Edinburgh, for the interesting Plate of
the celebrated Papin, after the original portrait in the Aula of the
University of Marburg.

GREENOCK, *August* 1856.

CONTENTS.

INTRODUCTION.

PART I.—LINEAGE.

CHAPTER I.

CHAPTER II.

PART II.—THE GREAT MECHANICIAN.

CHAPTER I.

CHAPTER II.

CHAPTER III.

CHAPTER IV.

CHAPTER V.

CHAPTER VI.

b

LIST OF ILLUSTRATIONS.

INTRODUCTION.

ORIGIN OF THE PRESENT WORK——GREENOCK LITERARY SOCIETY OF 1813——JAMES WATT'S
DEATH IN 1819——INSTITUTION OF THE WATT CLUB——ITS OBJECTS——FIRST PUBLIC
RECOGNITION OF WATT'S MERITS MADE IN THE TOWN OF GREENOCK——INACCURACY
OF THE FACTS THAT WERE GENERALLY CURRENT RELATING TO THE EARLY LIFE OF
WATT——IT IS RESOLVED TO PREPARE A MEMORIAL OF AUTHENTICATED FACTS FOR
THE CLUB——SOURCES FROM WHICH THE MATERIALS WERE DRAWN——NATURE AND
SCOPE OF THE COLLECTION.

THE collection of the materials which compose the present volume
is not a new or recent undertaking. It dates at least as far back as
the year 1819, and had its origin in a desire to contribute to the
gratification of a select circle of friends, who, as early as the year
1813, had been in the habit of meeting together from time to time,
for literary conversation and mutual improvement. The task was a
self-imposed one on the part of the chronicler. Originally, it was very
circumscribed in its design. Gradually, however, it extended itself,
and came to form a subject of more or less permanent attention.
Having opened up a field of investigation as agreeable as it was
instructive, the author found himself engaged in an inquiry which
offered many and peculiar attractions, and, at length, possessed of a
large accumulation of facts, of greater or inferior importance according to the point of view from which they might be regarded. To
many of these facts, the lapse of years—and, it may be added, with
greater force, the disappearance of the generation to whose memories
they belonged—had contributed to attach a certain degree of signifi-

1

cance ; and tended, if not to make valuable, at least, in many respects, to render interesting and worthy of preservation.

It is from these somewhat voluminous materials that the present selection has been made,—such a selection as has been deemed necessary to a clear exposition of the subject.   An attempt has been made to arrange and embody, in a consecutive form, such portions of the facts acquired as it has been conceived might be acceptable to the general reader.   At the same time, it is of some consequence that it should be understood, that this has been done, not with any idea of presenting a full *Biography* or *Life* of the philosopher whose history occupies the principal share of attention throughout the volume ; but rather, of rendering more available *for reference* an aggregate of data, which, indirectly or more immediately bearing upon the development of his genius, might be found contributive to the illustration of the character, AS A WHOLE, of this wonderful man.

As some statement, however, in regard to the nature of the work, more definite than that which has just been afforded, may still be desired, advantage will be taken of a few introductory paragraphs to give a succinct account of the special circumstances in which it had its origin ;—an account which will sufficiently indicate its character and objects, and afford, it is hoped, what apology may be necessary for any peculiarity of aspect which it may be found to present.

The year 1819, above alluded to, was that in which Mr. Watt's death took place.   The lamented event had given occasion, in a private society composed of about a dozen gentlemen connected with Greenock,[1] to advert in a particular manner to the splendid talents

[1] The original members of the Society, which afterwards became " The Watt Club," were, in 1813—

    George Williamson.
    J. B. Kirk, M.D.

George Blair.
Duncan Smith.
Their place of meeting at that time was, *The Masons' Arms*. For better accommodation, however, they removed to the respectable house in

of their departed townsman,—to the improvements which the peculiar display of these had introduced into the arts and conveniences of life, —and the benefits which the fruits of his genius were likely yet to confer upon the wealth and resources of his country ;—benefits probably more real and tangible than the combined results of the human intellect had hitherto succeeded in producing.

Merits of so transcendent a character surely claimed the unanimous testimony of his country's gratitude. As yet, however, no public recognition of them had been made. It was only natural and becoming that such a testimony should originate in the town, and in the heart of the community which enjoyed the privilege of numbering JAMES WATT among its sons. Beyond the general advantages derived from his prolific invention that were shared in common with the rest of the nation, the town of Greenock lay under signal obligations to the generosity as well as the genius of Watt. The adaptation of the steam-engine to the purposes of Navigation had given a remarkable impulse to its trade. The new requirements of this important branch of industry had caused the establishment of Foundries, Forges, and Engine-works, till then almost unknown in this portion of the country. A spirit of active enterprise had been evoked—not unobserved by the great mechanician himself; who, anxious that it might be rightly animated,—that the awakened ingenuity might be

William Street, known as *The Greenock Tavern*, kept by Mrs. Cunningham, and subsequently by Mrs. Lyle, and, in 1824, by Mrs. Fairlie. After their removal to the Greenock Tavern, several new members were introduced, at various periods ; the records of the Society shewing, at the date last mentioned, [1824,] the following, in addition to the original names above cited, to have been members :

Rev. John Dunn. (Librarian.)
J. Henderson.
Colin Buchanan. (Mathematical School.)
John Mennons. (Editor of the *Greenock Advertiser*.)
Alan Swan.
William Kerr.
James Mollison, M.D.
William Scott. (Bookseller.)
Andrew Lindsay.
James Caird.
John Fleming. (Artist.)
David Crawford.
J. L. Brown, [LL.D.] (Rector of Grammar School.)
James Watt. (Crawfordsdyke.)
Rev. Dr. Gilchrist.

based upon and guided by correct and scientific KNOWLEDGE,—had, himself, but a few years previous to his death, founded in the community a Scientific Library, with the express view of affording the means of instruction to its youth, in the essential, but at that time little understood, principles of the mechanical arts ;—thus giving the most direct proof possible of his liberal and enlightened zeal for the practical science, as well as the general prosperity of his native town.

In such considerations there were not wanting motives sufficiently powerful to induce a strong feeling of respect and even gratitude on the part of his townsmen towards the memory of Watt. The reflection was not without its effect upon the members of the Society which had made them the subject of its attention. Desirous as they had for many years been of rendering their corporate existence in some way publicly beneficial, they resolved to embrace the opportunity of associating themselves under a name so auspicious ; and, in adopting the appellation of THE WATT CLUB, to form a society whose special aim should be to *give permanency* to the interest and value which such a name might reasonably be expected to have upon the character and progress of the community to which it belonged.

With these views, the Club determined to avail itself of the first opportunity of giving public expression to its objects ; and the anniversary of Mr. Watt's birth was selected as a fitting occasion for this purpose. On the 19th January, accordingly, of the year 1821,—the first anniversary but one which occurred after his death,—a public commemoratory dinner was arranged to take place. At this assemblage the Chief Magistrate of Greenock presided, many of Mr. Watt's personal and intimate friends—among whom were Mr. Walkinshaw, Mr. Andrew Anderson, and Mr. Watt of Crawfordsdyke, for many years his correspondents—being of the number of the guests.[1]   A

---

[1] The original document, containing the signatures of the gentlemen present at this entertainment, is in our possession. As it may be interesting to some of our readers, we have subjoined a copy in Appendix A.

printed account of the entertainment, with the addresses delivered on the occasion, having been transmitted to Mr. James Watt of Soho, the following gratifying communication in acknowledgment was received from him, dated London, 3d February 1821 :—

" To JAMES WATT, Esq., Crawfordsdyke, Greenock.

" MY DEAR SIR,—Your very gratifying letter of the 23d ultimo, was forwarded to me here from Soho, but the *Greenock Advertiser* did not reach me until yesterday,—which will account to you for the delay that has taken place in the acknowledgment of both.

" I now beg you will undertake the office of communicating to the magistrates, and to the gentlemen of Greenock who attended upon an occasion so grateful to my feelings, and so honourable to their own, the deep sense I entertain of this distinguished proof of their regard for the memory of my father ; and I may be permitted to add also, of the kindness with which it was accompanied towards Mrs. Watt and myself. I shall be most happy to cultivate the connexion which has so long subsisted between my forefathers and their town, in which I also received a part of my earliest nurture."[1]

[1] The remainder of Mr. Watt's letter is as follows :—" It will be within your recollection that during the few days I had the pleasure of passing at Greenock last summer, I mentioned to yourself, as I did to other gentlemen, a wish to present the town with a *Marble* Bust of my father, executed by Mr. Chantrey, on condition of their providing a suitable place for its reception. The Town-Hall appeared to me objectionable, because the business and bustle of the place were not in character with the retired habits of the original, and also because it would not there easily be protected from injury. Other objections lay to the Church. Monuments are not usual in them in Scotland ; and this ought not to be considered in the light of a sepulchral one. The only other situation that occurred was the Library, which— as the appropriate seat of one who was no less distinguished for his extensive knowledge in every department of literature and of science, than for his inventive genius—would be entitled to unqualified approval, were the present (I presume temporary) edifice adapted to the reception and preservation of a fine work of art. Perhaps I shall be excused the expression of a hope, that the period may not be far distant when it may be deemed advisable to construct a building better suited to the tastes and wants of the increasing population and commerce of the town of Greenock ; and, in the meantime, I beg you will state from me that Mr. Chantrey has my instructions to proceed with the Bust.

" I have been informed that some of my father's friends are desirous also of having a Portrait

The town of Greenock thus had the honour of being the *first* to recognise by a public demonstration the merits of her great townsman,—of him, justly to celebrate whose genius was soon to become an object of highest ambition with the most illustrious and the most lettered of the age.[1]

Simultaneous with the institution of the Club, was the desire to form some collection of facts relating to the personal history of its distinguished patron,—to the incidents of his early life, his habits, education, character, with other correlative matters bearing upon his connexion with his native town. It was not overlooked that the *period* to which those details would refer—and in which the genius of Watt occupied so prominent a place—was, beyond dispute, one of the most remarkable and important that had occurred in the history of the commerce or of the social economy of this country; and the fulfilment of the assumed task might contribute in some degree to its successful illustration. A collection of facts of such a nature, even though it might not attract a more general attention, could not but be deemed of greater or less value to the Club, and might properly form the basis of its Records. It might tend to enhance, in its estimation at least, the distinction which the fact of Watt's birth conferred upon the community, and the claims which such a distinction might be conceived to entail upon it.

But even for purposes affecting a wider sphere there seemed grounds for making some attempt towards the elucidation of the

---

painted of him, for some public building; and that a young Glasgow artist of the name of Graham, now here, has been spoken of for that purpose. Should such intention proceed I shall be happy, not only to lend him the pictures I have by Lawrence and ——, but likewise to give any advice and assistance in my power.

"For the part you have personally taken in promoting the late Meeting, I beg you to accept my sincere thanks; and that you will have the goodness to present the same to Mr. Walkinshaw, and to all my father's friends.—Believing me, most truly, &c., JAMES WATT."

[1] It may be observed that this was *three years* in anticipation of the great public meeting in the Freemasons' Hall, London, which took place in 1824.

subject proposed. For recognised, to some extent, as were the merits of the great inventor, and known as his personal worth was, in the immediate circle of his friends here and elsewhere, this, at the period under consideration, [1820,] was by no means universal.

In regard to the first, as not unfrequently happens in similar cases, the claims of Watt attracted less of the notice and admiration of men while he lived, than they have done since his death. During a considerable portion of his life, or, more correctly, during the struggles of the new and mighty agent to emerge from its first crude state into the power and beauty of application which in our day it has attained in all the arts, it is not surprising that a certain unconsciousness of its importance, as THE great invention of modern times, seemed to have pervaded in some degree even the world of science itself. Happily, any very general insensibility of this kind could not be but of short duration ; and, accordingly, no sooner did the real splendour of the discovery break upon the world, than the greatest minds of the age, in our own and neighbouring countries, pressed forward to vie with each other in paying homage to the genius of him who had conferred such benefits on his race. Indeed, it is not perhaps too much to say, that never before in the annals of science were the pen and the eloquence of man taxed to so high a degree in duly signalizing the merits of an invention, felt then, universally, in regard to its endless adaptation, to be only in its infancy ; or was imagination, in its boldest flight, so baffled in the effort to measure in anything like its adequacy, the influence it was fitted eventually to exert on the destinies of our globe.[1] Such, at least, was the apprecia-

---

[1] See the orations delivered at the great metropolitan meeting, held 18th June 1824, in Freemasons' Hall, at which the Earl of Liverpool presided, and at which Sir Humphry Davy, Sir James Mackintosh, Lord Aberdeen, Mr. Secretary Peel, Lord Brougham, and many others equally distinguished for eloquence and for science, were among the speakers ; the object of such an assemblage of talent being to express their admiration of Mr. Watt's inventions, and to provide funds for the erection of a monument to his memory in Westminster Abbey.

tion, on a national scale, so to speak, accorded to the genius of Watt in 1824.

With respect to his private history, however, little pains had as yet been taken to render any of its published particulars accurate. Most of the floating information that was to be met with was of the most vague and indefinite description. Even the place of his birth was, at the date of the institution of the Watt Club, in 1820, not clearly known, or if known, was, in some quarters, not acknowledged. It is true, perhaps, that the fact of the town of Greenock having this honour was never seriously made matter of dispute. Still, it having been alleged in some publications that Glasgow had the distinction of being not only the place of his birth but of his education,—while, with not a few of his own townspeople, the impression seemed to prevail that Crawfordsdyke (until the Reform Act a burgh of barony independent, though within the parish of Greenock) was, in truth, the favoured locality,—it was evident that some record of facts of a more definite character than could be supplied by the then current sources of information was expedient,—such a record as, from its internal evidence, might be relied on. The state of incertitude and vagueness was, in every sense, undesirable, and the risk of its being perpetuated becoming every day more apparent. A long list, in proof of this, not of inaccuracies only, but of the most erroneous statements, might be cited, were it now necessary, from publications of the period of recognised authority. Even within the town of Greenock itself, the circumstances of his private history and the local reminiscences of his early life were fast fading away ; so that, unless something of the nature of the present undertaking had been, at the time, entered upon, it might at length have come to pass, that, in the very place of his nativity, the name of WATT, instead of being, as now, a household word, might have ceased to awaken even a passing interest, and in the course of years have been all but forgotten.

A first and essential point, therefore, was to discover, if possible, THE HOUSE in which Mr. Watt was born. This was soon satisfactorily done. It was ascertained upon evidence, both oral and documentary, that James Watt first drew the breath of life in a house which had stood upon the *site* of the tenement occupied in part, in 1820, as the " Greenock Tavern,"—the very house in which, in those days, the Watt Club meetings were held, and within which, by a singular coincidence, the inquiry which terminated in establishing the interesting fact was instituted.[1] A number of very interesting facts regarding Watt's boyish days were also at this time collected, chiefly from the communications of individuals still at that time alive, who had either been his schoolfellows, or of the number of his own or his father's personal friends, and upon whose testimony the most perfect reliance was to be placed ;—facts which, it is unnecessary to say, were carefully noted and preserved, together with the documents on which their authenticity rested.

For many years the author continued to prosecute his inquiries, as leisure presented itself, addressing himself to every source that was likely to reward research by adding to what might be known of so important a history. Much new and interesting matter was found to exist in the traditions as well as archives of the burgh, not only relating to the Great Engineer himself, but also to the particulars of his family and progenitors, who had, for more than one generation, occupied a respected position in the locality, and in different ways exerted a notable influence upon the welfare of the town of Greenock, during perhaps the most important period of its history. To these inquiries were added such as related to Watt's schools and schoolmasters,—to

---

[1] The concurrence of circumstances was the occasion of a change of the name of the House, which has long been known as *The James Watt* (Tavern); being by this means popularly identified as the *site* of the " House in which James Watt was born." For a detail of the original evidence collected by the author in regard to the house, the reader is referred to Appendix B.

2

his friends and correspondents connected with his birthplace,—to the circumstances immediately connected with his gift for the Foundation of the Scientific Library,—his general interest in the improvement of those arts to which the industry of his townspeople was most specially directed,—and, finally, to the influence which his great Invention had had on the development of the resources, manufacturing and commercial, of his native town, particularly in the rise and improvement of Steam Navigation, and the practical science of Naval Architecture with its subsidiaries.

Such is a sufficiently full statement of the circumstances in which the Watt Memorials originated.[1] With regard to the present structure and arrangement of the materials, the desire has been to leave a record of facts, illustrative, primarily, it is confessed, of Watt's connexion with his native town,—the probable influence of its early history upon the formation of his character and the bent of his mind, —the interest which, till his death, he manifested in its highest prosperity and progress,—and the significance which such a fact should have for his townsmen in animating them to perpetuate, by their intelligence and enterprise, the evidences of so distinguished a relation. Such a statement of the author's intentions will sufficiently indicate the natural limits of the undertaking. In the desire to give them effect, little apology, it is presumed, will be thought necessary for the attempt to afford such facts and incidents as relate to Watt individually, all the prominence to which it was felt they were entitled. In reference, however, to the earlier portions of the work—which bear upon the Lineage of the philosopher—it may be proper to state, that,

[1] It is proper to state that from time to time during the last thirty years, occasion had been taken to make public a considerable part of these papers, in an unconnected series of communications from the pen of the author to the *Greenock* *Advertiser*. Only selected portions, however, of these communications are now reproduced, together with a large quantity of new matter, existing only in the author's Memoranda and Notes.

in the wish to give permanency to this part of the inquiries, local historical subjects necessarily and unavoidably became wrought up with the materials. In the estimation of the Club, perhaps, and in view of the objects of its institution, it might not have been deemed a disadvantage to its memoirs to find even a large portion of the commercial and social history of the town intimately associated with that of WATT. Yet, as in the present arrangement, and even after considerable reduction, this local historical character may be imagined still to prevail,—it is due in some measure to the nature of the work more fully to explain, that, as some portion of these details was essential to the illustration of the period, and the kind of events amid which young Watt was reared,—only so much has been retained as was conceived necessary, in the first place, to the interest of that part of the subject itself, and, secondly, to the elucidation of principles which should afterwards come into consideration, in the particular view which is taken of the early life and development of the powers of the great mechanician himself. While, therefore, the details referred to have been made as far as possible *parenthetical* to the current of the narrative as a whole, it is hoped that the coincidences in point of character—the similarity in tastes, habitudes, and tendencies, which those chapters discover, may, in some degree, prove a compensation for their being retained, and justify to some extent the author's design in so doing.

Under such a representation of the motives which influenced the undertaking, the hope is entertained, that the Collection may not be wholly unworthy the regard of those who are disposed to value any contribution, however unpretending, the aim of which is to increase the aggregate of accredited facts which go to form the basis and the material of all authentic history.

MEMORIALS OF JAMES WATT.

PART FIRST.

LINEAGE.

CHAPTER I.

ANCESTORS OF JAMES WATT——THEIR CLAIMS TO CONSIDERATION——GREAT-GRANDFATHER
OF WATT——KILLED IN ONE OF MONTROSE'S BATTLES——DISASTROUS CHARACTER OF
THE PERIOD——GRANDFATHER OF JAMES WATT——HIS EARLIER YEARS——ACQUISITIONS
IN THE MATHEMATICS——SETTLES IN CRAWFORDSDYKE——PROBABLE REASONS FOR HIS
CHOICE——FIRST NOTICE OF HIM AS A TEACHER THERE——HISTORICAL NOTICES OF
THE TIMES——HIS SUCCESS AS A MATHEMATICIAN——THE MATHEMATICIAN AT HOME——
APPOINTED BAILIE OF THE BARONY——ACTS AND PROCEEDINGS OF THE "HEID COURTS"
——THE MATHEMATICIAN IN HIS LEGISLATIVE CAPACITY——AS A CRIMINAL JUDGE.

ANTIQUARIAN research, confining itself strictly to sources of information of an historical or otherwise perfectly authentic character, has
been unsuccessful in tracing the direct lineage of JAMES WATT farther
back than the great-grandfather of the philosopher. Even commencing here, however, it will probably be admitted that the homely
chronicles of the immediately intervening progenitors afford enough
to establish, for one who has thrown back such a lustre on their
character and name, a more enviable pedigree, than if, after having
ransacked the records of Heraldry, one had been able to submit to the
eye of the curious a long and imposing roll of armorial registries.   It
is for this, among other minor reasons, that it has been determined to
assign to these ancestral Memorials so prominent a place in the present collection.   Those progenitors of Watt, even within the narrowed
scope that has been afforded for tracing their lives, are found to have
been men of acknowledged integrity and worth,——notable, especially,
for scientific and practical attainments, though in spheres that were

limited and comparatively obscure ; as eminent for their industry in private, as for the ready devotion of their talents and time to the promotion of any object that might minister to the public good. There seems no reason, therefore, why a veil should be drawn over such a descent. For though Watt, undoubtedly, owed something to an external and favouring train of events,—to some of which occasion will present itself hereafter to advert,—that he owed incomparably more to the intelligence and worth of his sires, rests on evidence that is altogether indisputable. The details of this evidence will, it is hoped, illustrate some points not wholly without instruction in the personal history of so distinguished an individual. If in no other respect interesting, they will go to establish at least this far from unimportant fact,—that the invention, the wonderful practical genius of this great man—increasingly great as his life and philosophic character are subjected to examination—was not, in any sense, " the accident of an accident :"—that, however propitious to his great discovery events might have been, the happy germ had in vain unbosomed itself to him, had not the mental soil been previously stimulated by long and generous culture ;—and that his brilliantly successful career was the result, in an eminent degree, not of any merely fortuitous concurrence of circumstances, but far rather, of antecedents such as wise and thoughtful men may, in perhaps any age or condition, contribute to bring about, and that by means more or less within the reach of all ;—most happy confirmation of the apophthegm of the poet :—

> " Fortes creantur fortibus et bonis :
> Est in juvencis, est in equis patrum
> Virtus : nec imbellem feroces
> Progenerant aquilæ columbam.
> Doctrina sed vim promovit insitam,
> Rectique cultus pectora roborant."

Of the great-grandfather of James Watt, whose Christian name we are unable to give, little unfortunately is now to be known. He occupied, it is said, a piece of land in the county of Aberdeen, but having engaged (as most men were obliged to do, on one side or the other) in the wars, was killed in one of Montrose's battles. It is not ascertained on which side he fought, though the probability is that he espoused the cause of the Covenanters. The period in which he lived, and which is indicated by that of the birth of his son, was one of great trouble in Scotland, particularly in the county and city of Aberdeen. "In September 1644, (according to the Statistical Account of that city,) during the time of the civil wars, the Marquis of Montrose, with an army of about 2000 men, having approached the town, and summoned it to surrender, the magistrates, after advising with Lord Burley, who then commanded in the place a force nearly equal in number to the assailants, refused to give it up; upon which a battle ensued within half an English mile of the town, at a place called the Crabstone, near to the Justice Mills, where Montrose prevailed, and many of the principal inhabitants were killed;" and according to John Spalding, in his History of the Troubles and Memorable Transactions in Scotland in the Reign of Charles I., that country was left "almost manless, moneyless, horseless, and armless, so pitifully was the same borne down and subdued."

It was about this time, during the civil wars between Charles I. and the Parliament, that THOMAS WATT, the grandfather of the great mechanician, was born. From the age assigned to him at the time of his death—and there are two records of that event—he must have been born between the years 1639 and 1642. One of the records is to be found in the register of burials in the Old or West Parish of Greenock, and the other, on the tombstone placed over his remains in the West Church-yard of this town.

It is not ascertained where Thomas Watt spent the earlier years of his life, or by whom he was educated. Unfortunately no record exists from which might be filled up the long, and, as may readily be

3

believed, interesting period of his history between extreme youth and manhood. Judging by the type and character of his life, from the time when he first becomes known to us, there are many indications which induce the belief, that he was one of those who, though placed in circumstances the most adverse, have yet succeeded in distinguishing themselves by early ardour in the pursuit of knowledge. This, however, is certain, that though bereaved of his father at a tender age, and by the disastrous events of the times stripped of whatever patrimony he might otherwise have enjoyed,—whether from the native vigour of his genius, or from the care of those who had the oversight of his education,—he made solid acquisitions in learning of various kinds, and particularly in the science of the mathematics.

It is in the little town of Crawfordsdyke—about the middle of the 17th century, a small burgh in the parish of Greenock, and closely adjoining the town of this name—that we first meet with the name of Thomas Watt. At what period of his life he settled here, cannot now be known. Neither are we able to describe by what concatenation of events, romantic or otherwise, he came to find himself in a part of the country so remote from the place of his birth. His object, no doubt, was to establish himself in some locality where those branches of scientific knowledge, connected with the mathematics, such as astronomy and navigation, might be rendered available as a profession. Looking at the almost nameless village whither he had bent his steps, —not, certainly, as it is at the present day, as a portion of the town of Greenock, with its forges, and dockyards, and busy artisan population, but as it was some two hundred years ago, with its " forty-four houses that had outside stairs," and " forty-four that had none," the former being the more respectable,—it does appear at first sight difficult to account for his selection of this particular spot, as a place in which, with any adequate prospect of success, to exercise the duties of his calling. Thomas Watt, however, was a man of sagacity and foresight. A survey of the state of the Royal Burghs of Scotland at that time—and to them belonged by statute the exclusive privilege of "foreign trade,"—must have satisfied him that general decay and commercial inactivity was the characteristic of nearly all of them, and that they afforded little promise of immediate improvement. On the other hand, it was as evident that a vigorous movement was beginning to be made, by seaports which hitherto had been debarred from the enjoyment of foreign traffic, with the view of securing to themselves some portion of these benefits; and that foremost among these were the little towns along the River Clyde, whose multiplying harbours and growing enterprise were already opening up facilities for commerce of every kind, unequalled in any other estuary of the North.

One of these was the little Burgh of Barony of Crawfordsdyke.[1] It was situated in the Barony of Cartsburn, the lands of which bordered the left bank of the Clyde, about twenty miles below the city of Glasgow. According to George Crawford, the historian of Renfrewshire, it was erected by King Charles II. into a corporation, by charter in favour of Thomas Crawford of Cartsburn, dated 16th July 1669. It does not appear that Thomas Crawford granted any charter holding of himself, in favour of the feuars and inhabitants of the burgh thus created; consequently the administration of the law, so far as competent to the superior of the barony, and the management of whatever funds might be raised in the burgh, were intrusted to a *Bailie* appointed by the superior, and removable at pleasure by him.[2] The name, Crawfordsdyke, given to the town, was, in all probability,

[1] A *Burgh of Barony*, in legal language, is a corporation, consisting of the inhabitants of a determinate tract of ground, within the barony erected by the King, and subject to the government of magistrates.

[2] Robertson, in his Continuation of Crawford and Semple's History of Renfrewshire, assigns an earlier date to this charter of erection. His words are, "The town of Crawfordsdyke, or Cartsdyke as it is called, which was originally at a consider-

derived from the appearance or nature of its harbour.   The sea-board
of the barony being a deep, indented bay, protected from all winds
except the north-east, was found admirably adapted for trade, which
the spirited proprietor promoted and encouraged by building a long
narrow quay, or *dyke*, about the centre of the bay.   Hence *Crawfordsdyke*, abbreviated in common parlance into *Cartsdyke*, for the name of
the town, as contradistinguished from *Cartsburn*, the name of the
barony or estate.   The quay so built, which existed in a tolerable
state of preservation within the last thirty years, was formed after
the fashion of the old west quay of Greenock, and stretched into the
bay with a sweep to the eastward.   Hamilton of Wishaw, in a
description of the Sheriffdom of Renfrew, written about 1710,

able distance from Greenock, though now adjoining, was erected into a burgh of barony in 1636,
about fifty years before a similar form of internal
government was conferred on Greenock."   He
then goes on to say, " There can be no doubt of it
(Crawfordsdyke) being then the more considerable
place of the two."   I must take leave to demur to
both of these statements of the continuator of the
History, because, in the first place, George Crawford, on whose authority I have given the date
first above mentioned, who was brother-german to
the laird of Cartsburn, and may be fairly presumed to have had access to the best information,
gives the date of erection as 1669, and not 1636;
and because, in the second place, he is totally
silent on the relative importance of the two towns.
Crawford not only gives the date of the charter
of erection of Crawfordsdyke as above, but gives
the date of the charter of erection of Greenock as
about the year 1642."   On looking into the statute-
book, I find the date of the charter of erection of
Greenock into a burgh of barony, which he gives
hesitatingly, to be 5th June 1635.   It was ratified
in the Scots Parliament in 1641.   The ratification,
as the statute narrates, was made of the charter
granted in 1635, by Charles I., " for himself, and
as father and lawful tutor, administrator and governor to his hienes dearest son Charles Prince of

Scotland and Waills, Duke of Rothesay, &c., to
John Shaw of Greenock, and Helen Houstoune
his spous, and longest liewar of them twa in con-
junct fie, &c., . . . off the toune or village of
Greinock in ane frie brugh of Barronie, to be
callit now and in all tyme cuming the brugh of
Grienock, with all privileges, liberties, and immu-
nities at length mentionat and conteinit in the
said chartor."   With regard to the importance of
Crawfordsdyke, as compared with Greenock, I can
find nothing to justify the assertion that it (Crawfordsdyke) was then the more considerable place
of the two.   Crawford's account of the former is
the earliest I have been privileged to peruse, and
he describes it as at the east end of a large bay
" built of one street with a convenient harbour."
The time is not very remote when Greenock was
also a town of one street.   But then, if Crawfordsdyke, at any time, had the ascendency over
Greenock, in respect of population or trade, it
must have very rapidly lost it; for, in 1741, when
the population of the parish, comprehending both
Crawfordsdyke and Greenock, was first ascertained by a presbyterial census, Crawfordsdyke
contained a population of only 719 souls, while
Greenock had a population of 3381, making 4100
of all ages for the whole parish.

describes Crawfordsdyke as possessing " a very convenient harbour for vessels," and the town as being mostly subfeued to merchants, seamen, or loading men. On looking over a roll made up of the feuars and tenants of the barony in October 1712, (among the former of whom is to be found the name of Thomas Watt,) several persons are found described as " skippers and coopers," and many more as " sailors," from which it is clear that Crawfordsdyke was originally inhabited by a seafaring population. Among the tenants three or four are described as *Waiters*, and one of these is a tenant of Thomas Watt. These waiters, it may be presumed, were government officers, placed in Crawfordsdyke to protect the king's revenue. Its maritime trade was, so far at least as owned in the town, represented by a ship or two, and some boats. In a deposition emitted at Paisley by James Tailzour, merchant in Crawfordsdyke, before Sir John Maxwell, Lord Justice-Clerk, for the apportioning on the county and towns the *Free Trade* money, it is stated, " that there is two boats belonging to the inhabitants of Crawfordsdyke of nyne tuns per piece, item two oyr boats about nine tuns, ane thereof, and the other about six tuns, and that there is ane ship called the Nepptoune, ane part of as is reported, about ane third part, that is said to belong to James Galbraith, and this is truth, as he shall answer to God." Although the shipping of Crawfordsdyke, as thus represented, was very limited indeed, it by no means follows that there were not both ships and boats belonging to Glasgow and other places, which frequented the harbour. Its adaptation for trade, and the protection which its natural position was calculated to give to shipping, may easily induce the belief that the harbour would be one of favourite resort. Indeed, a very strong inference that such was the case, may be drawn from the fact of Thomas Watt's settlement in Crawfordsdyke rather than in Greenock, as a teacher of navigation ; as, had he not had sufficient encouragement in the way of his profession among the seafaring people of the former town, there is little likelihood that he would permanently have remained there.

The first notice obtained of this ancestor of Watt, in any public document, is during the dark period of civil commotion and suffering in Scotland, which intervened between the Restoration of Charles II. and the Revolution. Few were permitted to be merely indifferent, or to hold a neutral position in those infatuated times. Thomas Watt, from the nature of his functions, became involved under one of the propositions of the infamous " Test Act," and forthwith was publicly denounced as a " disorderly schoolmaster, officiating contrary to law." The delinquency was, of course, of a political, not of a moral character. The occasion was as follows :—The Scots Parliament, in which the Duke of York sat as commissioner for his brother Charles II., on 31st August 1681, passed an Act titled " Act anent religion and the test," by which a certain oath was required to be taken and subscribed by all persons " in public trust." As the statute was most arbitrary in its enactments, and the oath or test no less so, the Earl of Argyll, on the passage of the Act through Parliament, objected to some of its clauses, and afterwards declined to take the oath without an *explication*. For this explication, which was construed into leasing-making and high treason, the Earl was immediately afterwards indicted, tried, and convicted, and sentence of death was pronounced against him on 23d December 1681. Having been committed prisoner to the Castle of Edinburgh till the king's pleasure should be known, the Earl, having good reason to apprehend, from the vindictive and bigoted temper of the Duke, and his well-known influence over his brother, that the sentence would be carried into execution, effected his escape from the Castle, and fled to the Continent. On the accession of the Duke to the crown in 1685, under the title of James VII., the Earl headed a hostile invasion of Scotland, but his adherents having been dispersed, he was made prisoner near Renfrew, conducted to Edinburgh, and executed under his former sentence, no new trial or sentence being in the circumstances deemed necessary.

As if the Act 1681 were not sufficiently comprehensive and stringent, Charles, according to Wodrow, issued a proclamation " about *pedagogues*," on 4th June 1683, by which he strictly prohibited and discharged " all our subjects, of whatever quality soever, to entertain any person or persons to be chaplains in their families, or to be governors, teachers, or instructors of the children, or pupils, or minors, under their tutory or curatory, or to be schoolmasters within their lands or jurisdictions, &c., except such only as shall swear and subscribe the test foresaid, before their respective ordinaries" (Bishops.)[1] Several schoolmasters in the bounds of the Presbytery of Paisley having declined, or perhaps only delayed, to take the test, the matter was taken up by the Presbytery, who recorded the following minute, expressive of their resolution to act upon the proclamation :—

" February 7th, 1683.—This day, the moderator and bretheren, conform to ane act of Synod, gave in to Bayly Paterson, in Renfrew, ye Sherif-deputis substitute, ye following list of disorderly schoolmasters within the bounds, who have not taken the test, viz., [schoolmasters of Kilbarchan, Neilston, and Lochwinnoch] John Richmond, in Greenock, *Thomas Wat, in Carsdyke*, &c., which list the said baylie has promised to give into the Sheriff-depute, for officiating contrary to law."

So anxious was the Government that all persons designated in the Act of Parliament and proclamation should take the test, which was to be done upon their knees, that another proclamation was issued, by the Privy Council, in name of the King, on 13th April 1683, nominating certain noblemen and gentlemen as Commissioners, before any two of whom the test might be taken, and among these Commissioners is found the name of " Thomas Crawford of Cartsburn." Thomas

[1] Wodrow, Book III. chap. vii. sect. 1.

Watt had now no excuse for not taking the test, if he had formerly been disorderly or recusant, seeing one of the Commissioners for administering the Oath was his own landlord and patron. As little could Thomas Crawford excuse himself to the Government for neglecting, even had he been disinclined, to enforce the Oath on a teacher within his jurisdiction. Thomas Watt, it is feared, took the Oath. And it is scarcely to be wondered at if he did, as, in the event of his refusing to comply, he should, *ipso facto*, have been held incapable of all public trust, and been further punished with the loss of his moveable goods, &c.[1]

At this time, [1683,] when Thomas Watt was denounced by the Presbytery of Paisley for not having taken the test, the Laird of Cartsburn possessed the confidence of Government, as he was nomi-

[1] In this Royal Commission, I do not find the name of Cartsburn's nearest neighbour, Sir John Shaw of Greenock. Sir John himself had got into trouble, for on 10th December 1683, I learn from Wodrow that "he appeared before the Justiciary, and was with sixteen other persons *staged* [accused without formal trial] for treason, rebellion, and doing favours to the rebels," from which I conjecture he had perhaps helped, concealed, or, as it was termed, resetted some of the unfortunate men who had defeated and killed some of Claverhouse's troopers in the rencontre at Drumclog, or fought with the King's troops, under the command of Monmouth, at Bothwell Bridge; "but the Advocate," as the historian further states, "declared he is not ready to insist against them. The Lords oblige them to find caution to appear when called on, and liberate them."

This was the same Sir John who, when *younger* of Greenock, received, in 1683, the honour of Knighthood for fighting for Charles II. at Worcester, and was made a Baronet by James VII. in 1687. One would suppose that his treason could not have been of a very deep dye; but the Government was jealous of most of the landholders in the west country. The period referred to was signalized by many changes in political opinion, as well as in the personal history of the individuals who then took part in public affairs. *His son*, (afterwards Sir John,) when also *younger* of Greenock, made an offer in 1689, after the Revolution, to the estates of the Kingdom, to levy on his own expense, for King William, one or more companies of Foot, for defence of the coast against any invasion from Ireland. His offer is mentioned in a minute of the Committee of Estates. The committee, on 3d May in the same year, as they express it in another of their minutes, "reposing special trust and confidence in his fidelity, courage, and good conduct, have therefore nominated, constituted, and appointed, &c., the said John Shaw, younger, to be captain of the said company of Foot." The orders of the committee were somewhat pithy. They "ordain and require the said John Shaw, younger of Greenock, to be ready with the company under his command for defence of the said coast, *to pursue, fight, kill, dissipate, and disperse*, any persons who shall appear in opposition to the present government."

nated one of the Commissioners for imposing that oath. At the time of Argyll's invasion, two years later, Thomas Crawford of Cartsburn, according to Wodrow, was quarter-master of a troop raised by the heritors of Renfrewshire, under Lord Cochran. This troop was on guard at Greenock when the fleet, with the invading forces, came up the river, but retreated to the hill behind, on some guns being fired upon them from the ships. Wodrow states that " a landing," indeed, of some gentlemen took place on the shore below the kirk.[1] In levelling the ground of the new Cemetery, lately, an iron bullet was dug up, of the size of a swivel shot.[2] Its discovery on the hill opposite the landing-place may readily enough be referred to one of the shots discharged at Cartsburn's troop ; and, without any great stretch of imagination, may be held as a relic of an enterprise which had for its objects the freeing of the nation from a cruel political despotism, as well as the frustration of a scheme for subjugating the minds of the people to an enslaving superstition, under the pretence of a regard for " the true religion." But Thomas Crawford, although thus appearing on the King's side, entertained towards Argyll no personal hostility ; for, as Wodrow further states, " the Earl being taken, was carried into the town of Renfrew, and when at some refreshment there, he said (as I am certainly informed) to Thomas Crawford of Crawfordsburn—for whom he had a peculiar regard, and to whom, after his taking by the two countrymen at Inchinnan Water, he had given a silver snuff-box as a token of his respect :—' Thomas, it hath pleased Providence to frown on my attempt ; but, remember I tell you, ere long one shall take up this quarrel whose shoes I am not worthy to carry, who will not miscarry in his undertaking.'"

Argyll, in these observations, had no doubt in view the meditated invasion of Britain by the Prince of Orange, which took place three

[1] Wodrow, Book III. chap. ix. sect. 9.
[2] Presented to me by Mr. John Gray, the spirited projector of this beautiful work.

4

years afterwards ; and the Prince, most certainly, did not miscarry in his undertaking.

We have no means of learning whether Thomas Watt took any part in the resistance offered to Argyll's invasion. The probability is that he did, in some way or other ; and that he felt in conscience bound, as became a loyal subject who had sworn allegiance to the King, to oppose that measure. Be this as it may, there is evidence extant that he did take part in the memorable Revolution of 1688. It rests on the historical fact, that the abdication of James being held to have relieved all his subjects, " *pedagogue*" as well as those higher in authority, from their allegiance, not a few availed themselves of this liberty, to side with the Prince of Orange,—and that of this number were " *the men of Crawfordsdyke.*" " Crawford of Cartsburn, younger," was nominated an " overseer" for the new election of burghs, appointed to take place on the accession of King William and Queen Mary.

Thomas Watt, however, though thus so unceremoniously introduced to us as a " disorderly schoolmaster," was, nevertheless, from circumstances which his respectability and status about the time referred to abundantly evidence, already a person of some consideration in the little community to whose interests he had joined his individual fortunes. We have spoken of him simply as a teacher in Crawfordsdyke. To be more explicit, he was a teacher of the mathematics and of the principles of navigation. He was not the parochial schoolmaster, as shall hereafter be shown. Only once, indeed, do we find him styled " schoolmaster" at all. On all occasions where he is publicly referred to, he is designated " Mathematician ;" and on his tombstone he is styled " Professor of the Mathematicks."

Such seems to have been his success in his honourable vocation, that, after having married, he was able to become proprietor of the house and garden which he occupied in Crawfordsdyke ; and in addition to this house, in which he continued to live, to purchase another in the town of Greenock. This acquisition of property by him indicates sufficiently that his circumstances were easy, and his position comfortable. Nor is this, perhaps, surprising. For besides that native genius which he possessed, and which was calculated to advance him in any position of life, he would seem to have been without any competitor, either in Crawfordsdyke or in Greenock ; and Greenock being at that time even, one of the most important sea-port towns in Scotland, and rapidly extending its foreign trade, Thomas Watt's scientific knowledge must have been in considerable request, and his instructions valuable to those who desired to qualify themselves for the command of ships necessary for prosecuting the " trade beyond seas."

From all that can be gathered of " the Mathematician's " scientific attainments, these would appear to have been of a respectable order. His habits of thought, his general views and aims in life, may be similarly characterized, giving him, as they did, a recognised superiority among the men of his time. His disposition was meditative, perhaps reserved. He had brought with him sentiments enlarged and liberal ; and, without obtruding them, did not disguise them as the principles according to which all his conduct was regulated. There was nothing, it would seem, of the pedagogue about Thomas Watt, nothing indeed which indicated more than a quiet and thoughtful man of books, or a converse with those studies which ordinarily form an intelligent and well-furnished mind. "There is many a life," says Jean Paul, "that is as pleasant to write as to lead ;"[1] and from the occasional glimpses which the few and scattered remains of this good man's figure and influence, in the simple sphere which he graced so well, afford us, we can easily believe that a fuller supply of materials would have enabled us to present a picture of domestic and social

---

[1] Richter,—" *Blumen, Frucht und Dorn-Stücken.*"

worth, as agreeable as it might prove both instructive and entertaining.
He would appear to have been fond of home and its modest retirement.   His instructions in the several branches of his professed
knowledge were not publicly given, but communicated to those who
sought his aid in the simple familiarity of his own house and the
quiet of his study.   An honest and becoming industry filled up the
intervals of these returning duties, and gave dignity and enjoyment
to the occupations of each day.   It is true, the ordinarily tranquil
flow of those years, especially in the early part of his home and
wedded life, was not unbroken by trial and repeated family bereavement, the severity of which was nobly borne and shared with him by
a dutiful and loving spouse.   Still, those deep and passing shadows
of the spiritual picture serve only to heighten its other kindly lights,
and to render its living character at once more natural and pure.

But though conscious of the pleasures which such a retired, and
perhaps even learned kind of life was fitted to afford him, we are
bound to show that it was not in these alone—in the quiet in-door
pursuits of his calling, the more genial enjoyments of his study and
books, the increasing cares of his family, or perhaps the pleasures of
his garden—that the amiable Professor of the Mathematics was careful, or even desired, to pass the mature and most vigorous portion of
his days.   He evidently felt the claims of a more general and disinterested mission.   The little township would benefit by a wise and
judicious interest and interposition in its affairs ; and he had early
resolved to contribute what he could to its internal order and improvement.   But in a feudal lordship, and under such an administration as
this implied, any direct interference was not by every one attainable.
The requisite occasion was, however, soon afforded, the mathematician's
intelligence and general worth pointing him out to the superior as a
person eminently qualified to act as his representative in the barony,
—holding the baron courts, presiding in the town-hall, and adminis-

tering justice according to the primitive forms of investigation and summary trial in use in those times.

Thomas Watt was accordingly appointed to the functions of " Bailie of the Barony," a feudal office of importance and magisterial authority, which usually conferred upon its occupant respect and consideration, as well as influence in the community ; not only a large share, but also the most prominent direction of all its local affairs falling within its jurisdiction. Of the manner in which he deported himself in the discharge of the multifarious duties devolving upon him in this office, as well as in several others with which he came to be invested, the various public records of the time afford a not uninteresting picture ; presenting this worthy ancestor of James Watt in a light which will be found to have been eminently characteristic, and a family feature of all the Watts—a happy combination of qualities, a union of the speculative with the practical, of the reflective with the useful and active, and a judicious balancing of their respective claims, as bearing upon the aims and ends of life. This trait of character, indeed, in connexion with a name which now holds so distinguished a relation to Science and the Arts—and regarding which nothing can now be uninteresting—becomes so prominent throughout the course of our memorials, that did the simple but authentic memoirs of these estimable progenitors of Watt elicit no other fact of any moment than this, the task involved in the dusty researches of the chronicler would not, certainly, be wholly without its success and reward.

It will be seen that the " Bailie of the Barony" exercised both his legislative and judicial functions with consummate prudence and skill. A book containing a record of " Acts and Proceedings in the Heid Courts" (head courts) of the barony, as early as 11th November 1696, has luckily been preserved, of the interesting matter in which a few specimens will be given. This book shows that Thomas Watt was at

the commencement of the record " the baillie for the tyme." The
second act of court, which is titled on the margin, " Act anent the
church loft and bridge," &c., is as follows :—

" *Eod. die.*—James Sinclair, Archibald Murchie, Matthew Ramsay, James Rae,
and James Hugh, Thomas Watt, the baillie for the tyme, togyr. wt. the clerk, ar
appoynted to meitt with James Tailzeor, and advyse and consult among themselves
anent repairing the church loft in the west isle, and anent the raiseing of fyftein
pound Scots dew to James Galbreath, skipper, for pouther furnished by him to the
toun in December '88, and anent the expense laid out for *heids to the drum* and
dressing yrof, and the expense of building the bridge wider—the expense yrof sall
be paid out of the first end of what of the mortclaith money is in James Tailzeor's
hand ; or if they will lay it on the inhabitants be way of stent, and be publictlae read
in Court, the whole vassalls and tennants of the toun assented to and ingadged to
observ as it sall be declaired and appoynted by the comittee above named, who ar
appoynted to convein for the object foresd. betwixt and the twentie of this instant ;
also appoynts the sd. comittee to lay on the vassalls of Crawfordsdyke the propor-
tioun taken of by them of Carsburns valuatione, for the sds. ten months cess payable
at the terms mentioned in the former act, qch proportiouns of the vassalls extends in
money to the soume of twentie fyv pound Scots or yrby, and it is heirby declaired
that in caise of the neceser absence of any of the comittee that any fyv of the foirsd.
persones ar to be a quorum, and the cess is to be laid on betwixt and the twentie
instant, and the money when uplifted is to be put in the hands of Thomas Watt, and
to be payed out by him when requyred."

(Signed)   " WILL. CAMPBELL, Clr."

It will be remarked that one of the purposes for which " the baillie
for the tyme" and his associates were to " meitt, and advyse, and consult" about, was for raising fifteen pounds Scots (equal to twenty-five
shillings sterling) due to James Galbreath, skipper, for " *pouther*"
furnished by him to the town in December '88, (the very month and
year in which James II. took flight,) and anent the expense laid out
for " *heids* to the *drum* and dressing thereof."[1]   One would scarcely

_____

[1] The *drum* seems to have been an important   Crawfordsdyke, in their warlike demonstrations,
instrument in the hands of the good people of   for I find, in December 1716, a minute of the

have supposed that the remote and inconsiderable burgh of barony of Crawfordsdyke should have been called on to take part in the transactions which resulted in that most important event, *the Revolution*, even to the extent of incurring a debt of twenty-five shillings for powder, and for heads for a drum.

Such important financial deliberations, it should be remarked, however, formed but an insignificant portion of our mathematician's public functions. The bailie was eminently a person of versatile talent, and willing as he was able to render his services available in all emergencies. In a capacity, therefore, in which he was officially second only to the Superior or Baron himself, the duties of the burgh in his hands were of a character sufficiently miscellaneous. Besides his judicial engagements, his services were called into requisition for the adjustment of the public weights and measures, for collecting the government cess, the minister's stipend, the schoolmaster's salary, the assessment for the poor, and the funds for repairing the kirk, the bridge, the public clock, &c. &c. Crawfordsdyke, it may be remarked in passing, had then both a clock and a bell ; at a time, too, when the town of Greenock possessed neither of these public conveniences, so essential to the comfort of a well-ordered community. A regular assessment was laid on the inhabitants, or vassals, for defraying the expense of keeping the clock in repair and ringing the bell. Greenock, at the time referred to, had only the old or *west kirk* bell, which was then as remote from the town as was the Cartsdyke bell : and as a substitute for a clock, the inhabitants were content with a *sun-dial* placed on the corner of the house forming the north-east

---

head court in reference to "the militia money that was laid out in the tyme of the late insurrection," (the rebellion in 1715,) "payed by the laird and fewars and tenants," so much was laid out "for a gun, sword and belt, and oyrways, and for the outreech and wages of John Gray *alias* M'Glashan, militiaman, outreched for the barony of Cartsburn ;" and so much "debursed in the time of keeping guard, for coall and candle, peel and dressing of the town *drumm*."

angle of the High Street and Cross-shore Street, then about the centre of the town, where that primitive *orlege* may still be seen.[1]

No apology is made for adding a few more examples of the " Acts of the Heid Court."   On 18th March 1697, there is one marked on the margin, " Act anent the visitation of Weights and Measures," by which the skill and exactitude of the mathematician were put into requisition, for the adjustment of the *Elnwands* (yard-measures) of the burgh.   It is as follows :—

" 18th March 1697.

" *Eod. die.*—Forasmuch as it is represented that the mesurs and weights wt. in the burgh of Crawfordsdyke hav not bein tryed this long time bygain, and it bein necessr that the same be tryed and marked, for preventing the damnage that may be sustained throw fals weights and measurs in tyme comeing.   Thairfor it is statut and ordained that the wholl inhabitants wt' in this burgh bring their wholl stoupes, pouther, and timber, to the work-house of James Ramsay, couper, to be tryed by him, and if they be found aggrieable to the standard that they may be by him marked as just measurs ; as also, that the wholl weights be brought to the cellar of James Tailzeor, merchant, to the effect the justness yrof may be tryed by him, and if just, to be marked accordinglie ; likeas that the wholl elnwands be taken to the house of Thomas Watt, mathematican, that they may be tried as afoirs'd ; all qch is to be done betwixt and the first day of May next to come.   Certifieing such as sall faill herein, that they sall be proceided against as accords in law.

" WILL. CAMPBELL, Clr."

The records of the head courts contain no acts prior to the date on which those above recited were enacted, which bear the official signature of the bailie.   The first act of court, which is subscribed by him and his clerk of court, is under date 20th November 1697.   His signature occurs afterwards in the book referred to, about thirty times

---

[1] In a pictorial view of " Greenock in 1768," a *steeple* is shown at the Bell Entry, but without a clock.   It was reserved for the *son* of Thomas Watt to superintend the placing of a clock in that steeple.   It was not till 1787 that a clock was placed in the Steeple built in Cathcart Square, the dial-plates of which were removed in 1850 to make room for the illuminated faces or bull's eyes which now adorn that edifice.

between 1697 and 21st December 1717. The act now to be quoted is for the disposal of the fines to be levied from delinquents in court, and is as follows :—

" The qlk day Carsburn desyred that it may be recorded in the court books, that what fynes sall be laid one and uplifted, that the one-half yrof sall be at the disposall of the sd. Carsburn, and the fourt pairt to the clerk, and other fourt to the fiscal and officers, with the express provision that it sall be in the power of Carsburn, to remitt and give down any of the fynes in haill or in pairt, notwithstanding any thing contained herein to. the contrair, and this to continue in all tyme comeing.

" THO. WATT.
" WILL. CAMPBELL, Clr."

In the same session of the head court, the bailie proceeds by a series of statutes to provide, under the sanction of fine and subjection to civil damages, for the economic and domestic reform of several prevalent abuses in the burgh. One of these relates to the damage perpetrated by the " *hens*" belonging to some of the good people of the town, and is in the following words :—

" *20th Nov.* 1697.

" *Eod. die.*—It being complained that seall wt. in the toun keips hens to yr. neighbours prejudice, Thairfor it is statut and ordained yt. in all tyme comeing if any persons keip hens, and they doe prejudice to any neighbour that the owner sall mak up the damnage attour lyable in fourtie shilling *toties quoties*. This act extends to all sorts of taim foules.

" THO. WATT.
" WILL. CAMPBELL, Clr."

Exactly a year and a day after the passing of this act, another act by another bailie, was passed, in which hens are again denounced. The following is the statute :—

" CRAWFORDSDYKE, 21st Nov. 1698.

" *Eod. die.*—It is statut and ordained yt. in caise any horses, as, or mair, be found wt'in any mans inclosed ground or yeard that the owner yrof is not onlie to pay for

5

the skaith done but lykeways fourtie shilling scots *toties quoties;* as also, that heir-after if there be any *hens* upon thatch houses or yeards that the owners of the house or yeard justlie shoot the same attour the former fynes.

"JAMES TAIELZEOR."

Another act was passed in the head court to regulate, *not to forbid,* the drawing of *kail* out of yards on *Hallow-e'en night.* It is as follows :—

"*20th Nov.* 1697.

"*Eod. die.*—It was complained upon that seall of the young ones does upon that night called hallowevin night abuse severall yairds in drawing of kail. Thairfore it is *statut* and *ordained* in all tyme comeing that non upon any pretext, at any time nor night heireafter, draw any kaill out of any yeard or yet cut them w'tout libertie from the owner under the pain of fourtie shilling scots, *toties quoties.*[1]

"THO. WATT.

"WILL. CAMPBELL, Clr."

These acts, it is suspected, have long ago become inoperative, or fallen into desuetude, although the "*Hen nuisance,*" which one of them was enacted to abate, and the *kail-yard* depredations, which the other was intended to regulate, continue nearly as much as ever to be the

---

[1] Local superstitions and national pastimes take a deep root in the minds of the lower orders of society. The observances of Hallow-e'en are, even at the present time, scarcely less popular than when our national poet penned the following verses, so faithfully descriptive of the proceedings of that night of fun and frolic :—

Then first and foremost, thro' the kail,
    Their *Stocks* maun a' be sought ance ;
They steek their een an' graip an' wale,
    For muckle anes and straught anes.
Poor hav'rel Will fell aff the drift,
    An' wander'd thro' the *bow-kail,*
An' pou't, for want o' better shift,
    A *runt* was like a sow-tail
        Sae bow't that night.

Then straught or crooked, yird or nane,
    They roar an' cry a' throu'ther,
The very wee things, toddlin' rin
    Wi' stocks out-owre their shouther ;
An' gif the *Custoc's* sweet or sour
    Wi' joctelegs they taste them ;
Syne coziely, aboon the door,
    Wi' cannie care, they've placed them
        To lie that night.

The produce of the gardens of old bachelors and old maids—persons in general very sensitive and intolerant under any depredations in their kail-yards, are supposed by the votaries of Hymen to possess peculiar virtues, and therefore obtain an unenvied and undesired preference.

subjects of complaint among those who have gardens. We are not aware that the Police Act of the town of Greenock, which has merged the burgh of barony of Crawfordsdyke within the *embrace* of its sections, contains any penal enactment *anent* such important matters. Still, what regulations a future provident magistracy may see it to be their duty to submit to the wisdom of Parliament, to remedy these apparent omissions, can only at present be surmised.

Having given some of the acts passed by the "Bailie" in his *legislative* capacity, it may not be without interest to exemplify some of his proceedings as a *criminal judge*. The following is an exact copy of the proceedings in a criminal court, held by him on 29th September 1697 :—

    " *Curia legittime affirmata.*
    " Thomas Watt, Baylie, *pro tempore.*
    " William Branchel, pror.-fiscall.

" Complains the pror.-fiscall and one Robert Caddel, merchant in Port-Glasgow, and Alex. Mitchell, merchant in Greinock yt. qr. the saids persones on the 25 instant, did in the most unchristian meaner violently set upon others in the open street of Crawfordsdyke, and did beat and strek each other in comtempt of the laws, and yrby did break the peace, qrefor they ought to be punisht according to law, to the terror of others to commit the lyke in tyme cuming.

" Both the sds parties confesses the lyble as to a batterie, and yrfor the Baylie fines each of them in the soume of five pounds Scots money, and ordains them to be put in prisone till they make payment of the saids fines, or find caution yrfore.

    " THO. WATT.
    " ALEXANDER MITCHELL.
    " ALEX. PARK, Clk.
    " ROBERT CADDELL.

" Complains the pror.-fiscall on James Taylor, merchant in Crawfordsdyke yt. qr. on this instant day the sd. James did set upon, bruise, and wound the sd. Robert Caddel to the effusion of his blood, qch is a manifest contempt of the laws and breach of the peace, and yrfore the sd. James ought to be severely punisht for the terror of others to prevent the lyke in tyme cuming.

" The defender confesses the lybel as to the batterie, but denies the blood.

" JAMES TAILZOUR.

" The Baylie discerns the defender to make payment of five pounds Scots money, or find caution for the same.

" THOMAS WATT.
" ALEX. PARK, Clk."

Sometimes the laird himself sat in the Criminal Court, with the bailie, for the purpose, perhaps, of mitigating the rigour of the law. We find him exercising his prerogative of mercy in the following case :—

" Court holden at Crawfurdsdyke, upon the third of May, 1700 years, be the laird of Carsburne, and in respect of Archd. Murchie, bailie, his absence out of the kingdom, who gave his oath *de fideli*, when he should be at home, Thomas Watt is chos. pren. bailie, *pro tempore*.

Curia l'time affirmata.
Wm. Easoune, pror.-fiskall.

" Complains Wm. Easoune, pror.-fisckall, upon John Smith, joyner in Daling, and William Boyce, glazier in   .   That qr. yesterday the third day of May instant, they having cast of all fear of God and Christian neighbourhood, did fall out in William Callwell, skipper in Crawfordsdyke, his house, and thair, and upon the hie streat, did streake, beat, and bruise uthers, with many sade and heavie blows, and stroaks to the effusion of ther blood to a considerable quantitie, and thairfor they, and each of them ought, and should be punished in their persone, and goods conforme to the laws and acts of parliament of this kingdome, to the terrour of uthers to comitt the lyke in tyme coming, and to find cau'ne for keeping of his majesties peace for the future.

" The persuar compeared who opponed[1] the lybell, and the defenders also compearing they deny the said lybell—admits the lybell to probatione, and for proveing thereof, aduced the witnesses afternamed, viz. :—James Ramsay, couper; Joseph Reid, his servant; James Walker, sone to Thomas Walker, couper; James Love, joyner.

---

[1] To oppone—to oppose.—*Againis* is sometimes subjoined.—*Jamieson's Dictionary.*

" The defendars desyreous the pror.-fisckall to pass from the witness's, they ingenuouslie confess to be guiltie of battery, and becomes in will theirfor, but denyes any blood.

" JOHN SMITH.
" WILLIAM BOYCE.

" In respect of qlk acknowledgement each of the defendars are fyned in fyve pounds Scots, and the laird declares that each of them instantly payeing, the half of the fyne to be divyded to the baillie, clerk, fisckall, and officers, as the laird shall appoynt—the laird remits and gives doune the other half, they paying the other half instantlie as said is, and in case of refuseall, ordains ther persones to be comitted to prisone, whill they pay the wholl.

" THO. WATT.
" J. M'INTURNOUR,
no. pub. cler."

This is the only occasion in which any part of the fines imposed upon delinquents was appointed to be "divyded to the Baillie," and other subordinate officials of the court.

Passing over several Head Courts in which the proceedings are not characterized by anything out of the ordinary course of affairs in a modern court of police, and before closing our notice of the criminal court of the barony, we shall give a copy of the proceedings in a court which was held on 13th July 1703, in which Thomas Watt acted as "Clerk" pro tempore. These proceedings are recorded in a peculiarly neat hand, different altogether from the handwriting of the other enactments and proceedings in the old book. The handwriting is not that of Thomas Watt, though the record is subscribed by him as "clerk." The signature is in the ordinary handwriting of the Mathematician. No apology need be made for the length of this curious document, so illustrative of the manners of a bygone period. It is as follows :—

" Court holden att Crawfurdsdyke the 13th of July, 1703.   Arch. Murchy, baylyie, Wm. Geils, fiscall, and Thomas Watt, clerk, *pro tempore.*

" Curia affirmata legittime.

" Complains, Wm. Geils, pror.-fiscall, on Jon Henry, carpenter.   That whereon
ane or oyr of the days of May last past, the said Jon Henry did beat and bruise Jaur.
M'Neil, taylor, for w'ch the said Jon ought to be punished according to law to the
terror of oyrs to comitt the lyke—and sicklyke complains on Robert Gardner and
Archibald Miller, both servitors to John Watson, shoemaker, That whereon an oyr
of the days of June last past, the said two persons did most unchristianly and bar-
barously beat and bruise on ane other for wch they ought to be punished according
to law to the terror of oyrs to commit the lyke in time coming,—and sicklyke complains on Jean M'Vicar, spouse to Josias Thomson, skiper, and Jonet Scot, widow,
and Margaret Urie, that wher yesternight being the 12th inst., the saids three persons did most unchristianly flyt and scold on against the oyr by many bitter reproach-
ful and invective speeches to the prejudice of the fame and good name of each oyr,
for wch all of them ought to be punished according to law and custom in lyke caises
to the terror of oyrs to comitt the like in tyme comeing,—Sicklyke complains on
Jonet Erskine, servitor to James Ramsay, coupar, and Elspeth Galbraith, spouse to
Robert Erskine, and moyr (mother) to the said Wm., and on Archibald Miller, servitor to Jon Watson, shoemaker; That, whereon this present day, on the forenoon,
on the hie street, the said Wm. Erskine and Archibald Miller did most unchristianly
and unneighbourly fight with on an other, and did beat and bruise on another, and
particularly the said Wm. did by the help of his said mother, wound and beat the
said Archibald Miller to the effusion of his blood on two places of the head, for wch
the said persons ought to be punished according to law to the terror of oyrs to do the
lyke, and particularly that the said Wm. over and above the fyne be decerned to pay
to the said Archibald, such a sum as you shall think fit to be modified for curing of
his wounds.

" The Baylyie having heard and considered the lybell does find the same relevant
to be proven *prout de jure,* and therefore refers the verity of the lybells to oath,
particular defender's oath, and the said Jon Henry acknowledges the lybell, so the
baylyie fynes him in fyve pounds Scots to be given down by the laird if he please;
Jonet Scot being called, the fiscall and the pairties pass from the lybell as to her;
and Margaret Ury being sworn as to the lybell against her, finds it not proven against
her; as to Mrs. Thomson, the fiscal and Margaret Ury passes from the lybell as to
her; and Archibald Miller having confessed his rugging of Robert Gardner's hair and
casting him down; and Robert Gardner confessing his rugging the hair of Archibald

Miller, and casting him down, the baylyie fynes each of them in fyve punds Scots, to be given down by the laird if he please; and as to the libell against Elspeth Galbraith, the fiscal and Archibald Miller pass from the lybell agt. her; and finds Archibald Miller guilty of a battery by his own confession agt. Wm. Erskine, and fyne him in fyve pund, to be given down by the laird if he pleases, and ordains him in presence of court to promise to keep the peace, and certify him that the first fault of this kynd he shall be found in to be banished the toune; and Wm. Erskin having confessed the blood and battery, the baylyie fynes him in twenty shil. Scots, to be paid to Archibald Miller for his cure, and in four pund to be paid to the fiscal, to be disposed of as the laird shall please to order it, and ordains Wm. Erskin to be imprisoned till he satisfie the said Archibald of the twenty shil., and the fiscal of the four pounds, to be disposed of as said is.

"Archibald Murchie.

"Tho. Watt, Cleark, *pro temp.*"

CHAPTER II.

THE MATHEMATICIAN AS AN ELDER OF THE PARISH—THE SESSION RECORDS—THE
PARISH AND THE PARISH SCHOOL IN 1697—THE MATHEMATICIAN'S FAMILY—HIS
ELDEST SON, JOHN, BECOMES MATHEMATICIAN AND SURVEYOR—JOHN WATT'S MAP
AND SURVEY OF THE RIVER CLYDE—ITS HISTORY AND VALUE—HIS YOUNGER SON,
JAMES — HIS TRAINING AND APPRENTICESHIP — THE MATHEMATICIAN'S HOUSE IN
CRAWFORDSDYKE—HIS PROPERTY IN GREENOCK—HIS DEATH—HIS BURIAL-PLACE
IN THE OLD WEST CHURCHYARD—THE FAMILY REGISTER.

In the last chapter allusion was made to public duties of another
kind, quite different from those which devolved on the mathematician
as " Bailie of the Barony," although cotemporaneous with the latter.
The more important of these pertained to his office as an Elder of the
parish of Greenock, this parish embracing the town of Crawfordsdyke,
in which the Bailie was resident. It is interesting to note in passing
Thomas Watt's official connexion with the old ecclesiastical regime,
into the spirit of which he so warmly entered,—not only because of
the relationship of " the Elder" of 1695 to " the great modern Inventor ;" but because of its illustrating a state of society which the
prodigious revolution effected by the instrumentality of the latter has
well-nigh caused entirely to disappear from the organization with
which we are now familiar.

For the office referred to, the good mathematician possessed qualifications that were likely to point him out as one of the " fittest"
personages of the community to be vested with the responsible charge,
such as it was in those days ;—his respectability as a householder
and head of a family, the " competency of his knowledge," his gravity

in public as a chief magistrate or as a judge, as well as, it is added, "the blamelessness of his life and conversation" in private.[1]

On 10th January 1695, a minute is entered in the Session Books, in the following words :—

> "The Session, taking into their consideration the great inconvenience they laboured under, by reason of the paucitie of elders now present in office, and that they stand in need of many moe [more] to joyn with them in overseeing the manners of the people, appoint a list to be given in by the elders, of those whom they may judge fit both to be elders and deacons, for the better ordering and regulating the affairs of the congregation in town and country, against next diet." And on 16th of the same month, the list which had been made up, "after mature deliberation," was given in to the Session. Among one or two other persons whom it "made mention of as fittest" for these several offices, "Thomas Watt" was named for the eldership. "The minister," on 7th February, reported that he had "convened the persons designed as elders and deacons, and after trial found them to have such a competency of knowledge as might make them capable of that charge, the elders declaring that they were blameless as to their lives and conversation."

These "Acts of the Session" belong, it will be observed, to that interesting transition period in Scottish history immediately subsequent to 1688. They refer consequently to those wise and earnest measures which followed in the wake of "the glorious Revolution," prominent among which were the provisions made for the moral and intellectual instruction of the population, the alleviation of the wants of the poor, and, above all, the appointing "a school for every parish" throughout the country, so far supported by the public funds as to render education accessible to even the most indigent. So successful

---

[1] It was out of regard to such principles of personal character in the worthy mathematician as those above referred to, and which in all probability were the results of early parental instruction,—as well as from the fact of his accepting office in the eldership, that we ventured to infer, when speaking of the great-grandfather of Watt, that the old Presbyterian had fallen fighting on the side of the "Covenanters." The grandson of the mathematician, the great James Watt, is known to have maintained a lasting attachment to the historical Presbyterianism of his forefathers.

were the efforts having this view which were made, that the happiest effects were soon everywhere visible. " Poverty, degradation, and immorality," says a historian of the period, " almost disappeared ; and peace, intelligence, comfort, and purity spread their blessings over the land ;"—a testimony confirmed in the strongest manner by the remarks of an acute and impartial observer, the celebrated De Foe, who came to Scotland at a subsequent period to aid in promoting the Union of the two kingdoms.[1] The Acts of the Session prove that the " town and parish of Greenock" was among the first to give effect to the proposed measures, in appointing, or rather adding to the machinery by which they were to be carried into operation. The objects aimed at sufficiently indicate the nature of the duties connected with the ecclesiastical office to which we find Thomas Watt nominated and elected. Among these, the " over-seeing the manners of the people, regulating the affairs of the con-gregation in town and country, visiting the sick and attending to the necessities of the parish poor," afforded scope for much persevering and assiduous labour on the part of the " elders and deacons." And that these offices were not in those days purely honorary appoint-ments, is abundantly manifest from the records of the period. Several " cases of discipline" are recorded ; and the evidence afforded seems to indicate that they were conducted with considerable solemnity, and that the effects were beneficial and salutary. Many curious instances might be cited ;—the following, which occurs in a minute recorded 5th March 1696, may be given as an example :—

" The Minister having informed the Session that mountebanks having come to the place, had erected a stage for a stage-play to be acted thereon, and proposed they should fall on some effectual method for suppressing the same. The Session con-sidering the thing to be unlawful, and inductive of much sin and looseness, appoint some of their number, to wit, James Crawford, John Clark, and Thomas Watt, to go

[1] De Foe's Memoirs, p. 328.

to the Doctor, in name of the Session, and discharge him to use rope-dancing, and men simulating themselves fools, or women exposing themselves to public by dancing on the stage, or any indecent behaviour, allowing him only to expose his drugs or medicines to public sale."

The Session also took cognizance of persons who frequented public-houses on *Friday and Saturday* nights, as appears from the following minute, dated 23d May 1695 :—

" The overture anent the abuse of sitting at unreasonable times, &c., coming under consideration, it is appointed, that sitting in and haunting taverns, on Friday and Saturday nights, be abstained from after nine of the clock, at which time the bell at the kirk is allowed to be rung to give advertisement to all to repair to their own houses, except in case of necessity ; and that this may be the more effectual, the elders are required to be observant in their respective quarters, and report as they shall find ground ; and public intimation hereof to be made next Sabbath, in order to the more due observance."

The original Act, of the 13th Parliament of King James I. of Scotland, section 144, is as follows :—

" *Item.*—It is ordained, that na man in burgh be foundin in tavrenes of wine, aill, or beir, after the straike of nine houres, and the bell that sall be rung in, in the said burgh. The quhilkis founden, the alderman and baillies sall put them in the kingis prison. The quhilk gif they do not, they sall pay for ilk time that they be foundin culpabill before the chamberlane, fyftie schillinges."

At the period of the mathematician exercising the office of an elder, the records abound with cases of " Sabbath breaking," of a more or less aggravated character, to the correcting and prevention of which great vigilance on the part of *both* the civil and ecclesiastical authorities would seem to have been directed. Two of the elders, accompanied sometimes in their praiseworthy travels by the officers of the " Lairds of Greenock and Cartsburn," were in the habit of perambulating the town, occasionally during, but generally after, divine service, and censuring such persons as they found "vaging" about the streets and quays. One or two examples from the records may be given, in which Thomas Watt was called on in his official capacity to act. One of these is dated 4th April 1695 :—

"The minister informed the Session [that] Mr. Petticroe, minister in Govan, had told him, Anna Patterson, daughter of John Patterson, seaman in Cartsdyke, had on the Lord's-day carried into Glasgow a burden of pease openly. The business is referrd to the enquirie of Matthew Ramsay and Thomas Watt, appointed to report to the next diet."

"*April* 11*th*.

"Matthew Ramsay and Thomas Watt, according to the last day's appointment anent Anna Patterson, report she resides in Glasgow, wherefore it's appointed a letter be written to Mr. Petticro by the clerk, that he make his application to the Session there for discovering her."

Another example occurs, under date of 5th March 1696, in these words :—

"Informed, James Rae, skipper in Cartsdyke, had loosed his ship, *being sufficiently moored in a safe road*, on the Sabbath-day, which gave great offence, and its appointed Alexander Lees and Thomas Watt speak to him, and know what induced him to do so, and report to the next diet."

"*March* 9*th*, 1696.

"Alexander Lees and Thomas Watt report that, after discoursing with James Rae anent his taking the ship to seaward on ye Sabbath-day, they found him really affected and concerned for his breach of the Lord's-day, and that he would come to the Sess. and acknowledge his guilt. The Session considering his guilt thought he could not be passed without a sessional rebuke, which they appoint him to be censured with."

"*Sess. March* 27, (1696.)

"Qlk day after prayer, the Session being met, James Rae, of his own accord, came to the Session, and acknowledging his guilt by breach of Sabbath, is censured with a Sessional rebuke, and admonished to carie [carry] more tenderly on the Lord's-day for the future."

Looking at the deference paid to ecclesiastical procedures, and even to the censures of reverend courts in those days,—a deference not easily comprehended in our more liberal times,—one cannot fail to be impressed sensibly with the greatness of the *change* which society must have undergone in this country, even within less than the last century. How little, for example, could Thomas Watt, while piously pacing the lanes and harbours of Greenock and Crawfordsdyke, in 1695, with a view to the repression of even minor acts of "sabbath-breaking," foresee the inroad that has been effected on the day of rest, since the introduction of machinery! How little could he anticipate, while reprehending "James Rae, skipper in Cartsdyke, who had loosed his ship, being sufficiently moored in a safe road, on the Sabbath-day," that in the person of his own grandson was to arise one, the results of whose splendid genius—*so incalculably productive, in one point of view, of physical and moral benefits to the human race*—were *indirectly* to contribute more to the desecration of that day on a gigantic scale, through "excursion trains," steamboats, and a thousand other subsidiary means, than all hitherto existing causes combined had done!

But while it may hardly be disputed that reverence for the sacred principle of the day of rest has suffered a marked declension in the national mind since the times of our forefathers, it is, we think, equally indisputable that, in other essential points affecting the common good, a very decided *improvement* characterizes the spirit of our own times. Not to speak of the general benefits which have resulted from the abolition of class privileges, and from a better understanding of the great laws of toleration, this progress is perhaps nowhere so obvious as in everything that relates to the all-important matter of Public Instruction. Reverting to our "Records," it has already been observed that the good "Bailie of the Burgh" was not a schoolmaster, still less, we are bound to add, "the parish school-

master."[1]   That the *bona fide* schoolmaster of those days was a very
different person—not in point of qualification but of status—there is,
unhappily, but too good reason to believe, if one may judge from a
minute which occurs about this time in the Records from which one
or two quotations have already been made.

Crawfordsdyke being locally within the parish of Greenock, *one*
schoolmaster was deemed sufficient for " both towns ;" (so in the
original.)   Strange as it may appear, the heritors and kirk-session
prohibited there being any more !   At a meeting of the latter court,
held 27th September 1697, they recorded the following minute :—

" Qlk day, after prayer, the Session being met, its ordered, with consent of the
heritors, *no school be kept in the parish except the publict school*, they considering that
private schools were prejudicial to it, providing always the said school be in a commodious place of the parish."

From the same minute we learn what was the munificent allowance
made to the parish teacher.   It goes on to state " the small encouragement the schoolmaster had arising to him by the publict sallary,
which was only Forty pounds Scots, [Three pounds, six shillings, and
eightpence, sterling,] paid by the foresaid heritors," and their agreeing to add other Forty pounds to the salary, " making four score in
all, besides other casualties belonging to him as beadle and clerk of
the Session."

The teacher for whom this provision was made was, it is presumed,
John Richmond, denounced by the Presbytery of Paisley, along with
Thomas Watt, as one of the " disorderly schoolmasters," for not having
taken the Test in 1683.

---

[1] Whether the more dignified designation of
" Mathematician" was a cognomen to which he
himself attached importance, or rather was a title
accorded to him by common consent, from the
superior nature of his calling, is immaterial to
decide.   In all probability it was of this latter
character, conferred upon him originally by way
of honourable distinction, as indicative at once of
the exact and scientific habitude of his mind, and
of his profession in the town, as a teacher of so
important a branch of science as that of navigation was then especially considered to be.

Eight years after this minute of the Session, another is found, of the " Heid Court" of *Cartsburn*, dated 17th November 1705, as follows :—

" *Eodem die.*—Forasmuch as John Wallace, schoolmaster of this parish, has never gott any additional sellury, and it being thought reasonable that in pursuance of yᵉ 26 Act of the sixt sessione of K. Wm. Parliat. that there be somewhat settled one him, payable yeirly from the inhabitants, that shall be thought able living under Carsburne in the paroch of Greenock. Therefor its enacted that there be Five pounds Scots [Eight shillings and fourpence] of yeirly additionall sellury and otherways settled on the said John Wallace during his services of schoolmaster in this paroch, and whilk Five pounds yeirly is to be in satisfactione of all he can demand for additionall sellury and house rent, from and out of Carsburnes lands in the paroch of Grenock and the town of Crawfurdsdyke."

It is not to be wondered at, that the said unfortunate John Wallace intimated to the kirk-session, in March 1711, his resolution of laying down his charge in May following. It is probable that he was starved out of office. We do not know whether he had an assistant or not, but the Session paid the sum of *two shillings* sterling " to one Alexander Watson, for teaching poor scholars, which," as the record takes care to state, " compleats all due preceding this date." Thomas Watt, who was acting kirk-treasurer in 1711, paid the money to Watson from the kirk funds.

The reproach of discouraging learning to this extent is sad enough, certainly, in the case of the " Laird of Cartsburn," and " the people of Crawfordsdyke." But what is to be said for the " Laird of Greenock," and the people of this more opulent town, who were fully more deeply implicated in the illiberal resolution to have only *one schoolmaster* in the parish, and who, in thus preventing generous competition, contributed most to starving learning in his person? Still more extraordinary, if possible, is the fact, that in 1697, the year in which the above minute of the Session was recorded, the Reverend John Stir-

ling, formerly minister at Inchinnan, and afterwards Principal of the
University of Glasgow, was minister of the parish of Greenock! And
yet, such a system of policy was not altogether without high pre-
cedent, it would appear, in those days. Examples are furnished by
entries in the Council Books of the City of Edinburgh to the following
effect :—" November 1660. Vulgar schoolmasters were discharged
from teaching Latin. There was a similar prohibition in May 1661.
In August 1668, there passed an Act prohibiting any person from
teaching Latin, except the Masters of the High School. In March
1679, there was issued a proclamation prohibiting single persons from
keeping private or public grammar schools within the city or suburbs
of Edinburgh. These prohibitions were repeated in December 1693,
when the doors of private schools were ordered to be closed; and
again in June 1694."[1] It is to be hoped that such illiberal views, in
regard to the all-important subject of education, have long ago everywhere been exploded; and that in the communities of " both towns"
in the present day, a more liberal and enlightened spirit animates the
minds of both heritors and inhabitants.

Besides the duty of overseeing the manners of the people, which
devolved upon him as an Elder of the church, Thomas Watt was
more than once appointed Presbytery elder, as well as employed in
his sessional capacity in other matters connected with the Session.
It would appear that the office of Kirk-Treasurer was at that time a
gratuitous appointment, for on 9th December 1708, he was appointed
to that office in the following terms :—" The Session this day nominate
and chose Thomas Watt treasurer, and he nor any one after him shall
be obliged to continue in that office above a year." The Session, notwithstanding, it would appear, found his assistance too valuable to be
dispensed with, and prevailed upon him to continue longer than a
year in office ; for, on 20th March 1711, at a meeting of the Session,

---

[1] Chalmers' Life of Ruddiman, p. 90. 1794.

a vote " is taken whether or not Thomas Watt, present Treasurer, should be continued, it was carried in the affirmative, to be continued for another year." On 3d July of the same year, however, a minute of the Session states that " Thomas Watt, Treasurer, desired his accounts might be taken off his hand, in regard his circumstances could not allow him to continue Treasurer any longer." He was relieved accordingly of the office, and on the 17th of the same month, the Session recorded a minute in the following words :—" Reported by those who were appointed to revise the treasurer's accounts, that they find he has been *deligent and faithful* in the management of his trust."

It is scarcely to be wondered at that Thomas Watt should have been urgent to be relieved of his treasurership, seeing that he had imposed upon him at the same time the equally onerous office of Session-Clerk. John Wallace, the Session-Clerk and Schoolmaster, having in pursuance of his previously intimated resolution resigned his charge as Schoolmaster, with which, it would appear, the office of Session-Clerk was conjoined, the Session on 29th May 1711, appointed " Thomas Watt to officiate as clerk, till a schoolmaster and precentor be settled according to law." He held this office till 12th September 1711, when " Mr. John White, parochiner here and student of theology, being by the heritors' special advice and consent of the Session, called to be schoolmaster, was admitted precentor and session-clerk, he having given his oath *de fideli.*"

It was customary for two witnesses to subscribe the entries made in the register of baptisms. Thomas Watt's signature as a witness is frequently found, as well before as after he ceased to exercise the duties of Session-Clerk. One example of the former may suffice, in what follows :—

" 1707, Elizabeth, lawfull daughter to Archibald Yuil, skipper in Greenock, and

Jean Ferguson, was born May 11, and baptized ye same day, as witness Thomas Watt, mathematician in Carsdyke, and Hugh Montgomerie, sailer there.

"THOS. WATT, witness.
"HUGH MONTGOMERIE, witness."

After this there are several entries where John Watt, designated "son to Thomas Watt, mathematician in Carsdyke," attaches his name as a witness; and there are two or three instances where John Watt and James Watt, the two sons, subscribe as witnesses to the same entry. The following, holograph of the Mathematician, is so subscribed :—

"John, law'll son to John Speir, mercht. in Greenock and Anne Cuningham, was born 28 September 1711, baptised September 30, 1711, as witness John Watt and James Watt.

"JOHN WATT, witness.
"JAMES WATT, witness."

Besides making the entries of the births which occurred within the term of his holding the office of Clerk, he also made the entries of the marriages celebrated within the corresponding period : these only amounted to fourteen between 7th June and 20th November 1711.

After Thomas Watt was relieved of the office of clerk, by the appointment of the parish schoolmaster, the witnesses ceased to subscribe their names to the entries, in the register of baptisms, the names of the witnesses present at that official act being only given. It is difficult to explain how he and his sons came to be so often called on to witness these entries, unless it arose from the general superintendence we have so frequently had occasion to notice, which the professor of the mathematics took of the ecclesiastical as well as civil and criminal concerns of the parish.

Passing allusion has already been made to the domestic life of the Mathematician, and to the family bereavements which he and his worthy spouse had sustained during the early part of their wedded life. Besides the loss by death of two daughters, Margaret and Catherine, and one son, Thomas, all in infancy, a third daughter, Doritie, was cut off at the age of eighteen. Two sons, however, remained to them, John and James, both of whom survived their parents. To the education of his boys the worthy father seems to have devoted much attention and care. John's preparatory training, especially, would appear to have been very thorough, designed as he was, probably from the first, for the profession of a mathematician and surveyor. How long he continued under his father's roof cannot be very accurately ascertained, though, in all likelihood, he did so until he had attained early manhood; and during part of the intervening period assisted his father in teaching mathematics and navigation, thus improving himself in what would appear to have been his favourite department of scientific study. From notices of him, however, at this time in the public records, he seems to have acted formally as "Clerk" in the head court of the Barony of Crawfordsdyke, where we have seen the father during so many years officiating as bailie. The following is copy of the minute of court appointing him to the clerkship; the original is in the handwriting of the newly-appointed clerk:—

"Att the manner place of Cartsburn, the 25 day of October, 1712 years. In an heid court holden by Arch. Campbell, Baylie for this head court.
"The court fenced and rolls called.
"The qlk day John Watt, eldest lawfull son to Thomas Watt, mathematician in Crawfordsdyke, is admitted clark to the barrony of Cartsburn, and brugh and barrony of Crawfordsdyke, which office he is to continue during the laird's pleasure, and on condition during his service as said is, that he serve on the terms on which Andrew M'Inturner, notour in Greenock, was admitted clark, and in particular that he furnish and make up ye court rolls and precepts of warning and removing by the laird against his tenants when he shall be desired, and that gratis, and that he furnish and form the stent rolls for additionall stipend and trade money when desired, and that also

gratis, with the exception as to the additionall stipend and trade money rolls, that if the stent-masters think fit at casting of those stents to appoint any part of the excrescens of these stents as they shall be laid on, he may accept any part thereof the stent-masters shall think fitt to give him ; and Robert Eton is admitted Proct.-Fiscal, to continue during the laird's pleasure.

"Jo. Watt.
"A. Campbell."

At a subsequent diet of the head court we find Thomas Watt acting as bailie, and John Watt as clerk, in framing a most wholesome enactment against brewers who received pledges from women who had husbands. We should like to see some enactment in the same spirit introduced into every Police Act in Scotland, to correct, if possible, the prevailing intemperance in the use of every kind of strong drink among the lower orders of women. The following is the enactment, in the handwriting of John Watt :—

"15 *November* 1712.

"*Eodem die.*—It being represented as a grivance that severall brewares within this burgh do take in pledge, or buy from some persons within this barrony or burgh, severall pieces of housall furniture or weiring apparel far within the value, and from persons who have no right to sell or pledge the samen, whereby severall persons are exceedingly prejudged. For preventing whereof its thereby enacted that no brewar or any or other persons shall take in pledge or buy any such goods from any woman having an husband without consent of her husband. It being hereby enacted that all such brewars or others who shall controveen this act shall be obliged to restore all such goods as are above mentioned to the husbands of the women pledgers or sellers of such goodes, and that without anything to be payed by the sds. husbands therefor, and that such brewar or others that shall be convict of the breach of this act shall be layable in ten pound Scots money of fine *toties quoties*, and that over and above restoring and delivering up the goodes in manner fors'd.

"Tho. Watt.
"Jo. Watt."

John did not, however, long continue in office. He had higher views than such as belonged to the incidental discharge of the duties of a clerk in a baron court. Having early yielded to the family bent, and devoted much time to the study of the mathematics, and, subsequently, of hydrography, he determined on leaving Crawfordsdyke and establishing himself in Glasgow, with the view of prosecuting the profession of a mathematician and surveyor. Unfortunately an early death terminated at once his labours and his promised usefulness. One important result, however, of these still remains, in the form of an accurately drawn map or survey of the River Clyde,—a work which, even at this day, although it has been succeeded by several elaborate surveys made by eminent engineers, is, in many respects, not without high value. As this map is now exceedingly rare, not more than two copies of it, or at most three, being known to exist, a few particulars regarding its history may not be here inappropriate.

One of these copies, in the author's possession, bears on its ornamentally engraved shield the title as follows :—

THE

RIVER OF CLYDE,

SURVEYED BY

JOHN WATT.

As it conveys no further particulars regarding its history, and especially bears no *date*, nothing more than an approximate period could be assigned to it as that of its execution. Indeed, for many years, little farther was known in regard to its origin than that, its author having died shortly after its construction, it had been published some time afterwards by a member of the family. In the Article WATT in the *Encyclopædia Britannica*, the publication of John Watt's map is ascribed to his *brother*, that is, to James Watt, father of the Improver of the Steam Engine. This, however, is now ascertained not to have been the case. From evidence furnished by a *second* copy of this interesting work known to be extant, and which was in the possession of Dr. Davie, one of the Town-Clerks of Glasgow, the map, it now appears, was published by the surveyor's *nephew*, John Watt, the younger brother of the great James Watt. On Dr. Davie's copy there are certain additions made with a pen, and which, to one accustomed to the handwriting of the great Engineer, are easily identified as having been made by him.[1] These additions are very valuable, giving us information not only as to the authenticity of the map, if that could ever have been doubted, but also the period to which the survey is to be referred, the editor or publisher of it, and the date of its publication. To the name of " John Watt," in the title, is added, for example, with a pen, the word " Senior," evidently with the view of distinguishing the surveyor from his nephew of the same name ; " 1734" is added as the date of the survey ; and " Published by John Watt, junior, 1760," subjoined, gives the name of its publisher, and the year when its publication took place. The information thus conveyed is invaluable, as scientific and nautical men have now the means of ascertaining, by a comparison of the soundings given on John Watt's map with those of the present time, whether, by the natural action of the currents, or the sand sent down by the operations of the River Trustees, any changes have been occasioned in the

[1] It was in 1841, while in attendance, officially, at the Autumn Circuit Court of Justiciary, at Glasgow, that I first had an opportunity of inspecting this second copy of John Watt's Map, in the hands of my esteemed friend, Dr. Davie, well known for his interest in antiquarian literature. Dr. Davie had mentioned to me some time previously that he had this map, which he had purchased at a book sale. When I saw it, I at once said that the manuscript markings upon it were in the handwriting of James Watt, the great Engineer. Mr. Muirhead, the translator of M. Arago's " Eloge," and subsequently the editor of the " Correspondence of the late James Watt on his Discovery of the Theory of the Composition of Water," happening at the time to come into the Court-house, I suggested to Dr. Davie to show the map to that gentleman, feeling convinced he would corroborate the opinion as to the handwriting, which he at once did. The Doctor then made a present of the map, which was in a state of beautiful preservation, to Mr. Muirhead, in whose possession it is now understood to be.

depth or direction of the channel, and to what extent these may have taken place in the course of upwards of a century.[1]

The "John Watt, junior," who here appears as the publisher or editor of his uncle's map, was, as already noticed, the younger, and, it may be said, only brother of the Improver of the Steam Engine. It is singular that little more of him is known beyond the fact of his undertaking with regard to the map. From this circumstance, however, it is probable that he too was devoted to pursuits similar to those of his uncle. Whether on a voyage undertaken on account of his health, or for other reasons, is not ascertained, but he perished at sea in 1763, at the early age of twenty-four. His connexion with the map affords another example of the remarkable tendency of the Watts towards mathematical and scientific pursuits,—from Thomas Watt, the grandfather, who prided himself on the designation of "Mathematician," down to the younger grandson, who edited the "Map of the River of Clyde."[2]

[1] The substance of the above details relating to John Watt's Map appeared in a paragraph communicated by me to the *Greenock Advertiser*, of 12th April 1842. The occasion of its being prepared was as follows :—

A copy of the map which had been presented to the Town of Greenock, by the late Mr. John Turner, bookseller in Liverpool, having gone amissing, and being then supposed to be lost, Mr. Robert Buchanan, Master of the Mathematical School, had obligingly presented me with a copy which had belonged to his father. My copy being supposed to be the only other extant, was written for by Mr. Gray, the Town-Clerk, then carrying through Parliament the "Greenock Harbour Bill," and I accordingly sent it to him to London, accompanied by the Article I had prepared for the *Advertiser*, to shew the *value* of the information to be derived, by the Parliamentary Committee on the Bill, from a Map of the Clyde, constructed by the uncle of James Watt.

The article was copied into the *Glasgow Courier*, and I believe into other prints. On the 21st April, I received anonymously by post, some slips containing it. Dr. Davie, it appeared, had circulated some of these, and, among other persons, had transmitted a few copies to Soho, and to Mr. Muirhead, who sent me the following letter :—

"*Edinburgh, 30th April* 1842.

"MY DEAR SIR,—I conclude that I am to thank you for some copies of a notice of John Watt's Map of the Clyde, which reached me anonymously some days ago, and if I am right in the supposition, you will please receive my acknowledgments for your attention. I know that Mr. Watt was also gratified by receiving some copies of the same notice, also sent anonymously.—I am, my dear Sir, yours truly,

"JAS. P. MUIRHEAD."

[2] Since the above was written it has been re-

The few preceding paragraphs embody all, unfortunately, that can be collected of the life and remains of this eldest son of the Mathematician,—John Watt, the early surveyor of the River Clyde. In the early history of the younger son, James, the only member of the family who survived, we naturally feel an interest proportional to his after-relationship to the principal subject of these memoirs.

James appears to have been designed by his father for a more ordinary sphere of usefulness. While his elder brother's training might perhaps have been the more elementary and regular of the two, that of James, there is no reason to doubt, was on a scale sufficiently liberal both for his station and for the times. Besides the ordinary branches of learning supplied by the parish school of the day, he received under his father's instructions as much knowledge of figures, mensuration and geometry, as it was deemed might afterwards be helpful to him. As might be expected also from the character of the old "Elder," much care was bestowed on James's moral training ; while, in the choice for him of a profession, and in seeking to give to his outset in life a fair direction and aim, the same shrewd and judicious motives are observable, which have already so often been remarked in the life of the Mathematician. In choosing for James some craft or trade in which, equally with his elder brother, it might reasonably be believed he would rise to some degree of independence and usefulness, there is no ground for supposing that his father intended this to be the ultimate extent, or rather limit, of his son's business in life. Much more in conformity with the Mathematician's general views is it to believe, that such a course was adopted with James, as the most direct and most effective method of attaining the end he had in contemplation, namely, the giving his son a thorough and practical knowledge of some one trade or calling, to begin with ;

solved to have this interesting map re-engraved, on a slightly reduced scale, for the present work. The additions made by the pen of James Watt, however, are a fac-simile.

and that that was selected, which, in a seafaring town, and busy thriving community, was, in many of its aspects, as important and promising as the more scientific profession to which he had devoted his brother. With such views on the part of the old man, added to the natural temper and sagacity of the boy himself, James's outset in life promised fair of success. He might not, perhaps, turn out a philosopher or a genius, originate any great scheme to immortalize his name, or pile up a fortune that might make him the wonder of the vulgar. But he might become a wise and useful citizen; he might exemplify and give currency to principles of personal probity and rectitude, such as are the only solid framework for a virtuous society; he might show himself a good husband and a judicious father;—and so, eventually contribute more to the wellbeing of his fellows, than if he had been taught to value influence and wealth as the highest good, and to follow self-interest and self-aggrandizement as the sole end of existence. James was in due time apprenticed to the business of a general Carpenter or Shipwright.

The old Mathematician had thus the satisfaction, ere he was gathered to his rest, of seeing both of his sons established in life. Of John's undertaking—the Survey of the Clyde—it is probable that he witnessed the successful termination, though he was happily spared the sorrow of its author's death, [in 1737, only two years subsequently to the completion of the work,]—an event which probably deprived the practical science of his time of many useful contributions. To the notices of the life of the younger son, James, we shall presently return. In the meantime, we have to gather up here the few particulars which remain, relative to the grandfather of the great Mechanician.

The House in which the Professor of the Mathematics resided in Crawfordsdyke, is well ascertained. Indeed, it is easily done from the public records, a description of the house and garden, with their locality and boundaries, being found in the Charters granted by " Thomas

8

Crawford," the superior of the Burgh. The house was situated on the
east side of the bottom of the street known by the name of *"the
Stanners,"* [1] and had a slanting front to what was then, and still is, the
chief street or thoroughfare leading from Greenock towards Port-
Glasgow. [2] To the house and garden here mentioned he acquired
right by Charter from the Superior on 6th March 1691. The life-
rent of the property was conveyed by the same instrument to Margaret
Sherrer his wife. [3] The house was, about 35 years ago, pulled down
and rebuilt. [4] Besides this property in Crawfordsdyke, Thomas Watt,
as before stated, was proprietor of another house in the town of
Greenock, which was situated at the " Open Shore," and occupied part
of the site of the large fabric, fronting the short lane leading to what
is now Shaw Street, from the new Graving Dock.

After a long and exemplary life, the worthy Mathematician was
gathered to his fathers, at the advanced age of ninety-two. The
death of his estimable spouse took place the year after. The register
of burials of the old or west parish of Greenock, contains the following
entry of the time of his death :—

[1] A lady whose ancestors resided in Crawfordsdyke, mentioned to me a fact, which I think serves
to fix the etymology of the Stanners. It was here
the weigh-house was situated, and the weights or
standards were kept for weighing out the salt
used of old in curing herrings, of which trade
Crawfordsdyke had at one time a considerable
share. Nothing was more likely than that the
word Standards should be changed into Stannars,
according to the Scotch way of pronouncing the
word : hence the Stanners. In corroboration of
this authority, I find an old charter to one Robert
Bethune has the word spelt thus, " Stenders,"
and it is a fact that Robert Smith, the king's
weigher, dwelt in the street in question, next
door to Thomas Watt.

[2] Adjoining the ground on which are now certain erections connected with the premises occupied by the eminent marine engineers, Caird
& Co.

[3] John being the eldest son succeeded to his
father's property in Crawfordsdyke, to which he
obtained a charter, or what is technically called
a precept of *clare constat*, dated 28th August
1736. His brother James subscribes as a witness to the instrument of sasine which followed
on the charter to John. In these instruments
John is described as a teacher of mathematics in
Glasgow.

[4] Now the property of Mrs. M'Farlane and her
children.

"*February* 1734.

"Thomas Watt, teacher of navigation in Cr., died the 27, aged about 95 years."

And the following is a copy from the same register of the entry made of the death of his venerable spouse :—

"*March* 1735.

"Margaret Sherrer, spouse to the deceased Thomas Watt, mathematician in Cr., died the 21st, aged 84 years."

On a flat tombstone in the kirkyard of Greenock, placed on the west side of the old Church, to record the times of the deaths of Thomas Watt and his wife, and several of his family, and to mark the spot where their remains are deposited, there is an inscription not a little curious. By whom the Inscription was prepared, cannot now be known. It seems to have been the production of various hands. That the introduction was not written by John Watt, who survived his father by two or three years, seems clear ; for it cannot be supposed that he would have committed the orthographical errors it contains, particularly in spelling of the surname Watt with one T, seeing we have his own and his father's signatures uniformly spelt otherwise. It seems almost as clear, on the other hand, that the very particular record which the stone exhibits of the days, months, and years, of the deaths of his children, could only be preserved by Thomas Watt himself. The probability therefore is, that the tabular form of these family bereavements was made by him, and after his death inserted by a less skilful hand into the middle of the Inscription as it now stands. The table of deaths, if we are right in assuming it to be the production of Thomas Watt, affords a curious proof of the methodical and somewhat punctilious habit which his mind had acquired from the nature of his pursuits. The following is an exact copy of the Inscription :—

T W.   M S

THIS IS THE BURIAL PLACE
OF THOMAS WAT PROFE-
-SOR OF THE MATHEMATIC
-KS IN CRAWFORDSDYK HIS
WIFE AND CHILDREN.

1701.

NAMES.	AGE.			TIME OF Death.
	Y.	M.	D.	
MARGT.	0.	11.	6.	OCTR 1683.
CATHREN	0.	00.	10.	DECR. 1687.
THOMAS	2.	4.	4.	FEBR.
DORITIE	18.	5.	20.	AUGT. 1706.

THOMAS WATT DIED FEB
28. 1734 AGED 92.
MARGRET SHERRER HIS
SPOUSE DIED MARCH 21. 1755 [1735?]
AGED 79. LIVED IN
MAREDGE 55 YEARS.[1]

[1] As before stated there are two records extant which give the time of the death of Thomas Watt, namely, the tombstone above referred to, and the register of the Kirk-Session. In the latter he is stated to have died upon the 27th, not the 28th February 1734, and to be aged not 92, but *about* 95 years.

We have said that the parish record as well as the tombstone states the period of the death of Margaret Sherrer; but although both agree as to the 21st March being the day and month of the death, they widely differ in assigning the *year*—the Session book recording it as in 1735, the year following the death of her husband, and in the eighty-fourth year of her age, and the tombstone giving it as 1755, twenty-one years after the death of her husband, and in the seventy-ninth year of her age. By the former statement Thomas Watt would be made out to have been *fourteen* years older than his wife, while by the latter he would be *thirty-four*. Of the two accounts the former is the more probable: besides, the time they are said to have lived in marriage makes the discrepancy still more palpable and even absurd.

We shall, however, hereafter have an opportunity of showing that an *error* has been committed in *renewing* or deepening the figures upon the tomb-stone—an operation which took place in 1808 by the direction of the illustrious grandson of Thomas Watt—by converting the 1735 into 1755, which might inadvertently be done by an inattentive workman.

Court Holden att Craw furdsdyke
the 23 of July 1705 Arch: murchy Baylyie Wm Goes Clk
all & Thomas wait Clk pro tempore. — Curia affirmata legitime

Complanie Wm Goes pror Fishall on Jon Henry Carpenter That wher
=on and or oyr of the days of may last past the said Jon Henry did beat Bruise
=Jain: me not law[ou] for wch the said you ought to be punished according to law to
=the terror of oyrs to comitt the lyke &r &r

The Baylyie having heard & considered the hy boee Jodge
find the same relevant to be proven prowl de jure & therfor
referre the verity of the lybees to each particular defendant[s]
oath &r &r

Archbald Murchie

Tho: Watt. Cloark, pro temps

Att The Manner Place of Cartsburn
The Martinmas Head Court holden there on the 15 of
November 1712 years
        By Thomas Watt   Baylie for this headcourt
The Court Fenced and Rolls called
The 9th day the Fevers Tenents and Subtenents being
called upon lawfull warning &c &c

        Ja Watt   Tho: Watt

Greenock March 23th 1748
        Recived from Mr
William Alaxander full payment
of & above two pounds Leven
Shillings Sterling as full of &
above Act   Ja: Watt

CHAPTER III.

LOCAL EPISODE——EARLY HISTORY OF THE TOWN OF GREENOCK——GREENOCK IN 1592——IN 1635——ROYAL CHARTER CREATING IT A BURGH OF BARONY——EFFORTS OF THE YOUNG BARONY TO SECURE A SHARE OF THE FOREIGN TRADE——JEALOUSY OF THE ROYAL BURGHS——THE BARON AND HIS "FISCHER" PEOPLE——NOT TO BE BAFFLED——STEAL A MARCH ON THE FORBIDDEN PRECINCTS, AND BUILD A SMALL HARBOUR——THE BARON FORTIFIES HIMSELF AGAINST PAINS AND PENALTIES——CONFLICT WITH THE ROYAL BURGHS——SKIRMISH AT PORT-GLASGOW——THE BARON GAINS HIS POINT——FURTHER EFFORTS UNSUCCESSFUL——GREENOCK IN 1700——ITS SHIPPING AND THAT OF CRAW-FORDSDYKE PRIOR TO 1700——SIR JOHN SCHAW RENEWS HIS EFFORTS TO GET A HAR-BOUR BUILT——THE UNION INTERVENES——NO GOVERNMENT HELP——FUNDS RAISED AT HOME——AND A HARBOUR IS BUILT——A PRODIGIOUS WORK FOR THE PERIOD——POPULA-TION OF THE TOWN IN 1740.

WITH the death of the old Mathematician, and, soon after, of his elder son John also, Crawfordsdyke, with its quaint old houses and outside stairs, retires into the background, and our attention comes to be directed to the town of Greenock, whither the Mathematician's younger son, James, after completing his apprenticeship, removes, becomes a useful citizen, and, to us, especially noticeable as "the Father of James Watt." By way of prefacing the more intelligibly such gleanings as we have been able to make respecting the character, habits, and occupations of this worthy progenitor of Watt, as well as of introducing the reader to the bustling little seaport, with its engrossing schemes and plans of improvement, in the centre of which the youthful Inventor was nurtured, and spent considerably more than his boyish days, we crave the indulgence of the reader during the following rapid sketch of the history of this enterprising town, intended as it is to bear directly on the more personal notices which follow, both of the father and of the distinguished son.[1]

From its easy access and safe navigation, as well as the security which it afforded to the small-sized ships of early times, the River Clyde has, even from a remote period, occupied a considerable place in the history of this country. Owing to its having the royal fortress and burgh of Dumbarton on one side, and the ancient royal burgh of Renfrew—the seat of the Stewards of Scotland, the progenitors of its sovereigns—on the other, this beautiful arm of the sea has been the scene of many events of national importance. The town of Greenock, however, does not participate in any of the distinctions acquired by either of these elder seats of authority. Although situated at the distance of only eight miles from the former, and about as many more miles from the latter, it derives no advantage from local or antiquarian associations. It is distinguished by no historical celebrity, such as that which places in the forefront of patriotic valour the otherwise unimportant town of Largs, for example, not far distant. No ruins, serving to record the barbaric grandeur or the sanctity or superstition of a former age, are traceable on its surface or in its vicinity ; and tradition points to no spot rendered memorable among its inhabitants by foreign invasion or domestic feud. Unchronicled and without name

[1] If any justification be deemed necessary in assigning so much space in these Memorials to such historical details, it may be found in the consideration, perhaps, that this local episode, besides affording a characteristic example of the spirit of the times—times which originated great emergencies and called into activity the energies of great minds—is felt to be necessary in some measure to the main subject itself. In reverting also to the early history of distinguished men, and tracing the first bent of their particular genius, it is not unfrequently found, that those ideas, tastes, and habits of thought, which contributed most to the shaping of their after fortunes in life, have been dependent in a powerful degree on the particular character of the scenes, pursuits, and occupations amongst which they were reared, especially when these have been of a lively, energetic, or spirited cast. As it would perhaps be difficult to find an instance of this more to the point than that of Watt himself, it is felt that such details as those alluded to do not bear to be altogether overlooked in a collection of the present nature.

in the annals of bloodshed and of war, its happier guerdon has been to find a place in the page of history, and be pointed to in future times, only in connexion with the birth of genius, the spread and progress of the arts, and the blessings of peace.

The town of Greenock, compared with others which have figured for centuries in history, though they have hardly a name in modern times, is, as it were, but of yesterday. Little more than two hundred and fifty years have elapsed, since, in a royal charter granted by King James VI., and ratified by the Scottish Parliament in 1592, we find the *parish*, for there is no mention of a *town*, of Greenock, spoken of in the following most primitive terms, in relation to the authority granted to "jonne schaw of grenok" to build a *church* for the people on his estate :—The said "jonne schaw of grenok" is given by the charter full power and license, "not onlie on his awin coist to erect and big ane parroch kirk upon his awin heretage, bot als to appoynt and designne mans and yaird to the samyn, w^t the haill proffits and comoditie he hes of tiend belanging to the kirk, for the helpe and supporte of the sustentation of ane minister thairat, sua that the puir pepill duelland vpon his lands and heretage, qlks ar all fischers and of a ressounable nowmer, duelland four myles fra thair parroche kirk, and having ane greit river to pas over to the samyn, may haif an ease in winter seasoun, and better comoditie to convene to Goddis seruice on the Sabboth day, and rest according to Goddis institution."

Still, the village of Grinok as a "harbourie and havening place," possessed points of rare excellence in many important respects. In a sheltered bend of the Frith, which here begins to narrow considerably, backed by an amphitheatre of hills that stretch eastward and westward, and facing the rugged crests of Argyll and the gayer slopes of the opposite shores, lay the "beautiful bay." Its ancient Celtic name of "Grian-aig," so called from its sunny aspect and deeply indented

curve, is suggestive of a locality of great natural beauty.[1] At the
period to which our sketch reverts, it certainly presented charms of
the nature indicated by its name, which the smoke and dust of commerce have since gone far to obliterate, or at least subdue.   Not far
from the beach lay the primitive hamlet, a straggling row of thatched
and low-roofed houses, the dwellings of the Laird's " puir pepill"
alluded to above.   A little further, and beyond, were the boat-way of
the laird, the deer park, the fish-pond, the Church also,[2] with other
appendages of the baronial house ; while behind, embedded in trees,
and on an elevated platform which the eye approached by a succession
of terraced gardens and walks, rose the Mansion itself, described in
the old charters as " the auld castell-steid, castell, tour, fortalice, and
manor place,"—a picturesque enough structure, conspicuous from around
by its high-peaked gables and pointed roofs.   Parks and tall elm
avenues flanked the house, and, stretching away to the woodlands and
hills in the rear, completed the view.   Upon the whole, it is far from
difficult to believe—from traditionary and other credible sources of information on the subject—that the " policies" or pleasure-grounds of

[1] I hold the name *Grian-aig* to be descriptive
of the *Bay*, and not of the *Town* of Greenock, and
to be compounded of two Gaelic words, *grian* the
sun, and *aig* a bay or creek, and this compound,
as thus translated, I take to be the origin of the
name Greenock.   The orthography of the word,
as found in the old Acts of Parliament, is Grinok,
Greinock, and in the records of Presbytery, Grenok.
It was not till about the year 1700, that the word
was written with the double *ee*, Greenock, giving
rise to the fanciful and absurd emblem of a green-
oak, which has been seen on the flags of some of
our ships in the harbour ; and which some sixty
years ago, no doubt under the direction of the
Bailies, emblazoned the brass badges of the town
porters !

[2] *This*, evidently, was the primitive, the original
Kirk of the place, and *not*, as has been erroneously
asserted, the " West Kirk," in the old West burying-ground, though it has now the character of an
interesting ruin.   The earliest discoverable date
connected with this last building, (upon the arch
over the entrance,) as well as that on the oldest
gravestone in the Churchyard, is 1675.   There
were persons living not long ago, who remembered
the ruins of a Church on or near the site lately
occupied by the East parish church.   In such a
locality it would be in convenient proximity to the
Mansion House.   The wall of the " Royal Close"
was the termination of the gardens on that side
belonging to the " auld castill."   It is beyond
question that there *was* here a church of ancient
date, as at no very remote period there was un-
equivocal evidence of a *burying-ground* of limited
extent being there, and it is well known that our
ancestors always buried their dead when they
could within the precincts of the ground attached
to the *Church*.

the ancient family and lairds of Grinok might well have challenged attention, and afforded a view of the elegance and simplicity of feudal life as romantic as it was remote and wild.[1]

Great, however, as might have been the external attractions of the place in point of beauty, nature had formed it with capacities for a higher utility. The "sunny bay," with its easy access and excellent anchorage, was admirably adapted for shipping. And although, perhaps, from time immemorial, neither adventure nor love of gain had tempted the simple "fischers" far beyond the lochs and bays of the western coasts, there were elements, both in the natural position of the place and the history of the times, which were to develop, on the part both of the Laird and his people, an enterprise and an energy hitherto little thought of, or indeed, till then, at all realized in the commerce of feudal Scotland.

Till some time before the union of the two kingdoms the "village of Grinok" had not attained to any such importance as to induce the Kings of Scotland to raise it to the rank of a Royal Burgh. It is true it had, in 1635, made a step in advance in being made a Burgh of Barony, by a royal charter, dated 5th June of that year, and confirmed in the Scots Parliament in 1641. In this charter granted by Charles I., as administrator-in-law to his son Charles, Prince of Scotland, then a minor, in favour of " Johne Schaw of Greinok and Helen Houston his spouse, of all and haill the lands of Wester Greinok Schaw with

---

[1] With regard to the terraces, and to the site generally of Greenock House, a comparative reference is found in the Letters of a traveller of taste and accuracy, Alexander Drummond, Esq., (brother of the distinguished Provost Drummond of Edinburgh,) characterized by Dr. E. D. Clarke, as " *vir haud contemnendus.*" Writing from Leghorn in July 1744, Mr. Drummond observes : "At Canonica we crossed the Adda, and ascended a hill to the town of Vabro. . . . Here the Count de Merci possesses a very beautiful House, that stands upon the top of the hill, with some fine terraced gardens sloping down to the river's side, which yield a delicious prospect to the eye : yet beautiful as this situation is, the House of Greenock would have been infinitely more noble, had it been built according to the original plan, above the terras, with the road opening down to the Harbour :—indeed, in that case, it would have been, perhaps, the most lordly site in Europe."

the auld castell steid," &c., a *novo damus* grant is made " off the toun or village of Greinok in ane frie brugh or barronie, to be callit now and in all tyme cuming the brugh of Greinok." Still, the place, as a burgh of barony only, was by law excluded from any participation in the *foreign* trade in which Scotland was then embarked. The fact however of its being so elevated, small as the advance was, seems to have occasioned some jealousy in the minds of the " Provost, Bailzies, Counsel and communitie of the brugh of Ranfrou," whose representative, John Spreule, protested in parliament that " ane ratification of the charter to the burgh of Greinok be in nae ways prejudiciall to our said brugh liberties and priviledges thereof, conteinit in our antient infeftments as accords of the law"—so early does alarm seem to have been taken at the faint indications of movement on the part of the young Burgh of Barony.

The old Act of the Scots Parliament, passed in 1488, in the reign of James IV., limiting, with such questionable policy, the privileges of foreign trade to the *Royal Burghs*, was to this effect :—" It is statute and ordained that in time to cum all maner of schippes, strangers, and uthers cum to the Kingis free Burrowes, sic as Dumbartane, Irving, Wigtoun, Kirkcudbricht, Renfrew, and utheris free Burrowes of the Realme, and there make their merchandice."

It would appear, however, that this Act—notwithstanding " the paine of tinsel of their lives and gudes," denounced against our " Soveraine Lordis Lieges," and " the paine of tinsel and confiscation of their schip and gudes," denounced against strangers who should " do in the contrair" thereof—had been contravened, as was almost to be expected, by the " unfree" seafaring people and others connected with the west coast of Scotland. For by another Act passed in the reign of Queen Mary, in 1555, described as an Act " Anentis libertie of Merchandes at the West Seas," it is statute and ordained, " That the Acte made be King James the fourth, anentis the cuming of schippes to free Burrowes at the West Seas, bee published of new, and the samin to be put to execution in all poyntes after the form and tenour thereof, and the breakers of the samin to be punished, conform to the paines conteined therein, with this addition, that na person take upon hande to bye onie merchandice fra the saidis strangers, bot fra free-men at free portes of the Burrowes foresaidis, under the paine of confiscation of all the gudes that they bye, togidder with the rest of their moveable gudes, to be applyed to our Soveraine Ladies use, gif they do in the contrair."

Other Acts similar to these, and as exclusive in their enactments, were passed in the reigns of James VI. and Charles I., which, in place of effectually securing to the Royal Burghs the privileges meant to be conferred, and excluding unfree men from a participation in the growing trade of the country, gave rise, as stated by an Act passed in the reign of Charles II., in 1672, " to controversies and debates," and as the same Act proceeds to detail, " to the great disquiet and expenses both of the Royal Burrowes themselves, and other incorporations and people of the Kingdom : which controversies have arisen concerning the extent of the privileges of the Royal Burrows, and how far the ratifications thereof granted by his Majesty and his Royal predecessors, and the estates of parliament, have been derogate and abrogate by contrair custom, or by Infeftments and Priviledges granted by his Majesty and his Royal progenitors." This statute, besides confirming the previous Acts above referred to, " statutes and ordains that if any man not being a free man in the Royal Burrowes, shall be found to have in his possession any goods or commodities, to be bought or sold, exported or imported by him contrair to this present statute, and the priviledge of the Royal Burrowes granted thereby, the saids whole goods shall be escheat—the one half to his Majesty, and the other half to the Burgh apprehender ; and that if the saids goods be apprehended within any of the saids Royal Burrows, or the suburbs, or appendicles belonging to them, or within their ports or harbors, the same may be summarily seized and secured as goods escheat in manner foresaid."

It is matter of strong probability that the young Burgh of Barony had begun to taste the advantages that would accrue to it from engaging in this trade, and to hazard exposure to the sanctions of these Acts. Be this as it may, efforts began seriously to be made by the Laird and his " fischer people" to improve their position. For at the risk of committing a grave feudal offence, in occupying without royal permission " any pairt of the King's domaine and proper lands"—for which offence, " he quha is convict thereof sall be in the King's mercie and punished in his bodie and in all his lands quhilk he halds of him," —even at such a risk, as it would seem, the superior of the Barony, the said Johne Schaw, had taken upon him *to build a small harbour*, and, moreover, to enter upon the forbidden precincts of " the foreign trade."   The step taken was a bold one ; and the stake nothing less than the forfeiture of his estate in the event of failure.

Meanwhile, however, the indefatigable laird was not idle, but set about negotiating for a *second* royal charter, which might fortify him against the pains and penalties he had, already, so audaciously incurred.

This charter was actually granted, in 1670, by Charles II., as Prince Steward of his ancient kingdom of Scotland, in favour of the laird and his son, and was another great step in advance. It fully answered the laird's purpose ; inasmuch as it gave full power to the inhabitants of the burgh of barony of Greinock " then present or to come, to be receaved and admitted *free burgesses* to the said umql. John Schaw and his said sone, and their foresaids, with full power, privilege, and liberty, to buy and sell wine, walx, pitch, tar, &c., and all uther kinde of merchandize, and staple goods, &c.   To whom it should be lawfull to use and exerce their saids airts and trades, als freely as any uther tradesman within this kingdom."

So bold a stroke of policy on the part of the laird was not likely to escape the jealous vigilance of the "Royal Burghs" in the vicinity; and before the *confirmation* of the charter by the Parliament (which was not till 1681) an occurrence of rather a serious nature took place, from the energetic schemes of the laird and his people coming into conflict with the use-and-wont privileges of their ancient neighbours —the royal burghs of Dumbarton, Renfrew, and Glasgow.[1] As the occurrence is highly illustrative of feudal times, as well as of the jealousy with which the young barony began now to be regarded,—of the impolicy and folly also of setting one portion of the population to watch over the other in matters of trade, which was the natural effect indeed of the old royal burgh acts,—we give the original document without abridgment. It was presented to the Lords of Secret Council in 1675, and is as follows:—

"Informatione for the Magistrats of the Royal Burghs of Glasgow, Dumbartane, and Renfrew. 1675. (MS.)

"The toune of Greinok being a burgh of barronie, and lying upon Clyds syde, in q'ch Clyde the saids tounes, and par'lar [particular] the toune of Glasgow are infeft in the haill harbors, creicks, roads, and ports yr'of from Kelvin [foott] to the Clochstone, notwithstanding of the severall acts of Parlia'ts in favors of Royall Burrows,

[1] The Burgh of Glasgow, besides being a Royal Burgh, possessed a jurisdiction, and claimed a right of levying dues on the River Clyde, "from the Burgh to the Cloch stane;" a jurisdiction which, however exercised at the period referred to, now chiefly pertains to the functions of the magistrate styled the "Water Bailie." The Royal Burgh of Dumbarton claimed a jurisdiction, and the right of levying dues in the same river, still more extensive than that of Glasgow, inasmuch, as by a charter obtained "by the said Town of Dumbartane, from King James VI., in the year 1609, they acclaimed the right and privilege of dues in the said river Clyde, solely and wholly to themselves, in so far as that the Town of Glasgow, and merchants therein, ought and should arrive at their burgh, and make entries, and take cocquets—there load, and there make sale of their commodities therein, and should in effect, and by necessar consequence, reside at, and incorporate with the said Town of Dumbartane." It is not known to what extent beyond its privileges as a royal burgh and statutory port, the Town of Renfrew pretended right to levy dues on the river. It is clear, that rights so incompatible in their nature could not well be asserted in good neighbourhood and amity; and "contraversies and debates," as stated in the document from which this information is obtained, arose "daily betwixt them anent the said privileges and dues of the said river."

and the prohibi'nes in them contained against unfrie men traders that are not burgess
of Royall Burrows, hes at their oun hand, to the great prejudice of the saids thrie
Royal Burghs, both exported and imported staple commoditie, q're [by?] the act of
Parliament ffrie men and inhabitants of burghs of barronie are only allowed to retaill,
and because the saids tounes lay at a considerable distance from the s'd toune of
Greinok, the merchants and inhabitants yr'of took the advantage, q'n ther ships came
in they would have repaired and entered in his majesties custome books at Glasgow,
ther wynes and ther salt, and other commodities, and after entering, would have disloadened ther ships in ther oun privat sellars, and disposed thereupon befor ever the
saids tounes could be any wayes advertised; ffor in one night's tyme after entrie they
would have disloadened ther wholl vessells, and put the goods out of the hazard of
seizure be the s'ds Royall Burrows, and greatly diminished his maj. customes; and of
lait the lairds of Grinok, Bannatyne of Kelly, and oy'rs, upon the twentie of July
instant, haveing brought in a vessell loadned wt. salt, wyne and brandie, q'ch is
staple commoditie, and allowed only to burghs royall, the Magistrats of the saids thrie
tounes did send doune to the Road for against the hill of Ardmoir, q'hin the said ship
wes, and finding none w'hin her save some boyes, they did take the said ship loadned
with the s'ds commodities from the said Road into their own harborie at Newark,
and they wer so tender of all persones interest in the said ship, and particularlie of
his majesties interest as to the custome, that they called for thrie waiters, and caused
lock and seall up the hatches; and expecting no invasions be the toune of Greinock,
seeing they had done nothing bot that q'ch be the act of Parlia't they were allowed
for making seizure upon all ships w'hin the bounds of ther burghs, harbories, roads,
ports, and pendicles.   In the night tyme, after the said ship and goods had been in
ther possessione for the space of 12 or 16 houres, the saids lairds of Greinock, James
Bannatyne of Kelly, at the leest the said James himself, with 100 or 150 armed men,
after they had made open a sellar within the said toune of Greinock, q'hin the Earle
of Argyll had a number of fyre locks for the use of the Argyll militia, to arme themselves therewith, and whill the keepers of the said ship were asleep, came with six or
sevin boats loadned wt. the saids men and armes, and ther commanded the persones
that wer akeeping the said ship to render, and in respect they wer refused upon the
accompt that it was the night tyme, and that it was not known what they wer, and
that they might be alsweel robars as any other persones, and fearing that the goods
might be imbazled, and becaus upon the accompt yt. the act of Parlia't in respect
that the owners of the saids goods were not frie men, the entered the s'd ship with the
number of 8, and the rest who did not enter shott and cruellie wounded a number of
the persones that wer in the said ship, and had almost caried the ship away, untill

by Providence the said eight [who] at first entered were turned out of her and the
ship caried to the toune of Dumbartane under the protectione of his maj. castle, ffor
q'ch ryott, both bruising and bleeding, convocating of his majesties lieges with
swords, dirks, gunns, pistolls, and other weapons invasive, the Magistrats of the saids
tounes hes comenced a complaint before your Lo'ps of the Secret Counsell, craveing
that the committers of the ryott, bruisings, blood and batteries, and the convocators
of his maj. leidges in maner above represented, may be punished in ther persones and
goods, and that your Lo'ps upon the accompt of the lawfullness of the forsaid seazure,
may find that the Magistrats of the re'xive burrows have done no wrong in seazing
upon the said ship loadned with staple commoditie of unfrie men, upon the foresaid
road, within ther bounds q'hin they stand infeft; and that yo'r Lo'ps may order ane
to receive the oy'r half of the goods as fallen to his maj. by escheit, seeing be the
very late act of Parlia't, viz., the 5 Act 3 Sessione 2 Parlia't Charles the 2d, all that
burghs in barronie and the inhabitants in them hath of privilege, is only to export
the naturall product of y'r oun manufactories, and as a returne qrof to import timber,
tarr, dealls, and other commodities propper for their own tilladge. But no power to
import the staple commoditie, viz., wyn, wax, and salt, q'ch is left only peculiar to
royall burrows; and be the same act ther is a cleir power given to the said royall
burrows to make seizure upon the ship and goods imported by unfrie men otherwayes.''

It cannot now be ascertained how the collision between the Royal
Burghs and the Burgh of Barony terminated, nor whether any judicial
proceedings of a civil or criminal nature against either party were
instituted. But it occurs that the burghs acting in aggression may
have pushed their pretensions beyond the spirit, if not the letter of
the law. On looking into the Act of Charles II. in 1672, on which
the royal burghs grounded their right of seizure of the goods of un-
freemen, it appears that there was a reservation from the operation
of the Act in favour of " Noblemen, Prelates, *Barones, and others*, of
their privilege of importing any of the saids goods, for the proper use
of themselves and their families allanerly." As the Laird of Greenock
was in the sense of the Act a baron, it might be maintained, and perhaps was maintained successfully by him, that the " salt, wyne, and
brandie," imported in the ship about which the contest took place,

were intended for his own proper use, and that of his neighbour the Laird of Kelly and their families allanerly, and that they had undoubted right to defend their property from a seizure, which, however qualified with the tenderness " of all persons interest in the said ship, and particularlie of his Majesty's interest"—which, by their construction of the law, amounted to one-half of the whole—seems to have been very little short of an act of piracy.

But besides the plea that the Laird of Greenock was a " Baron" in the sense of the Act, he was further fortified in his resistance by his royal charter of 1670, and still more by the confirmation of it in the Scots Parliament in 1681. This charter granted full privileges of foreign trade, and, in addition, renounced the casualty of the forfeiture of his lands which the clear-sighted laird had risked in building his harbour, giving, moreover, " special and full powers to the said umql. John Schaw, and his said sone, and their foresaids, to repair and build *free ports*, *Harbouries*, and *Havening places* upon any part of the ground of the said lands."

We cannot help thinking that considerable diplomacy and tact must have been brought to bear upon the king in securing this royal favour ; and we conjecture that it was the more readily obtained by the laird in gratitude for services rendered by his son to the royal cause at Worcester in 1651, for which gallant conduct in the field he received the honour of knighthood on 3d September of that year ; and in this conjecture we are confirmed by the fact of his having further, in 1687, obtained a baronetcy.

This charter is to be regarded as a great step in advance in the history of the town of Greenock ; as, besides the above privileges of trade, and sanctioning the harbour, &c., it conferred on the laird and his eldest son power " to elect, creat, and input Bailies, Clerks, Sergeants, and other officers needful for governing the said burgh, yearly, in all time thereafter."

Repeated attempts were made subsequently to this, and before the Union, both by the laird and his eldest son, who succeeded him, to obtain further harbour accommodation for the town ; but both died without seeing the accomplishment of their favourite object. The efforts made by them, however, though unsuccessful, were beyond all praise.[1] It was reserved for the grandson—whom, for distinction's sake, we must name the great Sir John, or the good Sir John—the last baronet of the name and family, to carry out his father's and grandfather's desires ; to whom, accordingly, in a signal degree, the community of Greenock is indebted for whatever progress it has made as a town and a harbour.

The nature of the unsuccessful efforts prior to the time to which reference has been made was, to obtain from the Scots Parliament an Act authorizing an impost on the inhabitants for building and repairing the harbour. The near prospect of the Union, however, and the troubles and distractions which then prevailed, together with the influence which the Royal Burghs were enabled to impart to their petty jealousies, at first retarded, and at length effectually prevented a consummation so desirable ; and it was not until the affairs of the nation were, by the Union, placed under the more enlightened and liberal policy of the British Legislature, that Sir John, aided and backed by his feuars, obtained that for the town which its active and enterprising inhabitants so much desired.[2]

[1] Johne Schaw, the Laird of Greenock, who succeeded to the ancient estate of the family in 1620, died in 1679. He was succeeded by his son John Schaw, who, as we have said, received, during his father's lifetime, the honour of knighthood, and was afterwards created a baronet. He died in 1702, and was succeeded by his son, Sir John Schaw, the last who bore the family baronetcy.

[2] The project of the Union was anything but popular in Scotland. It may easily be imagined that Lord Belhaven's celebrated speech in the Scottish Parliament in opposition to this measure, and which was by many considered prophetical, would in no small degree, in some quarters, influence the popular discontent. His lordship had, among many other topics introduced into his speech, made reference to the Royal Burghs of Scotland. "I think," said he, "I see the royal state of boroughs walking their desolate streets, hanging down their heads under disappointments ;

10

It may be interesting here to shew what was the state of the shipping about this time, and previous to the year 1700. An attempt of this kind may be made, although it is almost a solecism to speak of shipping in the plural number, seeing there was only *one* ship, the *John*, belonging wholly to Greenock—the others, viz., "the *George*, the *Nepptoun*, and *Hendrie*, and the two barks and traveller boat," (perhaps the ferry or river passage-boat,) having part-owners in Glasgow. Other "boats and barks"—though too insignificant most likely to have their names recorded—are said to have belonged wholly to Greenock. But first to give a view of the town itself about the year 1700. The following is by Hamilton of Wishaw, in his "Descriptions of the Sheriffdoms of Lanark and Renfrew," compiled about 1710, and printed for the Maitland Club :—

"About two miles down from Newark, upon the river of Clyde, is the house, town, and parish of Greenock. This parish is of no old erection. But the lairds of Greenock having given incouragement to build, leave, and inhabite there, that the town so increased as the laird was incouraged to build ane church there ; and gott severall lands disjoyned from neighbouring parishes, which makes up this parish of Greenock." [" Mr. John Layng, Minister at Greenock," appears in "1616." (Commissary Record, Glasgow.) He deceased there "in the moneth of Februar, 1639 years." Testament confirmed, December 25, following. (Ibid.) The inventory of his effects is "maid and gevin vp be Mr. James Lang, his eldest lawfull sone,

wormed out of all the branches of their old trade ; uncertain what hand to turn to." And again : "I think I see the honest industrious tradesman, loaded with new taxes and impositions, disappointed of the equivalents, drinking *water* in place of *ale*, eating his saltless pottage, petitioning for encouragement to his manufactories, and answered by counter petitions." The managers of the funds of the town of Greenock, however, appear to have taken courage at the prospect which was opening up to them ; as, within little more than twenty years after the Union, they *voluntarily* assessed themselves on *their ale*—of which, whatever became of that of the Royal Burghs, they had not been deprived—and subsequently obtained an Act of Parliament to make what was a voluntary act obligatory by statute.

and ex'r dative."] "And the town of Greenock is now erected in ane burgh of barronie;—hath ane good harbour for vessels, and is become a place of considerable trade, and is like more and more to increase, as specially if the herring fishing continue in the river of Clyde : for as that fishing necessarily follows the sweaming of the herring, so when they sweam in Clyde, or in the lochs adjoyning to it, as frequently they doe toward the end of the year, it occasions a confluence of many thousands of people to these pairts, which yearly continowes a considerable space.

"The last Laird of Greenock, Sir John Schaw, did wonderfully augment his fortune, so as he left one of the best gentlemen's estate to his sone in all that country.

"This family of Greenock is descended, not many ages since, of the family of Sawchy in Clackmananshyre, and is repute the next heir male of that family : and he hath lately purchased the estate of Sawchie. Ther is very expensive works lately built about the house, gardens, and parks of Greenock, which exceadingly beautify the place ; and he hath singularly repaired and beautifyed the church.

"Near to the town of Greenock is the town of Carsedyke, lyand upon the river of Clyde, a litle to the east of Greenock. It is erected in a burgh of barrony, and hath a very convenient harbour for vessells. It belongs to the Laird of Carseburn, Crawford, who is brother-sone to the Laird of Jordanhill, who hath a convenient house and dwelling ther, att Carseburn. The town is mostly subfewed to merchands, seamen, or loading-men, who have built very good houses in it, and is a very thriving litle place."

With regard to the *Shipping* of Greenock at this period. In the year 1700, the Commissioners of Supply of the Shire of Renfrew presented a "Report of the unfree traders' offers within the Sheriffdom of Renfrew to the Commission of the Scots Parliament for settling the communication of trade. The offers so made were to relieve the Royal Burghs of a

certain proportion of the cess laid upon them by the Legislature for
the privilege of trade.   Among others, " Sir John Schaw of Greenock
offered fyve shilling Scots, for freedome, as is above specified, to himself and tennants wt'in his haill lands belonging to him and inhabitants
of the Toune of Greenock."   " Item, James Tailzeour, merchant in
Craufurdsdyck, for himself, and in name of the town of Craufurdsdyck,
and the Laird of Cartsburn, his tennants in Greenock, for the freedom
above wryten, offered eighteen pennies Scots money."   To the offers
so made, the Provost of Renfrew, the only Royal Burgh in the county,
appeared, and objected that the offers made by " Sir John Schaw for
himself, vassals, tennants, and possessors," and by " James Tailzeour
for himself, and in name of the inhabitants of Craufurdsdyck, were
not proportionable to their rexive (respective) trade, and offered to
adduce probatione for that effect, and craved a competent dyet might
be assigned to him thereanent ; and for that effect the saide Commissioners appoynted Tewsday nixt thereafter, and granted warrand
for diligence against witnesses for that effect."

Accordingly, " on the threttie day of Aprile, 1700," certain witnesses
were examined at Paisley, before Sir John Maxwell, Lord Justice
Clerk, and other proprietors.   The depositions relating to Greenock
and Crawfordsdyke are as follows :—

" Compeared, Allan Speir, Bailie in Greenock, aged 40 years, married, who being
solemly sworne, purged, and interrogate—Depones, that there is ane ship called the
Nepptoun, that, as he hears, belongs to Greenock and Crawfordsdyck, but doth not
know what pt. thereof belongs to each of the saids towns and inhabitants thereof.
Depones also, that there is ane called the John that is called ane Greenock shipe, but
knows not whether there be any other partners thairin or not that dwells in any other
towne or not.   Depones also, that there is ane shipe called the George, qr'of Robert
M'Clearie is master, but that ane pt. of her belongs to Glasgow ; and in lyck manner,
that there is ane other called the Hendrie, and that ane great part thereof belongs to
Glasgow.   Depones also, that there is ane bark that is reported to belong to William
Rowand, but knows not whether there be any partners in her that resids elswhere ;

and also that there is ane other bark that is said to pertaine to James Johnstone. Depones also, that there is ane travellar boat that is sd. to belong to James Rankine. Depones this to be trueth, as he shall answer to God.   Sic subscribetur, Allan Speir, Jo. Maxwell.   Wm. Tarbat, Clk."

"Compeared, Alexr. Mitchell, mert. in Greenock, unmarried, aged 22 years or thairby, who being solemly sworne, purged, and examined—Depones, that their is ane shippe called the John that is said to belong *wholly* to the inhabitants of Greenock, as als the George, Nepptoune, and Hendrie, and the two barks and the travellar boat, contained in the preceding deposition, but that it is reported that the partners in them are Glasgow people ; to wit, the partners of some parts of the sds shipes is said to belong to Glasgow, and the boats and barks wholly to Greenock ; and this to be trueth, as he should answer to God.   Sic subscribetur, Alexr. Mitchell, Jo. Maxwell. Wm. Tarbat, Clk."

To return from this digression.   In 1702, Sir John Schaw—whom for distinction's sake we have called the great or the good Sir John— prosecuted, before the Scottish Legislature, his favourite scheme of having a proper harbour at Greenock ; and although meeting with small encouragement, from the causes before alluded to, he was yet far from abandoning an object so important to the welfare of the community.   He resolved to act independently of public aid.   A mutual contract was entered into with his *feuars*, according to which each party agreed to *advance money* to be employed in defraying the cost of the projected Harbour.   It is much to be regretted that this contract of 1703 is not extant, as a monument at once of the patriotism of Sir John, and the public spirit and energy of the town of Greenock.[1]

[1] Although the year 1705 is generally assigned as the period about which the Superior and the inhabitants began to raise money by voluntary subscription, there is evidence, in two of the bonds or money obligations granted at the time, that a regular contract had been entered into between Sir John and the feuars, in the year 1703. It is referred to in a bond or obligation granted to Sir John, by Allan Speir, treasurer of the fund for building the New Harbour, for one thousand merks, Scots money, advanced by Sir John, "to be instantlie and forthwith applied for the erection and use of the *new harbour* of Greenock, conform to ane mutual contract, betwixt the said Sir John Schaw and the feuars of Greenock, dated the —— day of ——, 1703 years." The date of the bond or obligation itself, is 25th May 1705, and on the back of it there is a regular discharge of the money, signed by Sir John, on 22d November 1720. On 28th February 1707, Sir John made another ad-

No materials exist, that we are aware of, from which to state the extent and description of the *original* harbour, constructed by the Laird of Greenock in 1670, by the daring stroke of policy already adverted to, failure in which would have cost him the forfeiture of his estates to the crown. Nor have we found any materials from which to describe the works, if there were any undertaken between the last mentioned date and 1703, when the *new* Harbour was resolved on. Of the progress of the works connected with this, for the time great undertaking, no record exists. It is known, however, that they embraced an area of 8 acres, 3 roods, and 10 falls, comprehended within two projecting piers, called the East and West Quay—a projecting tongue in the centre, called the Mid Quay, dividing the harbour into two corresponding divisions. The form of these works is shown on a small, but sufficiently distinct scale, on John Watt's Map of the Clyde, constructed in 1734 ; although, at that date, the breastworks connecting the quays had not been completed. In the interesting view of the town, however, taken in 1768, which we have the pleasure of preserving in our pages, the new harbour is seen in its finished state.

Such was Greenock as a Seaport some years subsequent to the period when James Watt's father first entered upon office in the little community. The sketch serves to bring the reader *au courant* of our subsequent memorials.

The new Harbour was a formidable work for those days—the greatest undertaking of its kind at that time in Scotland ; yet accomplished with indomitable perseverance, at a cost of more than 100,000 merks Scots. Diminutive as it is now to be considered, in comparison

---

vance of seven hundred and fifty-two pounds twelve shillings Scots. In 1710, 20th April, he made another advance of two thousand merks Scots; and on 25th of September 1714, he made a further advance of two thousand four hundred and thirty-nine pounds twelve shillings and three pennies Scots, all for the purpose of constructing the said New Harbour.

Lithographed for the Watt Club, 1856. by Schenck & M:Farlane, Edinburgh.

A View of

Academy Glasgow 1768 Rob.ᵗ Paul del. & sculp.

reenocke 1768.

with more modern erections in its neighbourhood, it had the merit of leading the way to the more perfect and magnificent structures which soon began to engage the skill of the most eminent Engineers in different parts of the country. It is said that the magnitude of the debt incurred at first alarmed the good people of the town. But such was the effect of the new works in increasing the trade and population of the place, that the assessment and port dues cleared off the whole obligation before 1740, and left, in that year, a clear surplus of 27,000 marks, or £1500 sterling, to be expended in further local improvements, which then became very necessary. The population of Greenock at this time, according to an enumeration of the inhabitants made in 1740, was about 3000 souls : namely, above eight years of age, 2433 ; under that age, 550.

CHAPTER IV.

FATHER OF JAMES WATT——HOUSE IN WHICH HE SERVED HIS APPRENTICESHIP——HIS
MARRIAGE——FIRST PUBLIC NOTICE OF HIM——PURCHASES PROPERTY IN GREENOCK——
EARLY SUCCESS IN BUSINESS——EXTENDED NATURE OF HIS BUSINESS OCCUPATIONS——
HIS FIRST PUBLIC OFFICE——GREENOCK UNDER THE FEUDAL RÉGIME, FROM 1635 TO
1741——MR. WATT'S MUNICIPAL ELEVATION UNDER THE NEW CONSTITUTION——VOTE OF
THANKS ON HIS RESIGNATION, IN HIS SEVENTY-SIXTH YEAR.

RESUMING now our notices of James, the younger son of the old
Mathematician, tradition supplies little or no information respecting
him during the period of his indenture, or indeed till some years
after that had expired.[1]   All that we have from this source consists
in our having had, many years ago, pointed out, as " the place where
he served his apprenticeship," a ruinous house situated on the north

---

[1] It is much to be regretted that, with the fullest desire to portray the " Father of James
Watt" with minutest circumstantiality, and, in
so doing, to render some clear representation of
the habits and principles of him who was honoured
by so near a relation to so great a man, to one
whose life was not more remarkable for its intellectual acumen than for the genuineness of its
virtues, and the dignity of its moral tone,—the
materials for such a purpose are, after exhausting
every source of information, really so scanty and
imperfect. It is attributable, no doubt, to the
fact of his life having worn the same private and
unassuming aspect, from its outset to its close,
even long after industry and personal worth had
raised him to credit, moderate fortune, and the
expressed regard and gratitude of his fellow-
townsmen and friends. Still, there is room for

something being said of the bearing which his
life is found to have upon several points in his
eminent son's history. It was the pious tribute
of that son to the memory of his father, as appears
from the inscription on his tombstone, that " HE
WAS A BENEVOLENT AND INGENIOUS MAN, AND A
ZEALOUS PROMOTER OF THE IMPROVEMENTS OF THE
TOWN." Some vindication of the simple eulogium
is in a measure imposed on the chronicler. If,
with the materials at his disposal, he should be
enabled, in any degree, to accomplish this, at
least, the " gentle reader" will doubtless sympa-
thize with him in the discharge of a task, which,
apart from some such consideration, might really
prove to the one as tedious, as it is in fact felt by
the other to be barren in a great degree of the
usually coveted attractions.

side of the High Street of Crawfordsdyke, having a window to the front, on the lintel of which were carved, in rude but bold relief, three dead-eyes, a pair of compasses, and a square or rule, with the initial letters, I. H. — A. R., and, underneath, the numeral figures 1677. The carved figures evidently indicated premises that had been occupied, and probably been built, by a shipwright and builder ; the letters being, doubtless, according to a custom at one time very prevalent, the initials of the builder and occupier of the house, and those of his spouse.   It is very probable that in the matter of " the House" tradition is here correct ; as it is undoubted that our young craftsman did acquire a practical knowledge of the multiform branches of business of which the above carved figures are the symbols,—the dead-eyes representing the making of " blocks," in those times an essential part of ship-carpentry ; though now, according to the well-defined laws of the " division of labour," in itself a distinct and separate art.

It is not ascertained exactly at what time James married.   There is reason, however, to believe that this took place about the year 1728 or 1729, when in his thirtieth or thirty-first year ;[1] and it is not unlikely that to the same date is to be referred his removal to Greenock. A document in our possession shows, that, as early at least as 1731, he occupied part of a tenement in this town as his dwelling-house, the house, in fact—now unfortunately no longer existing, having been long ago pulled down to make way for larger buildings,—in which his illustrious son a few years later than this date [1736] was born.

Although, with his young partner, he had removed from under the

[1] In the register of births in the Old or West Parish of Greenock, there is the following entry of the birth and baptism of the father of James Watt :—

" February 3d, 1699.—James, lawful son to Thomas Watt, mathematician in Cardsdyke, and Marg. Shearer, was born Jan. 28, and baptized Feb. 5, as witness, James Hill, son to James Hill, mert. (merchant) in Greenock, and Joseph Rankin, son to Thomas Rankin, mert. there.

" James Hill, witness.

" Joseph Rankin, witness."

11

paternal roof in Crawfordsdyke, there is at the same time little doubt
that James enjoyed, until the death of the old Mathematician, all that
the presence and society of that estimable parent could afford of
advice and example, and that he imbibed much of his father's spirit,
and no inconsiderable portion of his taste for science,—acquisitions
which afterwards proved extremely useful to him, and were made
available in a practical manner, when he came to feel his own
independence, and to take an active part in the public affairs of
his time. Probably the sage old man had, during his life, had the
guiding hand in whatever concerned the interests of his son. James
himself, however, in due time begins to act, and create for himself a
position.

It is perhaps only a coincidence of slight moment that this turning
point in his life takes place in the same year with his father's death.
However this may be, a document still extant, bearing the date
" November 1734," and having reference consequently to this period
of his life, indicates clearly his intelligent activity at this time.   The
paper referred to is one relating to an Incorporation or Society of a
benevolent nature, connected with the craft of which he was a member.
It purports to be the Regulations of an association formed three years
before, having for its object the raising of a fund for the relief of
decayed Members, and of the widows and children of such of them as
might fall into poverty.[1]   At the beginning of the document, and in
the handwriting of another, probably the person who acted as Clerk
to the Association, stand the words, " James Watt, Preses ;" showing
that even then he was the leading member, and had attained to
some degree of consideration among his fellows.   Ten individuals

---

[1] This Association, it would appear, was under
the patronage of Sir John Schaw, the feudal
superior of the town; and his bailies were wont
to be appealed to when necessary, for the judicial
enforcement of the obligations come under by
the parties to its laws. The paper, of the date
referred to, is in the handwriting of our young
craftsman, which is easily recognised.

subscribe the paper, and among these is the ordinary signature, "James Watt."[1]

The institution of this benevolent society connected with the business to which he had been devoted, is the first public act, so far as can be traced, of the Father of James Watt, and is as creditable as it is characteristic. He seems to have entered upon active life with commendable resolution, yet not without the proportionate prudence and sagacity which his excellent previous training would lead us to anticipate. Shortly before the death of his mother, having left Crawfordsdyke, as has been shewn, and gone to reside in Greenock, he, on 17th May 1734, three months after his father's decease, purchased a house and piece of ground close to the sea, one of the oldest feus in the town of Greenock, the original title bearing the date, "2d August 1682."[2] Two years afterwards the premises were enlarged by the purchase of additional ground from Sir John Schaw, with liberty, as the charter states, to the "said James Watt and his foresaids, to edify, build, and repair the foresaid tenement of land and others above mentioned, and to build office-houses upon any part of the ground, close, or weir, and additional ground above disposed." It may be mentioned here that on 10th August 1774, he conveyed this property to his son, "James Watt, junior," the great engineer, who thus became a Freeholder in his native town.[3]

There is evidence of an incidental kind, occurring in the Records of the parish of Greenock, 28th August 1740, where "James Watt's apprentice" happens to be mentioned, which goes to prove that the

[1] In the following year, 1735, the regulations so drawn up were put into technical phraseology and form by John Alexander, Sir John's law agent, and one of his bailies for the barony.

[2] This property is situated in what was then called the High Street, opposite to the foot of Longwell Close, and is described in the charter as "a tenement of land, yard, weir, and others."

[3] The property now belongs to the heirs of Gabriel James Weir, some time one of the magistrates of Greenock.

" Preses of the Wrights' Society" must have entered into business shortly after the expiry of his own indentures.   This he might be enabled easily to do, having come into the possession of considerable property in consequence of the death of his brother John.   While, on the other hand, his native good sense, his ingenuity, and the thorough knowledge he possessed of all the branches of his craft, seem at once to have secured to him extensive employment and influence ; as, only five years after his first establishment in life, he was called to hold office, as one of " the most wise, substantial, and best qualified of the burgh,"—that is, to be one of the nine Trustees who were appointed by the feudal superior, Sir John Schaw, for the management of the town funds.   Sir John, before his death, employed him in enlarging the western front of the Mansion House of Greenock, and the substantiality of the work evinces to the present day the fidelity with which the contractor discharged his duty.[1]   He was fortunate also in falling upon a period of great and almost universal activity,—an activity in which some of the details given in last chapter prove the town of Greenock to have largely participated.   Mr. Watt's business, accordingly, grew with the increasing trade of the place, which he no doubt contributed his due proportion of means and influence to foster. So much so, that although setting out originally as a builder and contractor, in which capacity he was frequently engaged on the public works then so spiritedly undertaken by the town, it is under the designation of " Merchant," that he afterwards comes to be generally referred to in the public documents of the time.   This designation, it seems, is to be understood in its widest sense ; for, besides his posses-

---

[1] In what particular year this enlargement took place, although it forms the most modern as well as most considerable portion of the present building, does not appear. A niche, evidently intended to contain a date, above the front entrance was never filled up. The original edifice, described in the old royal charter of 1635, as " the auld castell-steid, castell, tour, fortalice, and manor place new buildit," was probably a more imposing structure than the present remains would lead one to infer. A considerable addition was made to it, as would appear from the date on a door-lintel over the *south* entrance, in 1674.

sion of property in ships, and engaging in foreign mercantile transactions, his daily business appears to have embraced a set of occupations
natural enough, no doubt, in a young seafaring community, yet so
manifold, so seemingly heterogeneous, that it is not easy either to
enumerate them or specify what they exactly were.[1] To some of
them, however, his workshops, for example, we shall have occasion
afterwards more particularly to refer, when we come to speak of the
youthful occupations of the wonderful James.

Into his conduct in public affairs, Mr. Watt seems to have carried
much of the prudence and sagacity so largely inherited from his
venerable father, the Professor of the Mathematics, and to have been
a most useful member of the community in all undertakings of a
public nature, where such qualities, added to his practical knowledge
and sterling integrity, were essential. Having been in office under
the old or feudal régime, as well as afterwards, under that more liberal
constitution to which in the course of time it gave way, it may not be
without interest to some of our readers to have in this place some
short account of the more ancient regulation under which the affairs
of the burgh were ordered.

During the long period which intervened between the granting of
the first royal charter in 1635, and the year 1741—a period of 106
years—the village or town of Greenock had been under a system of
government completely feudal in its character. The superior, in his
own person, or by a bailie of his own appointment, and removable by
him at pleasure—the office so frequently held by Thomas Watt in the

---

[1] As illustrative of this, an account I find
rendered by him, against the town, is for all
sorts of work and furnishings supplied by him,
even to the article of "*spoons for soldiers*,"—
for the six years between 1769 and 1775, which
account, with interest, and £25, 12s. 0¼d., a
balance due to him as town-treasurer, amounted
to £227, 13s. 4¾d. We notice this account, more
especially, from the circumstance of its showing
his son—who is described as " James Watt,
engineer, late of Glasgow, now in Birmingham,
as having factory and commission from the said
James Watt, his father,"—to have subscribed the
discharge granted for the amount to the town,
22d July 1776.

barony of Crawfordsdyke—exercised within the burgh *all* jurisdiction, civil and criminal, competent under his grants from the crown, as well as administered its financial concerns. The *inhabitants* had no recognised right independent of the feudal laird.[1] Such a state of things, it may be readily supposed, was far from favourable to the development of local enterprise, and a change of policy began to be felt expedient on the part of the superior himself. Actuated by a liberal spirit, and encouraged by the growing trade of the place, which had received an impetus from at length freely participating in the "foreign trade," and from the general commercial activity consequent on the Union with England, Sir John Schaw divested himself of a portion of his exclusive right to levy and manage the revenues of the burgh; and by a charter, dated 30th January 1741, conferred on the *inhabitants themselves* privileges in this respect, which, though still very limited, were, in some essential points, of a positive kind. This charter purports to be " for the better government and management of the public funds allenarly [exclusively] that has arisen, or may arise from any assessment laid on by the inhabitants of the said burgh, *with my consent, on themselves,* on all malt grounded at the mills of westward Greenock." It then proceeds to give authority to the feuars and subfeuars, " to appoint *nine of the most wise, substantial, and best qualified of the burgh of Greenock, being feuars,* (the Bailie, or Bailies of the Barony for the time being, that shall be appointed and chosen by me, being of the said number of nine,) *to be managers and administrators* of the whole public funds already belonging to the said burgh and

---

[1] The *immediate* management of the funds raised for the public wants of the burgh, from whatever sources derived, was placed by the superior in the hands of an officer *of his own appointment,* called a Collector; besides whom there were other officials styled Examiners, who took an oversight of the public accounts. An account current is extant, made up in 1730, between Andrew Lang, as *Collector* of the harbour funds, and the town of Greenock, docketed by a quorum of the *Examiners* of the town accounts, and subscribed by John Alexander, John Hood, and others. Another account exists, made up to 10th April 1736, the docket of which bears the account to be subscribed by the " Bailies and Managers."

barony, or which shall hereafter pertain or belong to the same," &c.
The purpose for which the assessment was to be raised, was, by the
charter, with extreme and scrupulous exactness stated to be "exclusively for the support of the public use and benefit of the said burgh.[1]"

It cannot fail to be remarked, in passing, how very limited, after
all, and anxiously defined are some of the powers granted by this
charter, which was intended to be a great boon. Nor is it easy for
us in these days to construe into a *privilege* what to us appears to have
amounted to little more than a *permission* to the inhabitants to *assess
themselves*. It can only be regarded as exemplifying the tenacity with
which—even in the case of a liberal and patriotic superior, as Sir John
unquestionably was—ancient feudal prerogative was clung to, and the
reluctance with which even an inconsiderable portion of it was
parted with.

As was to be anticipated, perhaps, the "voluntary assessment" but
indifferently answered the purpose intended, and recourse was had to
another measure. Great plans of improvement for the port and town
were in contemplation. The Harbour was to be cleansed, other works
connected therewith were to be undertaken ; a Church was to be built,
a Town-house, Schools, Market-places, were to be erected. It is to be
observed that up to this time the entire amount of the large sums of

---

[1] An account kept by the treasurer under the charter 1741, is still existing. It is the earliest, following the granting of the Charter which has been consulted, and is titled "The account of Gabriel Lang's debursements and receivings as treasurer of Greenock, from Candlemas 1749, to September 1751, a period of two years and seven months." The gross revenue within that period was £922, 9s. 6d., arising from the seat-rents of the new church, dues for grinding malt at the mill, and storage of tobacco at the Royal Close, the community being then lessees from the city of Glasgow, at an annual rent of £10, of the premises long known as the Royal Close, on the site of which the large tenement in Rue End Street, called Ewing's buildings, is now erected. The treasurer's account appears to have been accurately and neatly kept, and occasion shall be taken to refer to some of its most curious items, as illustrative of the manners of the worthy managers and administrators of the public funds.

A balance or surplus revenue of £23, 18s. 3½d., arising upon the account, was paid over by the treasurer Gabriel Lang in 1753, to his successor Gabriel Mathie, and a farther ascertained balance of 19s. 2d. was paid over to "James Watt," who is therein described "present Treasurer in Greenock," on 12th February 1756.

money expended upon the Harbour and public works of the town
had been furnished jointly by Sir John, the feuars, sub-feuars, and
inhabitants, (in the case of the latter, by voluntary assessment on
themselves,) *without any aid from Parliament.*   It was now, however,
resolved, with the approbation of Sir John, to make an application to
the Legislature.   Parliament was accordingly appealed to, and the Act
24 Geo. II. was obtained, giving them power to lay an imposition or
duty on every pint of " Ale or Beer brewed, brought in, tapped or sold
within the town of Greenock."   As this was the first enactment made
by the Legislature in reference to the affairs of the town, and as its
preamble gives a view of the public works and improvements at the
time projected, it is inserted here without abridgment :—

" Whereas, the town of Greenock is very advantageously situated on the river
Clyde for carrying on both foreign and coasting trade ; and whereas the Superior of
the said town, with the Inhabitants thereof, did about the year *one thousand seven
hundred and five,* begin to raise money by a voluntary subscription for building a
Harbour there, and some progress hath from time to time been made in erecting of
the same, which, if completed, would be of great advantage to the said Town, and to
the trade and navigation of those parts ; but the produce of the said subscription has
been found insufficient to answer that purpose, and to defray the expense of cleansing
the said Harbour, and of performing other works in relation thereto, which are absolutely
necessary to be done, to render the said Harbour useful and commodious : And, whereas,
the building of a new Church, Town-house, Poor and School-houses, and also Market
places for meal and flesh, and also of a publick Clock, are extremely necessary, and
much wanted within the said Town, but the inhabitants thereof are not able to raise
money to answer the expense thereof, nor to complete the said Harbour, and to keep
all the said Clocks in repair, without the aid of Parliament, the Managers of the said
Town of Greenock's funds, and the other Inhabitants of the said Town and Baronies
of Easter and Wester Geeenock and Finnart, with the approbation and consent of Sir
John Schaw of Greenock, Baronet, proprietor of the said Baronies and Superior of the
said Town, do therefore most humbly beseech your Majesty that it be enacted, and be
it enacted by the King's most excellent Majesty, by and with the advice and consent
of the Lords Spiritual and Temporal, and Commons, in this present Parliament
assembled, and by the authority of the same, That from and after the first day of

June, *one thousand seven hundred and fifty-one,* for the term of *thirty-one years,* and
to the end of the then next session of Parliament, there shall be laid an imposition or
duty of two pennies Scots, or one-sixth part of a penny sterling, (over and above the
duty of Excise paid or payable to his Majesty, his heirs and successors,) upon every
Scots pint of ale and beer that shall be either brewed, brought in, tapped, or sold
within the said Town of Greenock, and Baronies of Easter and Wester Greenock and
Finnart, or the liberties thereof; and that the said imposition or duty shall be paid
or made payable by the brewers for sale, or venders, or sellers of all such ale and beer,
to John Alexander, Writer and present Baillie, Robert Donald, Robert Rae, James
Warden, Gabriel Mathie, William Gemmel, James Watt, and James Butcher,
Merchants, and Nathan Wilson, Surgeon, of the Town of Greenock, who are hereby
nominated and appointed Trustees for cleaning, deepening, building, and repairing of
the said Harbour and Piers, and for building a new Church, Town-house, Poor and
School-houses, and Market places, and also a publick Clock, and also for putting in
execution all other the powers in and by this act given."[1]

From the increasing importance of the place in population and
trade, as well as from the steady decline of the old feudal notions

[1] It is curious to observe how cautious, or it should be rather said how distrustful, the Superior and the Legislature were of the people of the Town of Greenock in regard to the management of their own affairs. To guard against "any misapplication of the monies" (so the act has it) "arising by the said act, or any other abuses of the powers and authorities hereby given the said Trustees," four noblemen, and ten non-resident gentlemen, with Sir John Schaw, and the Member for the county, were appointed "*overseers* of the said duty, and the receipts and disbursements thereof;" and these "overseers" had power by the Statute to deprive or displace any trustee, and to elect and appoint another in his room.

I have no means of stating positively who the *managers* were under the *Charter* 1741; but as they were nine in number, and as the *trustees* who were appointed under the *Act of Parliament* were also nine, the probability is, that the trustees under the one, and the managers under the other, were identical. Mr. Watt, we see, from the preamble just cited, was a "Trustee" under the Act, and, as a consequence, if my conjecture is right,

a "Manager" under the Charter. Certain it is, that while holding the office of a trustee, he acted for some time as "Treasurer" of *both* funds. The office of treasurer being then as now, purely honorary, the duties were performed by deputy. One of the accounts kept by the treasurer of these funds has been consulted. It is titled, "James Watt, and Gabriel Lang, his depute-treasurer and cashier, to the Managers and Trustees of the Town of Greenock, funds in account current for their intromission for the said funds during their treasurership, from the second Monday of September 1759, to the second Monday of September 1760." The produce of these funds for the year, including a balance from the previous year of £80, 11s. 7½d., was, from the old funds under the charter 1741, . . . £351 15 5½
And from the duty upon ale under the statute, . . 145 13 11

Making a total of £497 9 4½

The free available balance on this account for general purposes, was £236, 15s. 8½d.

12

which had so long prevailed,—the " most wise and substantial men of
the burgh" proving themselves also, no doubt, as trustworthy as they
were competent, Sir John soon saw it requisite to act upon more
liberal principles than either he himself or the Legislature had hitherto felt constrained to recognise.   He accordingly granted two new
charters to the town in 1751,[1] which we do not deem it necessary
here to specify more particularly than to remark, that the last of
them was of a nature so liberal as to leave little to be desired in
respect of the powers and privileges it secured to the community.   It
was, in fact, that under which the town was brought to the state of
prosperity in which the Reform Bill in 1832 found it.   This charter,

---

[1] A Memorial on behalf of the Magistrates,
Town-Council, and community of Greenock, was
about this time presented to Lord Cathcart,
(who had acquired part of the estate of Greenock
through Marion Schaw, his grandmother, and
only daughter of Sir John Schaw,) soliciting the
exercise of his Lordship's influence with the
Commissioners of Customs and Board of Exche-
quer, for legalizing the West and Mid Quays.
The East Quay had been licensed about 1714, the
year in which Greenock had been " made a member of the port of Port-Glasgow," the latter being
at that time the seat of the chief officer of Customs.   As one of the paragraphs of the memorial
gives a view of the extent and kind of trade
carried on in Greenock a hundred years ago, it
may not be uninteresting here.   " For some
years," the document referred to states, " after
the said three quays were built, the trade from
the river of Clyde to the American colonies did
not take place; and was for several years after
the union of the two kingdoms but in its infancy,
so that the necessity of declaring the Mid and
West piers legal ones was not near so great as it
has become for some years past, in which period,
with pleasure it must be remarked, that the American trade, from the river of Clyde in general,
and with it the trade of Greenock in particular,
has so much increased that there has not been
less than betwixt six and eight thousand hogs-
heads of tobacco imported annually at Greenock
by the merchants in Glasgow and others, which
importation does of necessity, not only create a
considerable exportation thereof, but also there
consequently follows an almost continual shipping
of great quantities of our home manufactures
for purchasing the said tobacco; and not only
the goods necessary for purchasing the tobacco
brought to Greenock, but the greatest part of the
goods for those that come to Port-Glasgow, are
shipt off at Greenock; the ships choosing for
conveniency to fall down the river from Port-
Glasgow to Greenock, and there take on board
the bulk of their outward cargo of goods.   The
herring trade, to the extent of several hundred
lasts yearly, is carried on at Greenock, from
whence they are not only exported, but the returns thereof centres all at this port: and, besides
the returns of the herrings, which is for the most
part in iron and deals, there are considerable
quantities of these commodities imported from
Gottenburgh and elsewhere.   The importation
of timber and deals from Norway is very noticeable, and salt from France, Spain, and Portugal
is no less so; so that from the whole the revenue
of the customs at Greenock through the year
must be something very considerable."

dated 2d September 1751, provided that the nine trustees appointed under the Act of George II., and their successors in office, during the thirty-one years of the Act's duration, were to have the government of the town, and the management of its funds,—two of them to be Bailies, one to be Treasurer, and the other six to be Councillors. After the expiry of the specified thirty-one years, the method of election, as the charter sets forth, was to be by each feuar, subfeuar, and burgess present, giving in to the Clerk a list signed by him, of the persons to be removed out of the Council, and of those he elects and chooses in their room. Nine was still to be the number of the body composing the Magistrates and Council.[1]

Under this new municipal constitution, which came into operation 9th September 1751, Mr. Watt was, from a trustee, promoted to the status of councillor. Four years later [15th September 1755] he was chosen treasurer of the burgh; and in 1757 raised to the office of Bailie or Magistrate.[2] His colleague in office, Mr. John Alexander, who was senior bailie, having died in 1759, Mr. Watt remained sole magistrate till the next election on 10th September of that year; on which occasion a majority of the votes of the feuars were tendered for his advancement to the office of chief magistrate—a fact sufficiently demonstrating the confidence reposed by his fellow-townsmen

[1] No burgess was ever created; consequently, the constituency before the Reform Act was composed alone of the feuars and subfeuars—the former being such as had their feus from the heirs of entail of the estate of Greenock; the latter, those who held their feus from Lord Cathcart.

Whatever benefits other towns may have derived from the Reform Bill, Greenock, perhaps, of all the constituencies in Scotland, may be said to have obtained the smallest number from that measure, beyond and in addition to those the community had already enjoyed for *eighty years* anterior to that Act—with the sole exception of their power to elect a Member to serve in Parliament, undoubtedly a very great boon. The constituency of Greenock, at the time of the passing of the Reform Act, was, so far as we are aware, the most numerous in Scotland, and enjoyed a franchise so extended, that it has not been surpassed by the more recent privileges, whether in regard to municipal elections, or to the choice of representatives to Parliament.

[2] As there were only two bailies under the charter of 1751, they were usually distinguished as *senior* and *junior* magistrate, according to seniority of election. Mr. Watt was junior magistrate.

in his wisdom and integrity. He declined however to accept the
proffered honour, for reasons which he assigned; but again took
office as treasurer, to the honorary functions of which, as it was by
the charter declared to be annual, he was afterwards repeatedly re-
elected—the last occasion being on 12th September 1768, although
he continued in connexion with town affairs as a councillor for several
years later.

It was while Mr. Watt was in office—a period of at least thirty
years, during which he discharged his several functions with acknowledged fidelity and zeal,—that the improvements of the town went on
in the most spirited manner. Ground was feued from Lord Cathcart,
westward from the Mid Quay for building the connecting breastwork;
the dredging of the harbours was vigorously set about; the new
breastwork was built; the quays were laid with flags and paved; a
new church, market-place, town-house, and council-chambers built;
the cellars or stores at the "Bell Entry" were commenced, and a
"bell-house" or steeple was erected upon the roof of that building.

On 24th May 1774, Mr. Watt—being then in his seventy-sixth year
—for the last time subscribed the Minutes of Council, in which year
his schoolfellow, Bailie James Gammell, was chief magistrate,—and
ten days after that meeting presented to the Council a resignation of
his office, when the following very gratifying minute of thanks was
entered in the records:—" COUNCIL CHAMBERS, 10th June, 1774.
—Which day the Magistrates and Council being met, Mr. James
Watt gave in to the meeting a resignation, dated 30th ultimo by
him, resigning the office of a Manager and Councillor, which the
meeting accepted of, and returned him thanks for the many good
offices he had done to the community while in said office."

It would be gratifying could anything like a consecutive account be
afforded of "the many good offices" here alluded to, in connexion
with the life of the worthy Bailie; and particularly of those public

works in which he took an active part, and displayed his practical, if not professional ingenuity and skill. It is in this feature of his character and capacities that we are most directly interested. There is incidental evidence, doubtless abundant, that Bailie James Watt's "foot-rule and plummet," as well as his accurate and experienced "eye," were often the standard of reference in regard to the merits or demerits of public works executed during his time; and that his sagacious estimate of the reasonableness or extravagance of "specifications" was of no small value in the opinion of his prudently economical fellow-councillors. But more than this, unfortunately, on such points, is not to be gathered from the materials which the records furnish. Still, unwilling to quit our subject after so meagre a sketch as has been afforded, and public as well as more private sources of information having left in our hands a considerable number of details relative to it, and which have not yet been disposed of, we are tempted to afford to these a limited portion of our space here, not so much because of their general interest, seeing they are purely local, as in the hope of their furnishing here and there some stray light, illustrative of the character of James Watt's father, and, possibly, in an indirect manner, of that of the distinguished son himself.

CHAPTER V.

TOWN AFFAIRS IN THE BAILIE'S TIME—THE PREACHER AND THE ROYAL CLOSE LOFT—
SUBDIVISION OF THE OLD PARISH—BUILDING OF THE NEW PARISH CHURCH—THE
BAILIE AND THE REV. MR. SHAW—THE MINISTER'S DEATH—THE MINISTER'S FAMILY
—MR. WATT'S MAGISTRACY—CRIME IN 1756—NOTES FROM TREASURER WATT'S
ACCOUNTS—THUROT'S FRENCH SQUADRON—RECORDS OF THE OLD COUNCIL-CHAMBER
—M'LAREN'S INN—THE COUNCIL'S FAVOURITE BEVERAGE—EXAMINATION OF THE
GRAMMAR SCHOOL—SIMPLE MANNERS OF THE TIMES.

ALTHOUGH the Bailie — for by this appellation Mr. Watt was
familiarly known in after life—did not at any time, like his worthy
father, the mathematician, accept of ecclesiastical office, he appears,
nevertheless, to have been not altogether indifferent to church matters.
He seems to have taken an active part, in the first instance, in procuring for the town an additional minister, the Rev. John Shaw,
A.M.;[1] and, thereafter, in promoting the subdivision of the parish, and
the building of a new Parish Church, to the presentation to which, Mr.
Shaw succeeded as its first incumbent.   As this reverend and estimable
gentleman was one of Mr. Watt's most intimate friends, the members
of whose family also long enjoyed in after years the friendship of the
distinguished son, some notices of the time, having reference to the
parties, may be admitted here, as pertaining to our local chronicles.

[1] Mr. Shaw was a licentiate of the presbytery of Forres, in the Synod of Moray. He was licensed on 22d August 1736. The extract of his license bears date at Elgin, 19th October 1736, and is subscribed by Robert Dunbar, moderator, and Daniel Munro, presbytery clerk. Mr. Shaw removed within the bounds of the presbytery of Edinburgh, from whence he came to Greenock, carrying with him a certificate, which bears date 15th March 1738, subscribed by fourteen ministers of the last mentioned presbytery. He obtained the degree of Master of Arts from the University of St. Andrews, on 18th September 1738.

The necessity for a second ministerial charge, and Mr. Shaw's consequent invitation, are entered in the Records, 21st June 1739, as follows :—

"This day Bailie Anderson, Mr. Watt, Mr. Weir, Mr. M'Cunn, and Mr. Mathie, merchants in Greenock, compeared and represented to the session, that many of the inhabitants of the town of Greenock, having, some time ago, petitioned the Hon. Sir John Shaw, for concurring with the session in having an assistant provided for Mr. Turner, the minister,[1] in the discharge of the duties of his office, Mr. John Shaw, preacher of the gospel within the limits of the presbytery of Edinburgh, had, in consequence thereof, been invited to this place."

The Bond granted to Mr. Shaw contains several curious particulars. It specifies scrupulously the amount of his stipend, which was to be " *Forty-five pounds sterling* each year," indicates the place assigned for public worship, and defines the extent of his parochial duties.[2] The locality assigned to the new minister and his congregation, was eventually the "Royal Close Loft."[3] The accommodations of such a place could not fail to be of a very inferior description, being merely the upper part of a common store or warehouse ; and, from its situa-

---

[1] Mr. Turner was minister of the old [West] Church of Greenock, the only church at this period in the parish.

[2] The following is the document in full :—" We, subscribers, managers of the funds of the town of Greenock, do hereby bind and oblige ourselves and successors in office, to pay to Mr. John Shaw, preacher of the gospel, the sum of forty-five pounds sterling each year, for three years, after the date hereof, and that in equal portions at each six months' end, in consideration of the said Mr. John Shaw's preaching in the *Royal Close Loft*, or any other place which we shall fit up for public worship, within the town of Greenock, and otherways to assist the Rev. Mr. David Turner, our minister, in the exercise of his ministerial office, in the said town, which the said John Shaw, by his acceptance hereof, obliges himself to perform, during the term of three years, after the date of these presents,

unless better encouragement be offered him. In witness whereof, these presents are subscribed by us at Greenock, the 21st day of June 1739, before the subscribing witnesses. The above being written on stamp paper, by William Skeoch, servitor to John Alexander, writer in Greenock.

James Lang, witness.
Jo. Campbell, witness.   John Shaw.
Samuel Taylor, witness.
Gabriel Mathie, witness.   John Anderson.
Joseph Tucker, witness.   Rob. Donald.
William Weir, witness.   Ja. Warden.
Jos. Lindsay, witness.   James M'Cunn.
Archibald Whyt, witness.   Ja. Watt.
John Ritchie, witness."

[3] The wall of the "Royal Close" was the ancient boundary of the gardens of the Mansion-house of the Lairds of Greenock.

tion, the disturbance to the preacher as well as to the worshippers, was a frequent subject of complaint. A curious illustration of such interruptions as occurred is found in the Records, the *Bailies* being appealed to for judgment in the case. It is thus stated in the record of the Court, 30th May 1753 :—" Mr. Shaw ag^t Stewart for charging people to work in the cellars below the new church in time of worship," &c. The case was not pushed to judgment, a promise having been made that the offence should not be repeated ; but the magistrates by an act of Court,—

" Express't their just indignation against so indecent and irreligious a conduct, and prohibited and discharged all coopers, porters, carmen, and others, upon any pretence whatever, from giving any disturbance upon such occasions, either by working in any of the cellars immediately below the place set apart for public worship, while religious exercises are there performing, or making any unnecessary noise in the entry or any part of the closs adjoining to the house, &c. The above was published through the town of Greenock by tuck of drum that none might pretend ignorance."

The population of the parish being on the increase, it became expedient to adopt measures for the subdivision of the old, and the erection of a new parish—since called the Middle Parish of Greenock —a decree in the Court of Teinds to effect which was obtained 15th July 1741, and Mr. Shaw ordained to its spiritual superintendence on the 11th November of the same year. It was not, however, till 1758, seventeen years after the creation of the parish, that plans were matured for the erection of the much desired parish church ; and on 6th April of the following year, the foundation stone was duly laid " in the east corner thereof." Two pieces of ground had been granted by Lord Cathcart, the immediate superior in this case, one for the church, the other for the manse. The event, it would appear, was to be regarded by the inhabitants as one of public importance, of all the public works in contemplation, none having excited so much the interest of the community as the building of a new church. On 3d

April 1759, accordingly, the minutes of the Town Council record, that "a general advertisement was given to the inhabitants of the town of Greenock to be present, that afternoon, at receiving infeftment of the ground for new church and manse, which was accordingly done in favour of the managers, councillors, feuars, sub-feuars, and inhabitants of Greenock, when a good number were present." The minute ordering this convocation of the inhabitants bears the signature of "James Watt," as Chief Magistrate, his colleague, Bailie Alexander, being then dead.[1] The main body of the edifice steadily advanced to completion, with the exception of the Steeple, the erection of which was delayed for the time. Lord Cathcart himself furnished the plan of the Church, which was designed after that of St. Martin's-in-the-fields, London.[2] Mr. Watt is usually understood to have executed the internal work, according to plan, and to have otherwise mainly superintended the undertaking.

The Bailie, as a matter of course, was one of the individuals who made pecuniary advances towards the building. He held his interest in the Church for about ten years. It is not known whether Mr. Watt was the only party who then withdrew, but a document extant, in his handwriting, and bearing evident marks of having been hastily written, refers to a sudden resignation of his interest, in the following terms :—

[1] The feu-charter contains the names of the principal men of the town at this time. They are "John Alexander, writer in Greenock, and James Watt, wright and merchant there, Bailies ; Gabriel Lang, ship-carpenter and merchant there, Treasurer; Robert Rae, Wm. Gammel, Hugh Crawford, and James Crawford, all shipmasters and merchants, Gabriel Mathie, cooper and merchant, and Nathan Wilson, surgeon, Councillors, of the town of Greenock, and their successors in office, managers of the funds of the said town." The money necessary for building the church, agreeably to a scheme then agreed upon, was estimated at £1200, and was proposed to be raised by borrowing various sums from the inhabitants, who, in return, were to obtain assignations of seats or pews in the church, which they were to hold at estimated rates until their respective advances should be paid up.

[2] The ground on which the church is built, and which was valued at £130, no inconsiderable sum at that time, was gratuitously conveyed by Lord Cathcart. The square on which the church is built had then no particular name. It has now, however, been named "Cathcart Square," in compliment most worthily to his Lordship.

"Greenock, 23d Ap. 1768.

" To the Honourable, the Bailies and Managers of the Town of Greenock's Funds.
Gentlemen,—I have no more occasion for the Seat I subscribed for in the new Church
of Greenock, No. 168, containing 7 sittings, and desire you may let said Seat at ye.
15th day of May next for behoof of the town of Greenock, and give me credit for the
remains of four pounds sterling that I lent the town at building sd Church. Sirs,
Your humble Servant,

"James Watt."

The explanation of this unlooked for proceeding on Mr. Watt's part
introduces some interesting particulars relating to the parties. The
drafts of a correspondence, in our possession, which took place at this
time—they are in the Rev. Mr. Shaw's handwriting—throw some
light upon the circumstances. From this correspondence, it appears
that the reverend gentleman had fallen into bad health ; that his
congregation had considered it necessary to promote a subscription,
with the view of raising a fund for an assistant, and that he himself
had named a Mr. Buchanan, as a very proper person for the duty. A
minority of the subscribers, however—for the nomination had been
made the subject of an angry discussion and a vote—objected to such
a course on the part of the minister, though on what particular grounds
does not appear. The draft of one of the Letters, bearing to be written
in August, is in the following terms :—

"Greenock, *August 30th,* 1768.

" Gentlemen,—I take this opportunity of acknowledging, with the highest gratitude, your unasked and unexpected generosity, in so cheerfully and seasonably providing a fund for an assistant to me, for some little time, either until it shall please God
to restore me to some measure of strength for discharging my duty among you, or put
an end to a life which I think I can say with truth, was sincerely devoted to the
promoting the best interests of the parish, and which, I thank God, I always found
to be not only my duty but my highest pleasure. This generous plan, formed and
executed by yourselves, I justly consider as a new and very substantial proof of your
disinterested friendship to me, a friendship which has, blessed be God, subsisted
during the long course of our connexions together, and which it shall be my endeavour to cultivate and preserve."

A second letter bears to have been addressed in the following month to the subscribers : but by this time it had come to the minister's knowledge that debates and divisions had arisen among them as to the assistant ; hence the resolution of the reverend gentleman so decidedly expressed in the first paragraph, which is as follows :—

"GREENOCK, *September —*, 1768.

"GENTLEMEN,—The kind and generous design which you formed of providing me in an assistant, for a few months, has been the unhappy occasion of such difference in opinion as to the means of making it effectual, that it has given me much distress, and I really cannot be easy until I do all in my power to put an end to such disagreeable debates, of which I can see no end. With this view, therefore, after making the most grateful acknowledgments of your goodness, of which I hope I shall never lose the remembrance, I think it my duty, now to inform you, that I am absolutely determined to take no benefit from your most generous contribution ; and that while it pleases God to spare me, I will endeavour, in the best manner I am able, to provide the parish regularly in sermon, without any assistance from that fund ; and, indeed, without such resolution, it does not appear to me possible, that ever the present differences shall come to a conclusion, for principles have been adopted in this debate, the most absurd in themselves, and subversive of the very foundation of all society, whether civil or religious, on which account I am persuaded many who subscribed a letter I received did not duly attend to its contents before signing. I appeal to any man of the most ordinary understanding if, after an honest acknowledgment of Mr. Buchanan's having carried the place by a considerable majority, it was competent to the minority to make any farther debate about it."

A concluding letter, written in October, is in much the same strain.

"It is very true," proceeds this virtuously independent clergyman, "I am not rich ; and such as have known my income and charge, ever since I set up house in Greenock, will not be surprised to hear it ; but I bless God, I am not yet reduced to that state of meanness and beggary as to take any aid from private pocquets, upon terms inconsistent, as I apprehend, with the generosity of the gentlemen subscribers to offer, and I will take the liberty to add, with the honour of my office to accept. I am sorry to observe, that though many parishes have with equal generosity paid assistants for their ministers, Greenock, I believe, is the first in the kingdom which has had any debates about who should be the man, and I am willing to hope will be the last also; and I cannot help thinking it is but a bad omen for a peaceable settlement, when I shall be removed off the stage."

As Mr. Shaw died on the 9th November 1768, not more than a month could have elapsed between the time of his writing this last letter and his death. And when, in explanation of the high-spirited tone of the lines last quoted, it is told that the worthy incumbent had six sons and six daughters born to him, and it is recollected that, by the terms of the bond, his stipend was only forty-five pounds a year; —which, only in 1742, was augmented to eighty, and in 1766, two years before his death, raised to its maximum of a hundred pounds, —the independent spirit of the good man, coupled with the feeling and grateful tone of the correspondence quoted, cannot fail to command respect for his memory, not in every generous breast alone, but even in the "head" of the most captious member of a church court, or selfish contributor to a benevolent fund.

Mr. Watt seems to have felt keenly the injustice so palpably manifested in the case, and to have resented it in perhaps the only way open to him—by withdrawing any interest he possessed in the corporation funds of the church.

It is pleasing to discover in these simple records of the father of Watt, some lineaments of sterling character that were finely reproduced in the life and manners of the eminent son; in whom, combined with much that was gentle and attractive in his character, a strong instinctive sense of justice, and a generous indignation at everything that was felt to be mean, unworthy, or unfair, were among not the least conspicuous of his many virtues.

Up to the time of the excellent incumbent's death—a period of thirty years—the minister's family and Mr. Watt's had been very near neighbours, and the several members of both in daily and familiar intercourse. A good feeling and friendship of so long a standing was not likely to be easily broken up. We find it, accordingly, outlasting nearly a century more, terminating only in the death of the last survivor of the once pleasant and intellectual circle. Mrs. Shaw died in 1815, after forty-seven years of widowhood, three of her daughters having survived her. On occasion of his visits to his native town, the distinguished Mechanician was wont to invite these amiable and accomplished ladies to dine with him at the inn where he put up, and it may easily be imagined that the pleasantness of old reminiscences was not a little enhanced by the excellent sense of the elder sisters, as well as enlivened by the ready and sparkling wit of the younger of the two, Margaret, better known during her life as Miss Peggy. Mr. Watt's last visit to Greenock was in 1816. Margaret, the last of the minister's family, died in April 1852, in the ninetieth year of her age.

Miss Margaret, with maidenly coyness, managed to her last hour to keep her age a profound secret. Even considerably after she had arrived at such a period of life as made it evident that she had passed at least the " threescore years and ten," a point on the attainment of which it is not often that the few so favoured are careful to conceal the fact, she parried every inquiry on the point, however indirectly made, with the address of a girl just passing her teens. The dislike to revelations of this kind she seems to have inherited from her venerable mother, of whom an illustrative anecdote is recorded. The late Dr. Scott,[1] for many years the respected incumbent of the new parish of Greenock, was in the practice of visiting Mrs. Shaw's family, and of introducing to those amiable and accomplished ladies such of his clerical brethren as preached for him. On one of these visits a venerable minister thus introduced, having in the course of conversation, designedly or casually, made some allusion to the subject of " ages," glancing perhaps at Mrs. Shaw's two unmarried daughters, Agnes and

[1] Father of Professor Scott, now Principal of Owens College, Manchester.

Margaret, the old lady spiritedly rejoined by a quotation from Allan Ramsay's "Gentle Shepherd," "Never ca' her auld that wants a man."[1]

It might be here not uninteresting, particularly with reference to the magisterial functions of Mr. Watt, to notice the state of the population at this time—just a hundred years ago—in respect of its police and of crime. During the *feudal* times, which may be said to have prevailed in the burgh down to 1751, when Sir John Shaw granted his charter for the election of burgh magistrates, no public record beyond that of the "Kirk-Session" is known to exist, from which might be ascertained either the nature of the prevalent crimes in those days, or how they were punished. If we give credence to tradition, the baron was in no way behind his neighbours in the exercise of his feudal prerogatives in criminal jurisdiction. Indeed the iron-grated windows which the removal of certain buildings a few years ago brought into conspicuous view as belonging to the lower apartments of the Mansion House, testify, that whatever the nature of the offences might have been, the best provision was made for the safe custody of the offenders. A single instance from the Session Records, already casually noticed, in which James Watt's name happens to appear, is illustrative of the *ecclesiastical* jurisdiction. It appears, 28th August 1740, thus:—"James Watt's apprentice and various other persons were accused of profaning the Lord's-day, by vaging about the streets and quays after sermons." The offence would of course be followed by a sessional rebuke; and perhaps the grave censures delivered by that reverend court would be felt with as much keenness, and be more

[1] "That wants a man;" that is still unmarried. The line occurs in a passage after the "tulzie," brawl, or rather battle between *Bauldy* and *Madge*, in which *Bauldy* had been rather roughly handled, in consequence of an unguarded remark having reference to her *age*. The line quoted is addressed by *Madge* to *Bauldy*, after the reconciliation, in the way of counsel and of gentle warning, as it were, for the future, in his allusions to a point so delicate, and so directly affecting the liveliest sympathies of the fairer sex.

corrective in their effects, than the severer class of punishments we find inflicted from the *magisterial* bench, when the "Bailies" came into power.

From the first institution of the magistracy, however, the record of their proceedings has been regularly preserved. One or two examples from this may be given, as illustrating the manners and habits of the times. The first criminal case on the record bears date 8th January 1752, Robert Donald being bailie; it is as follows :—

"The Fiskal of Court against George Miller, quarrier, for several thefts. The defender banished the town, under pain of transportation, and an enactment thereof signed accordingly."

Another case, bearing date 4th March 1752, before Bailies Alexander and Butcher, is thus entered :—

"John M'Kirdy, sailor, was, because of his committing several thefts, as mentioned in the precognition, banished the town and baronies of Greenock, by tuck of drum, never to return under pain of imprisonment, and being banished a second time, conform to sentence this day passed against him."

Under date 1st November 1752, and before the same magistrates, an entry is made, of which the following is a copy :—

"Sharp Nickol and the Fiscal, against Wilson, Lang, Forrest, and Hendry, journeymen shoemakers. The lybel proven, in so far as that the whole of them had been guilty of disturbing the peace of the place by strolling the streets in the silent watches of the night; that, in particular, James Hendry was guilty of breaking open Janet Nickol's door, and the rest were art and part therein; therefore the bailies amerciated and fined the said James Hendry in five pounds Scotts to the Fiscal of Court: and the other defenders, namely, Wilson, Lang, and Forrest, in four pounds Scotts each, for which ordained extracts, and all the defenders to be imprisoned unless, or until, they find caution to keep the peace, and the complainers harmless in time coming."

A case occurs on 1st December 1752, in which John Rae, a carman, was, for inducing a boy to steal from his father, "fined in twenty shillings to the Fiscal, and ordained *to stand in the pillory*, for the space of half an hour."

It is curious to observe, that, from the time of the institution of the magistracy, the Kirk-Session seems to apply itself for judgment to the *civil power*, in cases and offences of which they were wont to take cognizance themselves, anterior to that date. The first case of this kind, occurring 30th May 1753, was one for the correction of persons charged with the breach of the sanctity of the Sabbath. The prosecutor was the Rev. Mr. Turner, minister of the West Parish; the Record thus states it :—

"Turner against the Carpenters. The bailies having considered the lybel with the defenders' acknowledgments, finds the particular circumstances the ship Bess was in justified the defenders' trial to remove her on Saturday night, and because of their not caulking after eleven at night, and the workmen were so early at home as two o'clock in the morning, the bailies do therefore assoilze William Scott and his servants, but finds the breach of Sabbath lybelled against John and Walter M'Kirdy proven, and therefore fine each of them in ten pound Scots, to be applied to the pious uses of the parish."

We cite one case more, to show how the bailies disposed of charges of scandal. The entry is as follows :—

"Galbraith and husband against M'Alister and husband;" [the date of the trial is 22d August 1753, and the judges Bailies Donald and Butcher.] "The Bailies," the Record bears, "having considered the lybel, finds the scandal proven, and therefore fines her [Mrs. M'Alister] in ten pounds Scots to the Fiscal of Court, and ordained her to be imprisoned for twenty-four hours, and decerned her and her husband in payment of five shillings as the expense of process." [The case, however, was brought up before Bailies Butcher and Alexander, on the 19th September, and the following entry is made in the Record :]—"The pursuer pass'd from the imprisonment ordained by sentence of the 22d August last, upon the defenders, *acknowledging in open Court that her false tongue lyed, which she having this day done*, and paid the five shillings of costs, she was assoilzed."

No materials exist from which a judgment might be formed as to how Bailie Watt demeaned himself on the magisterial bench, in the punishment and repression of crime. Indeed, it does not appear that in 1757 and 1758 when he acted as magistrate, he had ever sat in court for the trial of causes, civil or criminal. There were in fact few cases of either kind; and the duty, such as it was, devolved on his colleague, Bailie Alexander, who practised the legal profession, and who, from documents extant, must have been a very judicious and accurate person.[1]

[1] Whether it was that the evil-disposed portion of the inhabitants were awed into a virtuous course of life by the new power which had then come into operation, or that there were really few cases of delinquency, very little practically was required in the way of correction it would seem. It may, however, be assumed that the extension of trade would afford opportunities to such persons to commit crime, whether overtaken by punishment or not. A paper indicative of this, and illustrating at the same time a method of remedy for the evil, as patriotic as it is novel, was some years ago put into my hands, by a gentleman whose grandfather was bailie in 1769. The following is a copy of this singular document:—

"Wee the inhabitants of Greenock hereto subsg., Considering that the manie theifts committed in the Town of Greenock is partlie occasioned by allowing the guiltie persons to escape unpunished when detected, and considering that there are six of the crew of the brig Union at present incarcerate in the Tolbouth of Renfrew for stealing a saill out of a sloop belonging to James Wilson, merchant here, and who will not be at the expense of prosecuting them without making the following contribution, and we considering that it will tend to discourage theift in the place to have the said sailors brought to condign punishment, we the persons after named have paid to
the person chosen by us for collecting the same, the several sums annexed to each of our names, to be paid in by him to the said James Wilson, to be applied by him for prosecuting the said sailors for the said theift:—

    pd. James Donald, twenty shillings, £1 0 0
    pd. James Watt, twenty shillings,   1 0 0
    pd. James Wilson, twenty shillings, 1 0 0"

This mode of raising funds for prosecuting criminals was more than once resorted to, and another example may be cited. Bailie Buchanan, on 9th July 1792, "reported (to the Council) that the subscriptions for carrying on the trial or prosecution of M. Gibbon, for stealing ropes, before the Sheriff Court (at Paisley), fell short of the expense of the said criminal trial in the sum of £18, 14s. 6d." Ordered to be paid by the Treasurer.

The paper is without date, but I assign it to 1769, because James Donald, who is the first person whose name is put down for twenty shillings, was senior bailie at that time; James Watt, who was Treasurer, or at all events a councillor, is the second subscriber, and James Wilson, who was junior bailie, and the sufferer by the theft, is the third subscriber. £12, 11s. in all was subscribed to be sent to Paisley, to defray, so far as the money would go, the expenses of prosecution.

Perhaps the case above stated was accompanied by some aggravating circumstances which do not appear in the subscription paper, otherwise the punishments then inflicted on culprits in the most summary manner, as shown in the Record, ought, one would think, to have been sufficient to deter delinquents from repeating these offences "in all time coming." The following

14

It is during the bailie's tenure of office as "treasurer for the town," that the Records indicate an occasion of public alarm and of serious military preparation on the part of the good people and authorities of the place. Expenses incurred with reference to sundry articles of a martial nature, as drums, muskets, cannon, guardhouses, and guards, expresses to Edinburgh, to Glasgow, &c., are of frequent occurrence. The chronicles of the time, however, throw all the light that is necessary on this portentous passage of the treasurer's life.

is an instance of the kind of punishment referred to, after a very summary trial before Bailie Wilson:—

"At Greenock, the 5th April, 1771 years, in presence of Mr. James Wilson, one of the present Magistrates of Greenock, compeared John Smith, a vagrant, and who had been incarcerated in the Tolbooth of Greenock, on an application from David Smith, candlemaker there, for stealing candle out of the said David Smith's shop; and the said John Smith being examined anent the said theft, judicially declares and acknowledges that he stole some pounds of candle out of the said David's Smith's shop, and the candle being produced and shown to the declarant, he acknowledges that they are the same candle which he stole in manner foresaid, and is willing to submit to any punishment the Court shall please to inflict upon him, and this he declares to be truth.

"JOHN SMITH.

"James Wilson, *Bailie.*

"The Bailie having considered the above John Smith's judicial acknowledgment, ordains him to be carried from the bar and put into the Jugs, there to stand bareheaded for the space of half an hour, *with some of the candles hung about his neck,* and a label upon his breast, with the following words on it in large characters,—'*Here I stand for stealing candles.*' After his *stance* in the Jugs, his sentence ordains him to be *drummed out of the town,* and thereafter banished from the same for life, with the usual certification.

"JAMES WILSON, *Bailie.*"

The above is the last of the few criminal cases which occur in the Record from which the citations have been made, and it is not easy to conceive that any punishment short of transportation could be more severe.

It is a trite observation that in proportion to the increase of population, so is the prevalence of crime. It is matter of experience, however, that there are periods when crime, from favourable circumstances in the condition of society, is less rife than at other times, when want of employment and other similar causes may be supposed to lead to its commission. But there are times, too, when crime prevails, and no principle can be assigned as accounting for such prevalence. A remarkable proof of the truth of the last observation occurred in 1817. On 10th October of that year, the magistrates issued a proclamation, of the first paragraph of which the following is a copy:—"At this time last year the magistrates had great satisfaction in looking back on the previous twelve months, during nine of which a single case had not occurred requiring the punishment of confinement in jail; in the course of the other three months, two or three trivial breaches of the police took place. A review of the last twelve months presents a most melancholy contrast; offences have abounded, and crimes of no ordinary dye have been committed to an extent unprecedented in any place of similar population. From this town no fewer than five men have been condemned to suffer the capital punishment of the law, *three* of whom are to be executed here this day."

The occasion was, the apprehended appearance in the Clyde of "Thurot's French Squadron," which, for a couple of years and more, had been causing considerable uneasiness in different parts of the kingdom, and had done much damage to shipping and property along the British coast.   Thurot appears to have been a man of great daring and bravery.   He began his privateering exploits on board his ship, the *Maréchal de Bellisle,* mounting 44 guns, and carrying 500 men. With this ship he had on 26th May 1758 engaged two British twenty-gun ships-of-war, off Redhead, and thus become formidable, if not to ships of equal force with his own, in the navy, at least to the mercantile marine of the country.   In the two years of his cruise he had taken thirty-four vessels in all.   In consequence of his exploits, M. Thurot had been introduced to the French king, and had received the command of a squadron of five ships-of-war, having on board about 1200 soldiers, fitted out for the purpose of interrupting the commerce, and annoying the coasts of Great Britain and Ireland.   A British squadron had been set to watch the Frenchman's movements.   Availing himself of a fog, however, he had escaped from Dunkirk on 17th October 1759, and got into Göttenburg on the 26th of the same month.   Some idea may be formed of the alarm created by this adventurer from the magnitude of the preparations made at Liverpool to repel his attack, should he have ventured with his armament to approach that port. "On receiving accounts at Liverpool," says a chronicle of the time, "on Sunday evening, November 4th, of M. Thurot's squadrons having sailed from Dunkirk, Laurence Spencer, Esq., the Mayor, convened the principal inhabitants, who unanimously resolved to enter into an association and subscription, for defending the town, and a committee of managers was appointed.   At their request, a return of the muskets in the hands of the merchants and dealers being made, it was found that upwards of 4000 men could be completely armed.   About 500 gentlemen proposed to form themselves into squadrons of light horse.

Pilot-boats were sent out and properly stationed to give the earliest intelligence of the appearance of the enemy ; and regular measures were taken in case of their approach, to destroy all the buoys, and blow up the land-marks leading into the harbour. On the 10th, the King's birthday, five new batteries were opened with a royal salute. They consist of two batteries *d'enfilade*, scouring the whole river, a battery *en écharpe* which plays obliquely ; a battery *par camarade*, so contrived as to fire at the same time upon one body ; and a battery in the zigzag form, making several angles, completely sheltering the garrison from being fired on in a straight line. By that time 70 heavy cannon were mounted on the platforms, and several hundred men were employed in completing them. The king has approved of this measure, and ordered a commission to be made out for arming his loyal subjects of Liverpool, in the same manner as was issued in 1745."

The alarm reached Greenock, where, indeed, the likelihood of an attack was more imminent, from the ascertained proximity of the enemy. As early as November and December 1759, there is evidence in Treasurer Watt's accounts, of the establishment of a guard-house and guard in the town ; and, doubtless connected with the guard, 2s. 2d. are taken credit for by the worthy Treasurer, as " paid John Clark, drummer, to buy *drum-sticks*." As the alarm became more urgent, the Magistrates find it necessary to get " a *new* drum for the drummer ;" and Treasurer Watt takes credit for 19s. as the price of that martial instrument. Nor was the apprehension excited altogether without cause. For on Saturday the 16th February of the following year, Thurot with three ships entered Aros Bay, in the Island of Islay, and landed 200 men for the purpose of procuring provisions, which were supplied by the country people, and paid for partly in cash, and partly in bills on the French King's cashier. An express was sent to Edinburgh on the 23d by Captain Hay, regulating captain at Greenock, advising that the French squadron left Islay on Tuesday, and on Wednesday had entered the Frith of Clyde, adding that a lieutenant whom he had despatched in a wherry to observe the enemy's motions, had sent him notice, that on Thursday he saw about a thousand men landed at Carrickfergus from the ships. This town and castle were taken and plundered. A ship belonging to the Clyde also was taken at the same place, and burnt, after being plundered of her entire cargo, consisting of tobacco and sugar.

It cannot be doubted that the city of Glasgow participated in the general alarm. Credit is taken by Treasurer Watt, 26th February 1760, for " 7s. 6d., as paid express for going to Glasgow," two days before Captain Elliot, of the British frigate *Eolus*, with the *Pallas* and *Brilliant*, engaged and captured the enemy's squadron, between the Mull of Galloway and the Isle of Man. After the alarm had subsided, in consequence, Treasurer Watt has an entry in his accounts for payments made to " twelve soldiers and a Sergeant, two days, carrying over the cannon, shot, and carriage, and other utensils from Fort Beauclerc to the proprietor, &c. ;" and again, " paid William Ireland, proof-master for work in taking in yᵉ cannon from Fort Beauclerc, £1, 19s." The fort so named—in honour of Lord George Beauclerc, then Commander-in-chief of the forces in Scotland—was a battery erected for the occasion near to the Ropework Quay. Its *inauguration*, at which Lord George was probably present, is alluded to in Treasurer Watt's account, April 1760: "Paid for an entertainment at Mr. Donald's, at christening the fort, £4, 9s. 5d." The battery seems to have been scientifically thrown up, as there are entries made of payments " for putting up the embrasures of the fort." It does not appear to what extent Mr. Watt put in practice his engineering abilities in the preparations made for giving M. Thurot a warm reception, had he ventured as far as the " Tail of the Bank." Doubtless there would be many opportunities for applying his well-known practical ingenuity ; and the probability is, that, on the occasion, he acted in the double capacity of engineer and treasurer, it being part also of his ordinary business to make gun-carriages.

Eighteen years afterwards, another alarm of a similar kind, during the American war, was the occasion of a second battery being erected at Greenock,[1] in consequence of the threatened appearance in the Clyde of the famous Paul Jones, who did not, however, approach nearer in this direction than the Rock of Ailsa. But by this time our worthy Treasurer, though still alive, had withdrawn from public affairs, and ceased to take any part, so far as can be traced, in the concerns of the burgh. Before taking final leave, however, of the period and of the men who had contributed so much to the *safety*, it would seem, of the town, as well as to the prosperity and comfort of its inhabitants, we are tempted to add one or two touches by way of giving something of colour and character to the picture of the good old times.

Reference has already been made to the building of a " Town-house," as, in the Bailie's time, next to the building of a Church, one of the objects considered most desirable for the improvement and respectability of the place. The attainment of such an object was long unavoidably delayed. Prior to the existence of the present Town-Hall and Council-Chambers, which were built by Bailie Watt, the usual place of meeting of the " Town-Council " was a large room in an *Inn*, that was situated in what was then called the High Street, and kept by a well-known and respectable individual, named John M'Laren. A locality so reputable in the annals of the ancient corporation merits a passing description.

---

[1] This second battery, which does not appear to have received any distinctive name, was on the site of the former, or possibly on the ground which was afterwards occupied by *Fort Jervis*, erected during the French war, and consisting of twelve twenty-four pounders. It occupied part of the space now filled up, and extending seaward, forming the area of the splendid esplanade, the Albert Quay. This fort was named in compliment to Sir John Jervis, afterwards Earl St. Vincent. A stone bearing the inscription, " Fort Jervis, 14th February 1797," placed in the Ropework Wall, at once marks the spot where that battery stood, and serves as a memento of the great naval victory off Cape St. Vincent.

The principal entrance to the Inn was from the east side of Cross Shore Street. A stone placed in the front, towards the High Street, bearing the figures 1716, indicated the period when the house was built. It was one of the three or four houses covered with slate which the Town of Greenock could boast of prior to the year 1720. A sun dial, for ascertaining the hours of the day, retains its place on the western corner ; and opposite to the Inn, and consequently to the Council Chamber, in the High Street, stood the public prison, an ill-looking thatched house, from the front of which, the *jugs* were suspended by a chain, to the terror of all evil-doers. On the street, in front of the latter building, a Cross, and the date 1669, formed of white pebbles, pointed out that locality as the centre of the town or market-cross,—hence the " Cross Shore," or market-place of more modern times. The windows of the room in which the Honourable the Town-Council met, from being formed of strong astragals of wood, and small squares of glass, are yet in great measure entire ; and the various inscriptions still legible on the latter, demonstrate conclusively that the house had formerly been one of public entertainment, though no traces remain of its more dignified civic appropriation.[1]

Besides giving accommodation to the fathers of the town and trade of Greenock, for their Council meetings, M'Laren's was the place in which all other meetings of a public kind were held. The *riding of the fair*, for example, was always inaugurated here,—a ceremonial demanding a display of all the pomp and circumstance which might be imparted to it, for the purpose of impressing the minds of the Highlanders resorting hither, with due respect for and submission to the

---

[1] The following are specimens of the original window-pane inscriptions :—

" Unlucky fellow, I have lost my mistress unless Neptune should favour me, and swallow up my too powerful rival."

" Miss Nelly Boyd of Irvine :—
   " Sure never was before in nature
   So elegant, so fine a creature."

" Miss Susy Smith :—
   " La plus belle fille en Bourdeaux,
   Est Mademoiselle Belfont."

authority under which it was held.   These Highlanders drew up their
boats on the beach, with their prows to the High Street, at that part
of the harbour which now forms the West Breast.   The greater part
of the High Street, at that time, had no intervening buildings between
the south side of it and the sea.   Each boat had a plank or gangway
between it and the shore ; the people belonging to the boats lodging in
them at night, the houses in the town being too few to afford accommodation to the multitudes who thronged it on such occasions, and it being
necessary, for the security of the townspeople as well as of strangers,
that order should be preserved.   To preserve this order, and if necessary
to enforce it, was the duty of Sir John Schaw as feudal superior, in
whose favour an act of the Scottish Parliament had been granted " for
holding fairs."   Accordingly, on the first day of the *gathering*, Sir
John was accustomed to convene the dignitaries of the town and
deacons of trades at M'Laren's, and, after drinking the king's health,
and throwing their glasses among the populace, to issue thence in
formal procession, and perambulate the streets of the burgh,—exhibit-
ing at once a pageant to challenge the admiration of the rustics, and
to infuse into their minds a profound sense of the respect due to his
authority.

On ordinary occasions, and after the despatch of business, the
Council were wont to regale themselves with such cordials as Mr.
M'Laren's house afforded.   The expenses thus incurred were extremely
moderate, and were charged by the Town-treasurer against the town
revenue.   The reader is presented with a few items in this official's
accounts as follows :—Under the date 26th May 1749, the worthy
Treasurer Gabriel Lang takes credit in his account for 3s. 4½d., " for
expenses paid with the meeting of the Town-Council at Mr. M'Laren's."
On the 30th of the same month 1s. 6d. are put down for " expenses
incurred in agreeing masons to build cellars."   This was probably for
a social cup taken by the Treasurer himself, the mason contractor, and

a Trustee, or it might be a Bailie, at making the agreement. The quality of the favourite beverage of the Council at these meetings may be gathered from another entry under date 10th August 1749 :—" To cash paid John M'Laren *for punch* with the Council meeting, 2s. 6d." Surely the most sensitive stickler for economy in public expenses could find no fault with an expenditure so very reasonable and so moderate.

But even in those days of thrift and economy, there were occasions when the Council adventured upon a greater expenditure. Under date 10th May 1750, probably in connexion with the fair-day, there is the following entry :—" Paid John M'Laren for charges by the Town-Council, as per account, £4, 15s. 1d." Still farther, and shewing the Town-Council to have been possessed of some spirit, credit is taken for a much more imposing amount, thus :—" April 17, 1751.—To an account paid John M'Laren for the Town of Greenock's treat to my Lord Cathcart and Dromore, [Lord Dromore, one of the Supreme Judges of Scotland,] and other expenses with the Council meeting, as per precept drawn by the bailie on me, £15, 4s. 4d."

How long the Town-Council had made M'Laren's their " Council Chamber" cannot be precisely determined. But after Sir John had granted the charter 1751, so often already referred to, and when those in authority were entitled to call themselves "the Bailies and Town-Council," these functionaries, as early as 1753, deemed it necessary to provide some place other than the Inn, where the affairs of the town might be transacted. A minute of Council of 2d February 1753, sets forth, that " it was resolved that a little bit of ground belonging to Lord Cathcart, upon the east side of the New Street, [called William Street in 1775,] betwixt it and James Wilson's feued ground, be enclosed, and a shed laid thereon, for lodging therein *the water works*, which, in confidence that Lord Cathcart would agree thereto, the treasurer was ordered to get it done." The Shed was accordingly built, but was destined to be converted to a more important use, as appears from

15

another resolution of Council, on the 6th day of August in the same year. We here give the minute, which indicates the place chosen for the first *Post-Office*, as well as the first *Court-House* for the administration of justice. It is as follows :—"John Alexander [the Bailie] represented that, as Lord Cathcart had been pleased to interest himself in procuring a separate post-bag established here, and had also, at the desire of the Bailies and Councillors, recommended John Paton to be Postmaster, which would be a saving to the town, in respect they behoved otherways to gratify him for his services in the town business, necessary it was that he should be accommodated in some proper apartment whereat he might attend in the giving out and receiving the letters with such care and accuracy as becometh ; and the little Shed, originally built for the reception and preservation of the water-engine, being judged sufficient for serving both purposes, the northmost part thereof was therefore ordered to be fitted up as a Post-Office, whereat the *Bailies* and *Council* might also meet on occasions to doe business, and likewise the Bailies might hold their weekly Courts there till better provided." The probability is, that it was at this place the Bailies dispensed justice to the lieges till the present Town-Hall was built.

Finding themselves however again straitened in point of accommodation for public affairs, the Magistrates and Council, on the 3d August 1765, feued from Lord Cathcart the piece of ground occupied by the Town-Hall and Public Buildings now in use. The building of the Town-House was at length proceeded in without delay, Bailie Watt being the architect and contractor ; but it does not appear whether the Magistrates then used the *Hall* on Court-days. It is more than probable that they did not, and that the Courts were for the most part, if not always, held in an apartment on the *ground floor* of the building, several years ago converted into a shop, the Hall itself above, being occupied occasionally as a ball-room, and ordinarily as a news-room, until the Exchange Buildings were erected in 1814, when the members removed thither, and the Magistrates took possession of the Hall, where they have ever since continued to hold their sittings.[1]

But it must not be supposed that the Town-Council, after they were entitled to take the designation of the "Bailies and Council," thought it derogatory to their dignity longer to patronize their old snug retreat, or that it was at all necessary to give up their economical social meetings at M'Laren's. On 13th November 1759, there is an entry in the worthy depute-treasurer's account of that year as follows :— "By paid expenses with James Watt and James Crawford at settling his treasurer's accounts, 1s. 2d. ;" immediately afterwards :—" By paid John M'Laren for an entertainment which the Magistrates gave Mr. Charles Brown, Lord Cathcart's doer, £1, 9s. 3d. ;" on 24th January 1760 :—" By expenses with James Watt and John Paton in getting the two pennys from Mrs. Monroe, 1s. 2d. ;" and, to instance only one more, 7th April 1760 :—" By expenses with the Council at qualifying the Bailies, 5s."

And as it was in nowise considered disreputable that the *Town-Council* should meet at the principal inn of the place for the despatch of public business, so it need not cause surprise that after so important an affair as an examination of the *grammar-school*, for example, the worthy examinators, who reckoned among them several retired shipmasters and plain unpretending merchants, should—to relieve the *ennui* experienced in listening to Latin, and, what was still worse, perhaps Greek examinations—make a refreshing draught a thing rather to be desired than otherwise. The items quoted as paid on all

[1] Many of our readers will recollect the shed occupied on the east side of William Street by the late Mr. Matthew Glassford as a clothier's shop, and now the site of a handsome building. Here were cumulated, in the infancy of Greenock, the house for " lodging" the fire-engine, the first Post-office, and the first Council Chamber, "whereat the Magistrates and Council might also meet on occasions to doe business, and likewise the Bailies might hold their weekly Courts till better provided."

occasions by the authorities to the innkeeper, were all that he received
for the accommodation he gave, and the *generous* officials might naturally find themselves obliged to do something—and certainly that
something was moderate enough—" for the good of the house." It
need not be matter of great wonder, then, that an entry should be
found in the Treasurer's accounts, about midsummer, 11th June 1772,
to this effect :—" By paid for *punch* after examination of Latin-
school, 2s. 4d. ;" or that as late as 1783, the date of the founding of
the Greenock Library, the inn, probably with its wonted accompaniments, should be the place of meeting of the committee for the discussion of matters connected with that institution,—or that even up
to a date considerably more recent one of its regulations should run
as follows :—" That the Society shall meet the second Friday of
January and July at the house of James Stewart, vintner in Greenock,
to transact the business of the Society." [1] The simple and social
habits of the people did not forbid such usages. Indeed, about the
period under review, the affairs of the town generally—whether of a
purely public nature, such as the encouragement of trade by additional harbour accommodation, the building of a new church or a
school-house, a market or a prison ; or of a less formal character, as
the examination of the town grammar-school, or the literary business
of the town-library—were conducted in the friendly spirit of social
meetings much more than, as is not unfrequently the case in proceedings of the public " Boards" of modern times, in the temper and style
of debating societies. Every considerable community had not then
as now its public journal of intelligence, with its staff of busy

---

[1] A note appended to this regulation in the
Catalogue of the Library, published 1792, indicates an improvement in the customs and manners of the time, in its transferring the place of
meeting of the managers from an Inn or Tavern
to the Grammar School. It is as follows :—

" *Note.*—This fourth Rule is printed as in the
original Regulations ; but, by general consent of
the Society, the meetings of the proprietors of
the Library are now to be held in the Grammar
School of Greenock, where the Books of the Library are placed under the care of the Librarian."

" Reporters," ever on the alert for the instruction and gratification of " The Public." This branch of the commonwealth of letters had then no existence in the provinces. In that golden age of municipal life personal ambition had little to feed upon, and as little motive existed for display in the forensic efforts of oratory or cunning-of-fence debate. The fathers of the town were alike unstimulated and undisturbed in their homely deliberations by the presence of the " fourth estate," all-powerful in the days in which we live, when backed by its hundreds of " constant readers" out of doors, or attended by the ever-jealous vigilance of an argus-eyed public. Yet what should we not give for a " report" of such deliberations, of the length of an ordinary newspaper column, on any of the subjects that occupied the consideration of the magistrates and council of the town just *a hundred years ago*. How much light might it not throw on the municipal policy of those days! Sincerely, however, is it to be regretted that no such document of any kind, no such reported " speech," of any length whatever, is known to exist, even for the antiquary, by which he might, in so interesting a way, illustrate not only the mode of conducting the public affairs of the time, but also the character and spirit of the men who were the able founders of the town and its trade.

In relation especially to the present subject of our chronicles might it not have been hoped, that a deduction from such recorded facts, in detail, might have thrown light upon many features of the personal character, if not habits, of the Father of JAMES WATT ;—facts also which might have had their value as a reference to which to date back some of those fine qualities of mind that formed in after-days the wonderful assemblage of gifts and talent that so adorned the life and declining years of the matured philosopher himself.

It is useless now to lament the absence of any such data. Happily in the days in which we live, the task of the statist and chronicler is

rendered both more agreeable and more useful, by the almost endless
multiplication of channels through which even the minutest particulars
relating to public or social manners are made to flow, and that, with a
correctness and authenticity that leave little to be desiderated. In the
attempt that has been made to render some faithful representation
of the immediate ancestors of our distinguished townsman, a great
part of its acknowledged imperfection will be generously attributed,
it is hoped, to the scantiness of the materials at the disposal of the
chronicler ; even such details as have been given having been drawn
from sources in great part now accessible—perhaps it may with some
truth be added, now interesting—only to the antiquarian.

MEMORIALS OF JAMES WATT.

PART SECOND.
THE GREAT MECHANICIAN.

Partridge pinx.^t.   Schenck & Mc Farlane, Edin.^r.

JAMES WATT.

From an Original Portrait in the possession of Robert Napier, Esqre

CHAPTER I.

IF the appearance of the great Inventor be held, as it must, to form
an important epoch in our national annals, it cannot be here altogether
inappropriate to endeavour to mark, somewhat more distinctly than
has yet been done, the character and the exigencies of the period to
which the event belongs ; illustrating, especially, as these circumstances do, many points in our subsequent memorials. The period
was one of amazing energy and enterprise throughout the kingdom.
We have already seen what indications had been given, in the
north, of a national awakening to the importance of foreign trade,
and the value of home commercial enterprise to the country.
Hitherto commerce and industry in feudal Scotland had been prosecuted rather as a means of existence, than, as now, of princely
luxury and refinement.[1]

[1] In an official account drawn up in 1656 by
"Thomas Tucker, one of Cromwell's servants," a
curious and interesting view of the commerce of
Scotland at that period, in one of her "most considerablest burghs," is afforded. Thomas Tucker
had been appointed by Cromwell to arrange the

16

It was the beginning of a new state of things when, after the Union, the claymore and brand in one part of the country began to be exchanged for the pickaxe and the plough ; while in another, clanship with its endless feuds was all but forgotten in the frequent and peaceful labours of the anvil and the loom ; when private enterprise felt that it could extend itself securely ; when ships began to multiply ; when the arrival of foreign commodities rendered a reciprocation of trade both necessary and inevitable ; when the resources of the country became the objects of attention ; when, instead of the question with feudal lairds, How many belted men their estates could maintain ? a more enlightened and interested inquiry came to be,

---

" Customs and Excise" in Scotland. His report is dated November 20, 1656, and is addressed to the Right Honourable the Commissioners for Appeals. It is believed that a few copies of this Report were once printed privately. Our extract has been taken from a MS. copy in the Advocates' Library, Edinburgh. Its particulars are fullest in relation to Glasgow. The other trading burghs are more briefly alluded to :—

" Glasgow," proceeds the Report, " a very neate Burghe Towne, lying upon the Bankes of the river Cluyde, which, rising in Annandale, runns by Glasgow and Kirkpatrick, [Killpatrick ?] disburthening itself into the firth of Dumbarton. This Towne, seated in a pleasant and fruitful soil, and consisting of Foure Streets, handsomely built in Forme of a Cross, is one of the most considerablest Burghs of Scotland, as well for the Structure as Trade of it. The Inhabitants, all but the Students of the College which is here, are Traders and Dealers ; Some for Ireland with small smiddy Coales in open Boates from Foure to Ten Tonnes, from whence they bring Hoops, Ronges, Barrel staves, Meal Oates, and Butter ; Some for France with Pladding, Coales, and Herring, of which there is great Fishing yearly in the western Sea, for which they return Saltpetre, Rozin, and Prunes ; Some to Norway for Timber ; and Every one with

theyr neighbours the Highlanders, who come from the Isles and Western parts, in Summer by the Mul of Cantyre, and in Winter by the Tarban (Tarbat) to the head of Loghfyne, which is a small neck of land over which they usually draw theyr small Boates into the Firth of Dumbarton, and so passe up into the Cluyde, with Pladding, Dry hides, Goates, Kiel, and Deereskins, which they sell, and purchase with theyr price such Comodityes and Provisions as they stand in neede of from time to time. Here hath likewise been Some who have ventured as farre as the Barbadoes, but the losse they have sustained, by reason of theyr going out and coming home late every year, have made them discontinue going thither any more. The situation of this Towne in a plentiful land, and the mercantile genius of the People, are strong signes of her increase and growth, were she not chequed and kept under by the shallowness of her River, every day increasing and filling up, soe that noe vessels of any burden can come nearer up than within fourteen Miles, where they must unlade and send up their Timber and Norway Trade in rafts or Floates ; and all other Comodityes by Three or Foure Tonnes of Goods at a time, in small Cobbles or Boates, of Three, Foure, Five, and none above Six Tonnes a Boate. There is in this Port a Collector, a Cheque, and Four Wayters," &c. &c.

What were the agricultural, mineral, mercantile advantages of their lands?—when territory accordingly began to be cultivated, the bowels of the earth to be explored, and the produce poured into the eager hands of the manufacturer and the merchant. Population then rapidly increased, and as rapidly became concentrated,—in no part of the country more perceptibly than in the West, and along the shores of the Firth of Clyde, that splendid estuary, whose waters, skirting the coasts of Renfrewshire, and penetrating far into the richest mineral districts of Lanarkshire, were soon to become the great artery of foreign and domestic opulence to Scotland. Harbours then were built or enlarged, rivers and firths were surveyed ; roads, bridges, canals, required by the new inland traffic, were demanded ; and ere the lapse of the first half of the century, under the influence of a few sagacious men,[1] general intrepidity in many of the productive arts had begun to mark out those favoured spots which have since become the seats of unrivalled manufactures, and of all but unrivalled wealth.

In the south, on the other hand, Lancashire and Nottingham, with the contiguous districts, were making similar strides ;—there, as in the north, an almost absorbing interest attaching itself to the linen, cotton, and woollen manufactures, and to the improvement of the inefficient machinery that had long been in use in the structure of those important and staple fabrics. A prodigious thirst for *invention* stirred all classes ; and thoughtful men found their attention strongly

---

[1] "I once," says Sir John Dalrymple, "asked the late Provost Cochrane of Glasgow, who was eminently wise, and who had been a merchant there for near seventy years, to what causes he imputed the sudden rise of Glasgow. He said it was all owing to four young men of talents and spirit, who started at one time in business, and whose success gave example to the rest. The four had not ten thousand pounds among them when they began."—Memoirs of Great Britain and Ireland, by Sir John Dalrymple, Bart., vol. ii., Appendix, No. II., p. 48. Edinburgh, 1788. [The "four young men" referred to, are understood to have been Mr. Speirs of Elderslie ; Mr. Cunninghame of Lainshaw ; Mr. Glassford, after whom "Glassford Street" was named, afterwards of Dougaldston ; and Mr. Ritchie of Busby.]

forced in the direction of the great problems of the day,[1]—some to
elaborate their purely scientific principles, though by far the majority
to grapple hand to hand with the *practical* difficulties of the case,—
the perceptible and tangible defects of the machine, as these pressed
themselves upon observation.   Thus were the *spinning-jenny*, the
water-frame, the *mule-jenny*, worked out into admirable contrivances
by the untiring perseverance and ingenuity of the Hargreaves, the
Wyatts, the Hayes, and the Arkwrights of those days.[2]

But the arts and manufactures of this great country, or rather, the
progress and civilisation of the world, waited upon the steps of a far
loftier genius, of one whose mission was to be, by a single stroke as it
were at the fountainhead of mechanical power itself, to convey to the
commerce, the manufactures, the most ponderous branches of industry
as well as the most delicate of the fine arts of his country, a vitality
and an expansiveness, which, while they were to revolutionize the
interests of all classes, were at the same time to benefit every individual.   And for such an exalted calling, the *preparation*, so far as it
reveals itself to us, seems to have been adequate.   We think the
earlier portions of these Memorials reveal certain noticeable features of
character, appearing and re-appearing without interruption down all
the line of ancestry, which seem to warrant the idea of a preparation
in the case of the individual in whom those qualities should culminate.
The grandfather, we have seen, a man devoted to scientific pursuits
by taste as well as profession ; the uncle, following the same bent,
and giving promise of very extensive scientific usefulness ; the father,

---

[1] It is worthy of remark that the SOCIETY OF
CIVIL ENGINEERS dates its creation from this
period, 1760, a fact sufficiently significant. The
profession of CIVIL ENGINEER was unknown in
Britain prior to this epoch, and owed its origin
entirely to exigencies in the northern and south-
ern portions of the kingdom, such as those indicated in the text. See the very interesting historical preface, giving an account of the Society's
origin and formation, prefixed to the three quarto
volumes of " Reports of the late John Smeaton,
F.R.S., published by the Committee of Civil Engineers. London, 1812."

[2] Baines' History of Lancashire. Manchester
Memoirs. Second Series, vol. iii. *Encyclopædia
Britannica*, Art., Cotton Manufacture.

characterized through life by an eminently ingenious and practical turn of mind ; the younger brother[1] also giving the indications he did of the common family predilection,—an atmosphere of practical science could not fail to be that which the great inventor even from his earliest years inhaled, the very circumstances of his delicate youth appearing to have seconded the design of nature that he should come under the influence of hardly any other. All this forms a peculiarity in the intellectual history of the chief subject of these Memoirs, so striking, that it ought not to be overlooked in any view that may be taken of such a life ; producing, as the " conjunction" of the several "influences" did, just those very properties which were essentially requisite towards the complete furniture of the MAN for the WORK, —pure science on the one hand ; on the other, clever and ingenious experiment : in other words, the happiest union, in his individuality, of the THEORETICAL with the PRACTICAL,—points which will probably be admitted to have been the preponderating, certainly the most lasting principles of his philosophic character.

Had a portion of the family talent descended to him by a simple continuation of that intellectual succession which we have remarked in his progenitors and kindred, it would still not have been surprising to find that in his case, as in that of most of his cotemporaries, the occupations of purely abstract speculation should have absorbed the other active powers of the man, and that as a mathematician or natural philosopher he should have been content to resign to the rougher hands of the operative, the testing, by experiment and practice, of the results of his more subtle and ethereal conceptions. Nor, on the other hand, would his have been an exceptional case had he applied himself exclusively to the ruder efforts of the practical mechanics, and, without the pre-occupations of theory and of abstract

---

[1] John Watt, the younger brother of the Mechanician, was the editor or the publisher of his uncle's Chart of the River Clyde.

principles, felt satisfied when merely contrivance and a tolerable adjustment of parts to an end proposed, were found to yield the desired results of a visible utility. If, however, the following memorials bring into prominence any feature of character more distinctively than another, it is, the rare and even wonderful *combination* in Watt of these two opposite though not conflicting poles of genius, the elements of which are so fairly referable to his sires. His after-life, doubtless, exhibits the two great powers, each in its several *bearings*, so strong, and yet, in repose, so balanced and adjusted, that it is difficult to determine which of them, in action, commanded in him the greater reverence and regard. Yet this is nothing more than may be discovered in the *boy*, from his earliest years thoughtful, contemplative, studious of things in their first and most elementary principles, delighting in whatever was graceful and symmetrical in form among objects of skill and ingenious mechanism : a taste this which was not, however, a mere sentiment, or the source simply of *passive* enjoyment ; nature—as if to heighten and realize to him the secret pleasure he derived from forms of truth and beauty visible in the first instance only to the inward eye—having endowed him with the power of rendering the satisfaction *actual;* and in gifting him with a hand capable of the nicest and most delicate manipulation, aided a happiness which was only complete when he was able to *produce*, and that according to observed fundamental laws, the "working-model" of what had before been evolved in the inner chambers of the mind in the harmonious lines only of a beautiful problem.

We do not think we have touched here unnecessarily upon these ancestral influences, conceiving that they afford the key to much that is philosophically interesting in this eminent man's history; if, indeed, they be not found to contain the rationale of his whole distinguished career. But without further anticipating details, we resume with the reader the thread of our Memorials.

James Watt, according to the records of the Old Parish of Greenock, was born on the 19th of January 1736.[1] Unfortunately less is known of his early life, even in his native town, than either the curious in literature or the admirers of his genius could wish. The period spent by him under his father's roof at Greenock, extended no further than to his eighteenth year, an inconsiderable portion, in one respect, of his long and active life, yet, such a portion, nevertheless, as, did sufficient data in regard to those early years exist, could not fail to be pregnant with the deepest interest.[2]

Like most great men, of ancient as well as of modern times, Watt was much indebted, during more than the infant period of life, to the instructions and care of an affectionate and judicious mother. Previously to the birth of James, she had suffered severe family bereavement, in the loss of two sons and an only daughter. As might be expected—like the loving mother of Cuvier in very similar circumstances—her affections and solicitude centred in more than an ordinary degree upon her boy,—for whom, also, a certain delicacy of constitution, which early manifested itself and continued by him during almost the rest of his days, tended greatly to augment her anxiety and care. James, in this way, was much in her society ; and, by his gentle and engaging attentions, reciprocated the maternal fondness of which he was so continuously the object. In reference to the pleasure she enjoyed in this grateful companionship, his mother was often heard to say, that the loss of her daughter

[1] The particular house in which he was born has already been specified. See Introduction, p. ix, *supra*.

[2] Although the author's opportunities of collecting information in regard to his favourite subject have been in many respects advantageous, and although during the course of nearly half a century, facts have been from time to time added to his interesting collection, still no one can lament more than himself their paucity, even after exhausting every available source. Scanty, however, as, after all, the facts may be, these pages will contain a far fuller representation of James Watt's youth and education than any sketch or biography of the great man which has yet appeared, and, from their unimpeachable authenticity, cannot—if viewed apart from the execution and setting—be without high value to many readers.

was most fully made up to her, by the dutiful attentions of her son James.

The few particulars we possess in regard to this portion, or rather period in our Memorials, afford a not unpleasing glimpse into the indoor circle and fireside of our young but thoughtful invalid. They give the impression of a quiet family, in sufficiently easy circumstances, and enjoying, at least till some time later than this, perhaps more than an ordinary measure of social and family comforts. James was advantageously circumstanced in regard to both his parents. Of his respected father, we have hitherto had occasion to speak more in his public and out-of-door character. In private, as in his domestic life, he was equally worthy of esteem. The lady to whom he was early united in marriage, was Miss Agnes Muirheid, a gentlewoman of good understanding and superior endowments, whose excellent management in household affairs would seem to have contributed much to the order of her establishment, as well as the every-day happiness of a cheerful home. She is described as having been a person above common in many respects, of a fine womanly presence, ladylike in appearance, affecting—according to our traditions—in domestic arrangements, what it would seem was considered, for the time, rather a superior style of living. What such a style consisted in, the reader shall have the means of judging for himself. One of the author's informants on such points, more than twenty years ago, a venerable lady then in her eighty-fifth year, was wont to speak of the worthy Bailie's wife with much characteristic interest and animation. As illustrative of what has just been remarked of the internal economy of the family, the old lady related an occasion on which she had spent an evening, when a girl, at Mrs. Watt's house, and remembered expressing with much naïveté to her mother, on returning home, her childish surprise, that " Mrs. Watt had TWO candles lighted on the table!" Among these and other reminiscences of her youth, our venerable informant described James Watt's mother,—in her eloquent and expressive Doric,—as "*a braw, braw woman,—none now to be seen like her.*"

From a mother so endowed, with graces as it would seem both of person and of mind, the boy probably inherited something of those more than comely and massive features which the chisel of Chantrey has so happily immortalized. Be this as it may, there is little doubt that she influenced the physiognomy of his plastic mind. From her he received his first lessons in knowledge; and, although, by their very gentleness, he may have been rendered doubly sensitive under the ruder and more popular methods of the public school, to which he was afterwards sent, there is every reason to believe that the very aversion occasioned in his mind to the rough sports and hard usage of his less exquisitely refined playmates, conspired, with other causes, to further, rather than impede, the steady development of his future powers.

In course of time James was sent to the school of a Mr. M'Adam, of whom little more is known than that he kept what in those days would be called the commercial school of the place. The thoughtful gravity of the boy, induced in some measure by the severe constitutional headaches under which he suffered, though still more, perhaps, by the sober studies and hitherto feminine recreations of his home-culture, was found to comport but ill with the wild glee and thoughtless abandonment of his schoolfellows; and, with an ingenuity of persecution common to the petty tyrants of the playground everywhere, reproaches both abstract and concrete fell thick and heavy upon the ethereal yet passive spirit of the gentle boy! His sufferings—for such without any exaggeration may his feelings be styled, on being thus floated out from the indulgent haven of home-training into the boisterous surges of the public school—remind

17

one very forcibly of the experience related, in riper years, by the
sensitive Cowper in circumstances not very dissimilar.[1]

This softness of disposition and partiality for quiet pursuits and
rational conversation on the part of young Watt provoked those more
adventurous youths,—whose hazardous exploits in the harbour, or
along the sea-shore, offered little that was congenial to the boy's
mind,—to stigmatize him by foolish and offensive epithets, expressive
of what, to them, was a most dull and effeminate way of spending his
time. But this was not perhaps the severest part of the ordeal
through which the young philosopher was doomed to pass. Even the
gentler sex, which, according to the primitive arrangement of those
days, formed half the school, joined, it would seem, in the fray ; and,
with them, that debility which, with little intermission, hung over him,
and oppressed at times alike his faculties and his animal spirits,—
phases which the quiet observation of the parental eye knew so well
to manage,—passed during school hours for stupidity and a total want
of sense !

It is not conceived in any way needful to vindicate our young hero
from such unmeaning and undiscriminating persecution and judgments
on the part of those so little qualified to decide the merits of such a
case. But neither do we deem it incumbent to suppress facts, whatever they may seem to involve.[2] The truth in regard to young Watt's
first years in the public school is, that, owing doubtless to infirm health,

[1] "At six years old, taken from the nursery and from the immediate care of a most indulgent mother," he tells us, "I had hardships to conflict with, which I felt more sensibly in proportion to the tenderness with which I had been reared at home ;—my chief affliction," adds the poet with genuine indignation, "consisting in my being singled out from all the other boys by a lad of about fifteen years of age, as a proper object upon whom he might let loose the cruelty of his temper, to such a degree that he had, at length, by his savage treatment, impressed such a dread of his figure upon my mind, that I well remember being afraid to lift up my eyes upon him higher than his knees, and that I knew him from his shoe-buckles better than any other point of his dress."—Memoirs of the Poet Cowper by Dr. Memes. 1834. P. 13.

[2] "Quis nescit primam esse historiæ legem, ne quid falsi dicere audeat, ne quid veri non audeat ; ne qua suspicio gratiæ sit in scribendo, ne qua simultatis."—Cic. de Orat., Lib. ii. 62.

to the suffering and depression which affected his whole powers, he
was unfitted for a considerable time for displaying even a very ordinary
and moderate aptitude for the common routine of school lessons ; and
that during those years he was regarded by his schoolmates as slow
and inapt.   Although to some minds facts of such a nature may be
conceived to mar the romance of a great man's history, yet seeing
they rest on authenticity, which cannot be impugned,[1] there appear
no reasonable grounds on which it may be thought that they ought to
be passed over as if they had not existed, or were altogether un-
founded.[2]   They do not involve any moral, nor even, one may confidently say, any intellectual depreciation of the massive genius that, at
the very worst, was only slumbering in those early moments of life,
and gathering strength by its temporary repose.   Even if, however,
yielding in some measure to their pressure, one of their effects should
be to compel us to postpone by a year or two the marked development
of his great mind, and to date later by a year or two than has been

[1] Our authorities for the facts in the text are
as follows :—The late JAMES GAMMEL, Esq., who
was born 12th December 1735, and was, therefore, just thirty-eight days older than James Watt.
He was not only a contemporary, but a schoolfellow of Watt. Mr. Gammel, who was in all
probability a burly youngster, spent several years
of his early manhood in the pursuits of a seafaring
life, and afterwards became a devoted man of
business, and successful banker in Greenock. On
his retirement from business he purchased a large
estate in Aberdeenshire, where he died, having
survived Mr. Watt by several years.—Mrs. LEITCH,
a venerable lady, who lived to see two of her sons
successively fill the office of Chief Magistrate of
Greenock, with equal credit and respect. She
was born 10th August 1746, and consequently
was somewhat more than nine years younger than
James Watt, and well known to him. She died
25th May 1833.—Bailies JAMES DONALD and
JAMES WILSON, who were joint Magistrates of

Greenock in 1769. Bailie Wilson's daughter was
at school with James Watt. We might mention
others, but the detail would be only tedious. We
have considered it right to adhere to our facts,
as we conceive not only the veracity of the whole
narrative to be affected by the principle, but also
that the genuineness of the character of Watt, as
a whole, will greatly gain thereby, in the estimation of the ingenuous.

[2] In such matters one admires the ingenuous-
ness and sincerity of the amiable and elegant
Pliny the younger, in writing the events of a
portion of his life to his cotemporary Tacitus,
where, generously vindicating the historian from
any partiality of friendship in dealing with the
facts communicated by him, he adds :—" For
history ought not to exceed the bounds of truth ;
and honourable actions demand nothing more than
a truthful narration." "Nam nec historia debet
egredi veritatem, et honeste factis veritas sufficit."
—Pliny, Lib. vii., Epist. 33.

done, the birth of his mathematical talent,—what, may one ask, is lost either in point of interest or of power, in view of the whole brilliant career of Watt's philosophic invention ?   The child PASCAL, the great prototype of mathematical precocity,—by stealth, it is said, lest he should incur the displeasure of his father,—worked out at *twelve* years of age, with a piece of charcoal on the floor-tiles of his chamber, the thirty-second Proposition of the first Book of Euclid ; and that before, it seems, he had ever heard of a triangle, parallelogram, or circle, or knew the definition of a straight line.   But the recluse of Port-Royal would not, to our mind at least, have been less a great man, though the amiable Gilberte had not, by her manner of narrating the attendant circumstances, done it in terms which went to make a prodigy of her illustrious Brother.[1]   A modern Pascal,—a name hardly less honoured perhaps among the savans of the Institute, than it is familiar in the academic halls of our own country,—has no miracle of his infancy to point to : and yet CHALMERS is not surely the less conspicuous in the walks of science and literature, or less wonderful in the breadth and comprehensiveness of his majestic imagination, because the spark of his mathematical and intellectual genius was only struck out in the third term of his college life, and when he had attained his *thirteenth* year.[2]   No less, it is conceived, can NEWTON be thought to merit the title of The Immortal, because only in his *thirteenth* year did he begin to astonish his playfellows at Grantham by the effects of that passion for the mathematics, which soon became with him irresistible.[3]   The enduring frame of the great WATT needs no adventitious aid from the marvellous, in dealing with the facts of his early life ; and he whose little finger is thicker than the loins of any ordinary man, may surely

[1] Lettres, Opuscules et Mémoires de Madame Périer et de Jacqueline, sœurs de Pascal ; publiés sur les mémoires originaux ; par P. Faugère. Paris, 1845.

[2] Memoirs of the Life and Writings of Thomas Chalmers, D.D., LL.D.   By his Son-in-Law, the Rev. William Hanna, LL.D.   1850.   Vol. i. p. 11.

[3] Biographie Universelle ; Newton.   By M. Biot.   Translated by Society for the Diffusion of Useful Knowledge.

afford to hear, without being disconcerted, the boastful jargon of the pigmies around him.[1]

At thirteen years of age, young Watt, like that other giant of Timnath, when the Philistines were upon him, awoke up into something of his real strength, on being put to the study of the mathematics.[2] This we conceive to be the true date of his intellectual birth, —the happy moment when he took into his hands the mystic key of all scientific knowledge, with which, in after years, he was successively to unlock so many of the secrets of nature, and lead mankind to the participation of some of her most precious treasures.

[1] It will be evident to the reader,—from the allusions to the concurrent testimony of Watt's school companions, in regard to a certain mental dulness exhibited by him during the earlier period of his school days, to which we have adverted purposely, in implied rather than in direct terms, although from documentary evidence we might have followed the latter course,—that we are compelled to regard the story of the child's being chid, while drawing on the floor with chalk geometrical problems *at six years of age*, as apocryphal. The interesting myth, as we are forced to consider it, has, with other trivial inaccuracies respecting Watt's parentage, &c.,—natural enough, perhaps, in the absence of better authenticated facts,— already obtained a wide circulation in the passing literature of the subject. With regard to one of its sources, we cannot but think that the miraculous *age* assigned to the performance has been a slip of the pen on the part of the learned and eloquent Academician; whose acute and masculine understanding, of a character, in philosophical inquiries, strongly akin to that of his illustrious contemporary, Niebuhr, was the last to allow itself to be influenced by the fabulous. It is hoped that the light in which we have sought to place the authentic details of Watt's boyhood, while it is believed to detract nothing from the wonderful genius of the Great Inventor, will exonerate us from the imputation of any feeling inconsistent with a regard for the truth of history.

[2] Our authority for this fact rests—among other confirmatory evidence—upon a document in our possession, of which the following is a copy:— " My sister has a distinct recollection of hearing her mother mention that James Watt was educated at the same school as she, viz., at a Mr. M'Adam's, held at the Rue-end. He was thought rather dull at his lessons. His abilities began to appear when he was—about thirteen or fourteen years old—put into a mathematical class, where he made rapid progress." . . . The father of the lady whose statement is here cited was Mr. James Wilson, formerly referred to as one of the magistrates of Greenock, in 1769.

CHAPTER II.

THE PHILOSOPHER'S BOYHOOD——HIS SOBER PASTIMES——THE BOY BECOMES A SAGE——
MATHEMATICS AND ASTRONOMY——HIS MATHEMATICAL PRECEPTOR——HE IS SENT TO
THE GRAMMAR SCHOOL——THE GRAMMAR SCHOOL AND ITS RECTOR IN 1751——THE
SAME A FEW YEARS LATER.

FROM what has been said in the last chapter of the appreciation of
the young philosopher, when just entered upon the mingled and
salutary discipline of the public school, it must by no means be
inferred that Watt, in his boyhood,—though not, it would appear, in
his infancy,—exhibited no tokens of his future distinction, or rather
manifested none of those beautiful traits which were so eminently
characteristic of his riper years.   The noisy taunts of those mischief-
loving urchins must not weigh more than they really purport, or be
allowed to obscure, with us, the true merits of the case in this respect ;
—though it is maintained that the detail given in relation to such
matters is not to be considered entirely without point in our narrative, or devoid of instruction in the study of his life.   The grandest
operations of nature are those which have the most feeble and noiseless beginnings, and which least attract the observation of the crowd.
The early workings of the mind of Watt were of this character—slow,
silent, profound ; but in their very depth and silence consisted their
inherent strength.[1]   It was, indeed, already a manifestation which,
in the circumstances, could not escape attention, that, as early as
thirteen, he showed so decided a predilection for the mathematics.

---

[1] " Toute vie forte est une vie profonde."

This was almost to have been anticipated. But, even before this, disadvantageous as the circumstances of his health were, there had not been altogether wanting, to the discerning, marks unmistakable of a great mind,—a mind at once retiring, modest, and simple, the usual accompaniments of true genius, prosecuting the while, in its own way, its own earnest and grave speculations. The ponderous intellect had been already gathering momentum; but, in conformity with Nature's own laws, silently and slowly.

It would be gratifying could we furnish any very ample details in regard to the occupations of this boyish period. But the life of a philosopher, especially in its early portions, is proverbially barren of striking and startling incident, and rarely offers much that attracts the attention of the ordinary and unconcerned reader. That of the youthful Watt is particularly grave. Its colouring wears a sombre, sometimes even melancholy hue; but the effect produced is far from unpleasing, and its quietness of tone is in admirable keeping with the temperament of the sage. All his amusements even were of the soft and gentle order. By the side of his affectionate mother, drawing, cutting and carving with penknife or tools, not without ingenuity, had made to glide by many a noiseless and even delicious hour, in those otherwise depressed and sickly days, under the tranquil shelter of home. Of out-door pastimes, the only one in regard to which we have been able to gather any local information, deserves mention from its being so singularly characteristic of the bent of his mind. It was that " most honest, ingenuous, quiet, and harmless art of Angling," in which, according to good Izak Walton, " contemplation and action, the two elements of happiness, meet together, making it the most fitting pastime for quiet men and lovers of peace." However he might have pursued this engaging recreation along the solitary streams which traverse the upper moorlands of the vicinity, he is known to have practised it much nearer home, indeed within the precincts of his father's own property. It will be remembered, that, in our early notices regarding his father, allusion was made to a house and property which he purchased on the open shore at Greenock. This was not of course the house in which James was born. To the house and property just referred to his father removed only subsequently to James's birth, and it was here that the latter lived, during the sixteen or seventeen years which he spent at Greenock. It was in great part built by his father, and was on the north side of what was then called the High Street, with its rear to the sea, having a weir or jettee extending into deep water in that direction.[1] Here the meditative boy might be often seen, in the inviting stillness of the morning hours, occupied with his most honest art, and enjoying the freedom from interruption and annoyance which their solitude afforded. The pleasure derived from this pastime would seem to have been very great, as it was said to have been often resorted to by him, even in after days, when confinement or over-application to study had rendered a slight and temporary relaxation necessary to his constitution, when he no doubt found the gentle stimulus to "contemplation and action" as conducive to health as it was congenial to his mind.

But to return from this short digression. From the time when young Watt entered upon the study of geometry, for which he gave many indications of aptitude, and in which he made rapid progress, a new impulse and charm was added to his existence. Not so much is

---

[1] The following quotation from a paper describing the " Harbour of Greenock," in 1750, in the handwriting, if I mistake not, of James Watt's father, will shew how the studious boy might occupy an hour of relaxation in fishing without leaving his father's premises, doubtless, in his eyes, no small enhancement of the pleasure. The document quoted from, modernized a little in orthography, but not otherwise altered, begins thus:—" The town of Greenock on the River Clyde, from its situation and harbour, may truly be said to be amongst the most convenient in North Britain. The High Street is bounded on both sides with stone houses, and those on the river side, most or all of them, within the full seamark, having closes or quays falling a considerable way into the sea, so that vessels of fifty or sixty tons burthen can discharge at those back closes."

heard now from his schoolfellows of languor and want of parts. Indeed it may be believed that, as in the case of the great Port-Royalist, his bodily suffering was outweighed, and, for the time at least, forgotten, in the intensity of interest which the all-absorbing problem evoked. The thoughtful boy now questioned, read, remembered, but meditated and reflected more. The passion with him was, to know, to *understand* everything. The seclusion which feeble health had at first made necessary, soon became desirable and even loved, for other reasons than that it shielded the delicate spirit from the rude rebuffs of an idle or meaningless sport in which it found nothing worthy of it. The youth began to value solitude for its own sake, and wooed retirement for the secret joy and conscious intellectual strength it ministered,—the maxim being as true for the studious as it is for the devout, that "everything which distracts weakens us," and its converse.[1]

To the south of the town, and on the rising ground behind the church, at no great distance from his father's house, was a clump of trees of considerable extent, composed of stately elms and venerable beeches, part of what were, in former days, the retired and beautiful pleasure-grounds of the Old Mansion-house of Greenock. The planting referred to was, it is much to be regretted, more than forty years ago cut down, to make way for questionable improvements; but before that time, occupying a height which was on a level with the present Well Park,—its grey and moss-grown gateways are still standing,—it formed a background of great beauty to the elevation of the town when viewed from the sea. Here the young recluse found a genial retreat. To this spot he was wont to retire at night as well as by day; and, like another Ferguson, the astronomical herd-boy of Scotland, was known to spend hours lying upon his back, to watch through the trees the wondrous movements of the stars. Of a spot

---

[1] "Tout ce qui nous dissipe nous affaiblit."

18

so interesting, and thus rendered classical by genius, it is much to be lamented that no vestiges remain.

The prosecution of his favourite geometry now occupied habitually his thoughts and time ; and it is not surprising that Astronomy should have become with him a study as agreeable as it was fascinating to an imagination such as his.   In the repositories of his father were to be found abundance of optical instruments of various kinds, calculated to render his observations of the heavenly bodies both accurate and enlarged.   Of these the young astronomer sedulously availed himself ; and there can be little doubt that familiarity in the use, as well as construction of these scientific implements, in the way we shall have to allude to more particularly hereafter, contributed to form in him a taste for this species of delicate mechanism, which perhaps also went far in recommending him, at a later stage of his youth, to notice and consideration among those qualified to appreciate his ingenuity and skill in such workmanship.

Of the mathematical Preceptor of so apt and promising a pupil too little is unfortunately known that could be very interesting to the reader.   In regard to few particulars in the memorials of Watt's youth is one disposed to lament the scantiness of information more sincerely than in this.   His name was John Marr, a name not unknown to historical record.   He would seem to have been retained in some capacity in the household and family of the Lord of the Manor, Sir John Schaw.   We have seen his subscription as a witness to some charters granted by Sir John in 1751.   In these deeds he is designated "John Marr, Mathematician in Greenock."   He appears to have had a salary from the town, as, in the years 1750 and 1751, there are found in the accounts of the town-treasurer more than one payment made to him.[1]   Nothing further is known of him than what appears

---

[1] The worthy *Treasurer* designates him simply and shortly " English Schoolmaster."

The entries are as follows :—1750, Feb. 9.— To cash p$^{d.}$ John Marr, English Schooll-

in the Records of the Society of Freemasons known as the "Lodge, Greenock, Kilwinning, No. 11," of which he was a Brother, and in which he acted in some official capacity, having been initiated into the mysteries of the craft in the city of Glasgow. To be able to record more of James Watt's mathematical preceptor would be gratifying, not less on his own account than that of his pupil; and the gratification would be proportionably heightened could a relationship, by no means improbable, be happily traced up from him to another John Marr, who was mathematician in the household of King James VI., and friend of the great Napier of Merchiston. The following anecdote, in which the latter John Marr acts so dramatic a part, is so interesting in itself, and so graphically narrated, that we cannot resist the opportunity of quoting it. Lilly, in his Life and Times, thus relates the circumstances to Elias Ashmole :—" I will acquaint you with one memorable story related to me by John Marr, an excellent mathematician and geometrician, whom I conceive you remember. He was servant to King James First and Charles First. When Merchiston first published his Logarithms, Mr. Briggs, then reader of the astronomy lectures at Gresham College in London, afterwards of Oxford, was so surprised with admiration of them, that he could have no quietness in himself till he had seen that noble person, whose only invention they were. He acquaints John Marr therewith, who went into Scotland before Mr. Briggs, purposely to be there when these two so learned persons should meet. Mr. Briggs appointed a certain day when to meet in Edinburgh, but failing thereof, Merchiston was fearful he would not come. It happened one day as John Marr and the Lord Napier were speaking of Mr. Briggs,—' Oh, John !' said Merchiston, ' Mr. Briggs will not come now ;' at the very instant, one knocks at the

master, for on year and on quarter's cellery at six pound stg. per year, . £7 10 0
Again :—1751, May 7.—To cash pd. John Marr, English Schoolmaster, for his quarter's Cellery from Candlemass last till this date, ... £1 10 0

gate,—John Marr hastened down,—and it proved to be Mr. Briggs, to his great contentment. He brings Mr. Briggs into my Lord's chamber, where almost one quarter of an hour was spent, each beholding other with admiration, before one word was spoken. At last Mr. Briggs began,—' My Lord, I have undertaken this long journey purposely to see your person, and to know by what engine of wit and ingenuity you came first to think of this most excellent help unto astronomy, namely, the Logarithms ; but, my Lord, being by you found out, I wonder nobody else found it before, when now being known it appears so easy.' He was nobly entertained by Lord Napier ; and every summer after that, during the Laird's being alive, this venerable man went purposely to Scotland to visit him."[1]

The only other preceptor of Watt was Robert Arrol, the first Master appointed to the Grammar School of Greenock, his nomination having taken place at least as early as the year 1727, in which year he is mentioned for the first time in the town Records.[2] It is not known at what age our young geometrician was sent to the Grammar School, or how long he continued under the instructions of its zealous and learned pedagogue. There is, however, the best reason for believing that he made good progress, and attained to a creditable proficiency in Latin, and, most probably, the elements of Greek. And although we are not in a position to hazard in regard to him, what the great Lexicographer said of his own classical attainments,—that he should never have learned Latin if it had not been flogged into him,—we know that our young philosopher learned his so well, that he is found, in his eighty-second year, notwithstanding the contrarieties and

[1] For the above dramatic anecdote I am indebted to one of the many learned historical labours of my early friend, Mr. Mark Napier,—the "Memoirs of John Napier of Merchiston." 1834. P. 408.

[2] We have said, the *only* other preceptor, because it is accurately ascertained that James Watt received no other instruction, in the way of education, beyond that which he acquired in his native town ; being indebted for all the wonderful advances in learning of which his after-life bore such ample fruits, to his own unaided labour and insatiable thirst for knowledge.

occupations of a long and busy life in very different departments of study, making use of his Classics with as much discrimination as taste, and delighting even the circles of the Edinburgh literati, during its most brilliant epoch, with the extent and correctness of his critical and philological attainments.[1] But for such a fact we should not perhaps have felt ourselves amenable to the well-known dictum of Dr. Johnson, that "not to name the *School* or the *Masters* of men illustrious for literature, is a kind of historical fraud, by which honest fame is injuriously diminished."[2] Under the circumstances, therefore, we shall give here all that we have been able to ascertain of the character and history of James Watt's first and only classical master.

Arrol seems to have been a man of some pretensions and merit for the times in which he lived. In its scholastic or disciplinary aspects, the period was signalized by hot disputes and voluminous controversies among the Grammarians as to "the best way of teaching the Latin tongue;" one party contending for Ruddiman's and Lily's, or Lilius', Rudiments and Grammar, which were wholly in *Latin*,—the other, maintaining the absurdity of such a practice, and advocating the employment of these and other elementary works "in an *English* dress." The most prominent combatant and vindicator of the former system was our own Ruddiman at Edinburgh; while Clarke of Hull, supported by other scholars, asserted the reasonableness and advantages of the latter method. The controversy was carried on in the north with the usual *ingenium perfervidum* of our countrymen, and with great obstinacy; though, eventually, a compromise was effected, and the Rudiments rules came to be printed in *both* English and Latin. The concession, however, gave rise to a much more objectionable practice,—that of "literal translations" of the Latin school-books

---

[1] See, for example, the playful letter to Captain Clutterbuck, in the Introduction to *The Monastery*.
[2] Lives of the Poets: Addison.

used,—the cause of which was pleaded, with much ingenuity, by the learned Dr. Isaac Watts.[1]

Supported by such eminent authority—as even Dr. Johnson admits the Divine in matters of education to be, not to mention that of the judicious Locke, and, in more recent times, of no less acute and sagacious a scholar than Sydney Smith—the practice came to have numerous advocates, at least in England ; and, judging from some of Arrol's productions, he would appear to have contributed his share to the contraband stock. He was author of a translation of Eutropius, with notes, as well as one of the Select Colloquies of Erasmus,—a book then in common use in schools, and much admired on account of its purity of style and near approach to the ancient models. He executed also a translation of Cornelius Nepos, with a vocabulary, chronological table, and notes, having prefixed an Introduction in Latin—the whole showing considerable erudition and appreciation of his subject. Besides such employment of his talents and leisure, he appears to have been occasionally engaged as collaborator with some of his cotemporaries, furnishing contributions to their works, of a philological, geographical, and mythological character.[2]

Such were some of the qualifications of the master to whose instructions James Watt was indebted for his first introduction to the study of grammar and language, the elements of the profoundest study of the human mind. Under so zealous and capable a philologue there is every reason for supposing that he made solid advances, and acquired a generous taste for classical literature, in addition to his other attainments in the mathematics. It was a favourite axiom with the late

---

[1] Chalmers' Life of Ruddiman ; Essay on the Education of Youth in Grammar Schools, by John Clarke, 1720 ; New Grammar of the Latin Tongue, with a Dissertation on Language, by John Clarke, 1733 ; Supplement to the Art of Logic, by Dr. Isaac Watts, &c.

[2] In the title-page of Clarke of Hull's Metamorphoses of Ovid, Arrol's name occurs among other learned contributors :—" Notis fere integris, Cl. Virorum, *Thomæ Ruddimanni,* et *Gulielmi Willymotti:* quibus et aliæ partim Mythologicæ, partim Geographicæ, a *Roberto Arrolo* adjectæ sunt. Glasguæ, 1770."

Dr. James L. Brown, the somewhat eccentric, though most successful Rector of the Grammar School of Greenock,[1] that in proportion as a boy distinguished himself in Classics, in the same ratio would he be found successful in the study of the Mathematics. If the converse of this was held to be true, in regard to a boy who distinguished himself in the latter branch of knowledge, the inference would tell favourably in respect to young Watt's eminence in the former department of liberal education. Without, however, invalidating the conclusion so far as it might enhance the polite acquirements of the youthful scholar, we are disposed to demur to the universality of application of the learned Doctor's maxim. It may hold true, to a limited extent, in regard to the acquisition of the mere elements of the several branches referred to, where sheer industry or temporary application are the procuring causes of success. But, with reference to anything ulterior and permanent, with reference to the time when the mind, either spontaneously or by constraint, makes its selection of study, for the display of its powers, something more than merely general application is needed. The mental qualities demanded for distinction, in the higher mathematics on the one hand, and in philology and criticism in the higher classics on the other, are so exceedingly diverse, that a *many sidedness* of talent is required in order to an equal eminence in both; and adaptation for the one study is by no means correlative with adaptation for the other. And yet, such a comprehensiveness of mental power is just what,—on not inadequate grounds, we think, as we shall hereafter have occasion to illustrate,— we claim for James Watt, however circumstances, and the popular

---

[1] Of Dr. Brown's success as a classical teacher, the best evidence is found in the number of his pupils who have distinguished themselves—after a successful and often brilliant University career —in all departments of the learned professions. As most of these are still alive, it would of course be invidious to give what could only be a partial enumeration of such men. This, however, may be said, that while the number is large in proportion to the population, it will bear, it is believed, in point of success and merit, a favourable comparison with any other provincial town of Scotland.

estimate of this great man as an inventor in mechanics, may tend to make his other qualifications in letters only secondary. And such a claim is conceived to be due not only to the merit of the pupil but also to that of the preceptor.

We have in vain endeavoured to rescue further from obscurity this worthy instructor of Watt, or to discover how a man of Arrol's learning and respectability as a scholar came to be induced to settle in so small a community as Greenock.[1] Equally difficult is it to conceive how his literary labours, which were not unknown, should have been so much overlooked by other more important seminaries as to allow him to remain in comparative obscurity, and we fear it must be added also, in comparative indigence, during his life,—except in so far as that might have been irradiated by the honest sincerity of his studies, or the simple reputation which his various publications no doubt obtained for him. We have said comparative indigence. In regard to what were Arrol's circumstances, or what the extent of his moderate fortune, we have no means of knowing the exact state of the case. In all probability his honorarium was derived from more sources than one ; from the public records of the period we find the amount of his remuneration paid by the community, and from this an estimate may be formed of the rest of his combined salary. We quote from the worthy town-treasurer's account, from which it will be seen, that however the youth of Greenock may have been benefited by Mr. Arrol's labours, his own advantage in a pecuniary point of view could never have been considered by him, in the generous and self-forgetting, though far from enviable character of his position and

---

[1] At the time of his probable appointment, the population of the town, including Crawfordsdyke and the landward part of the district, must have been very inconsiderable, as, fourteen years later, in 1741, the detailed census amounted to only 4100 souls. [The population of Greenock according to the last census, 1851, was 39,391.]

It is probable that Arrol was invited to the charge of the Grammar School—with what promises of success we cannot tell—by Sir John Schaw, as nothing of any importance took place in the community without the superior being consulted.

functions.   The following is a verbatim copy of the entry :—" 1749, November 24th.—To cash p^d Robert Arrol, grammar schollmaster, for his year's cellery from Candlemes 1749 to Candlemess 1750, £4, 9s. 5⅓d."[1]   Although a century has elapsed since this payment was made, our wonder, shall we say our indignation, at the sum is not at all diminished ; nor can the astonishment be less, that this estimable individual was not called, or rather, did not feel compelled to seek some more generous field of labour, and consequently of greater usefulness as well as personal advantage.

Arrol seems to have been married, and to have had at least one daughter.   We can, however, only conceive of him as a quiet and unpretending but laborious scholar, devoted to letters and cultivating learning for its own sake.   In such ardour and devotion he no doubt enjoyed what he might consider an ample reward.   But while we admire the nobility of such a self-renouncing character, we cannot but deplore the unequal fortune which would seem to have been his lot. If anything, however, is wanting—beyond the attempt here made to redeem his memory from oblivion by faintly representing his merits

[1] Subsequently to 1741, after Sir John had granted his first charter to the town, we find that the Kirk-Session had a share in the nomination of the teacher of the grammar-school, and that his salary was paid partly by Sir John, partly by the Kirk-Session, and partly by the town or corporation ; and the fractional character of the sum paid here by the town-treasurer, induces the belief that the amount of Arrol's remuneration was made up in a similar manner. A curious example of how this joint-payment was managed we cannot help inserting here, as illustrative of many features in the character of those times. The document is dated 2d October 1751. It relates to Mr. Arrol's successor, Mr. John Woodrow, who had been invited to supply the vacancy in the grammar-school caused by poor Arrol's death. Twenty pounds sterling, it was agreed, was a genteel appointment for the new functionary. It was accordingly proportioned and agreed to be paid in the following manner, viz. :—" By Sir John Schaw and his heirs, Three pounds, one shilling and one penny, one-third of a penny sterling: By the said Archibald Crawford of Cartsburn and his heirs, One pound, two shillings and twopence, two-thirds of a penny, money foresaid: By the Old Kirk-Session, out of the session seats, Four pounds, nine shillings and fivepence, one-third of a penny: By the New Kirk-Session, Three pounds and sixpence, two-thirds of a penny, money foresaid ; and by the Magistrates and Town-Council themselves, in name of the town, to complete the foresaid twenty pounds sterling, the sum of Eight pounds, six shillings and eightpence, money foresaid."

19

and his virtues, to brighten the else rayless round of that generous obscurity in which he was content to pass his days,—it surely is the consideration, which is not without its price, that Robert Arrol has the privilege to be remembered as one of the preceptors of the immortal Watt.[1]

For the sake of those who may be curious in such matters, we may here take occasion, in alluding at length to Watt, Arrol, and the Grammar School of Greenock, to point out the locality of " the noisy mansion," as, however mean its actual aspect, it cannot but be regarded as classic ground,—a kind of *oasis* in a region then little cultivated. The old tenement at the foot of the west side of *Smith's Lane,* formerly known as the *Wee-kirk Street,* where it joins the Vennel, is the house in which the town-schools at the period alluded to met. It probably belonged at that time to one of the magistrates of the day.

By way of " tail-piece" to the present chapter on Watt's Schools and Schoolmasters, and as accounting for, though by no means palliating the neglect under which Arrol's inglorious days were passed, the chronicler cannot forbear a notice of one of his immediate

---

[1] As a last duty to the memory of poor Arrol, we cannot omit mention of the spot where his remains are deposited. He died in 1751, and was buried in the Old West Churchyard, in a lair, close to the south wall, purchased by him in 1732. A slab placed in the wall contained an inscription which appears to have been hewn off, and now bears in large Roman characters the letters A L. On 4th June 1785, thirty-four years after his death, the lair was transferred, by whom is not said, to John Leitch, Press Master in Greenock, and with it, of course, poor Arrol's remains; and again, on 17th November 1808, to Alexander Leitch, cooper in Greenock, heir to the former; the probable conclusion from which is, that the worthy schoolmaster left behind him no relations in Greenock to represent him.

Robert Arrol was chosen Session-Clerk of the parish on 29th June 1727. A rather curious minute of the Session occurs during his holding the office, 18th September 1729, as follows:— " The said day, William Smellie, yᵉ Thesaurer, having represented to yᵉ Session, That he has amongst yᵉ poor's money a good deal of bad halfpence that are not current,—yᵉ Session allow and appoint him to dispose of yᵉ said bad halfpence, to yᵉ best advantage, by giving twelve pence of yᵉ said bad halfpence to any yᵗ inclines to take yᵐ for eight or nine pence of current money, for yᵉ use of yᵉ poor,"—a measure sanctioned by the pious and prudent men then composing the Session, no doubt on the ground that the wants of the poor of the parish amply justified their project!

successors in the labours of the grammar school,—a man possessed of
more fire, though not perhaps of a more noble spirit of independence,
than his worthy predecessor, and who magnanimously retaliated under
the pressure to which a fate felt to be so ignoble exposed him.   Mr.
John Wilson, to whom we refer, succeeded to the mastership of the
Grammar School in 1767.   He was at once a scholar and a poet.   He
was author of an elegant poem, entitled " CLYDE," republished at
Edinburgh in 1803.   A very spirited biographical sketch of its author
is prefixed to this edition by Dr. Leyden, from which we extract the
following illustrative passage :—

" I have now," says Dr. Leyden, " to relate a singular transaction,
which I can scarcely believe would have taken place in any district
of Scotland but the West, so late as 1767.   Greenock at this period
was a thriving sea-port, rapidly emerging into notice.   In the beginning of last century it consisted of a single row of thatched houses,
stretching along a bay without any harbour.   In 1707, a harbour
began to be constructed, but the town increased so slowly that in
1755 its population amounted only to about 3800 souls.   About the
latter period, however, it began to increase rapidly, and continued to
flourish till the commencement of the American War.   Still, however,
its inhabitants were more remarkable for opulence and commercial
spirit, than for their attention to literature and science.   During the
struggle between Prelacy and Presbytery in Scotland, Greenock, like
most of the towns and districts of the West of Scotland, had imbibed
the most intolerant spirit of Presbyterianism ; a spirit which at no
period had been favourable to the exertions of poetical fancy, and
which spent the last efforts of its virulence on the *Douglas* of Home.
Induced by this religious spirit, and by a cool mercantile attention to
prudence, the Magistrates and Minister of Greenock, before they
admitted Mr. Wilson to the superintendence of the Grammar School,
stipulated that he should abandon " *the profane and unprofitable art*

of poem-making." To avoid the temptation of violating this promise, which he esteemed sacred, he took an early opportunity of committing to the flames the greater part of his unfinished manuscripts. After this he never ventured to touch his forbidden lyre, though he often regarded it with that mournful solemnity which the harshness of dependence and the memory of its departed sounds could not fail to inspire.

"He seems during life to have considered this as the crisis of his fate, which condemned him to obscurity, and sometimes alluded to it with acrimony. In a letter to his son George, attending the University of Glasgow, dated January 21, 1779, he says :—' I once thought to live by the breath of fame ; but how miserably was I disappointed when, instead of having my performance applauded in crowded theatres, and being caressed by the great—for what will not a poetaster in his intoxicating delirium of possession dream—I was condemned to bawl myself to hoarseness to wayward brats, to cultivate sand and wash Ethiopians, for all the dreary days of an obscure life, the contempt of shopkeepers and brutish skippers.'"

Costly and precious as was the holocaust thus offered on the altar of ignorance and prejudice,—which were, however, characteristics of those times generally rather than of this town in particular,—thanks to our happier stars, a POET, like any other good citizen, may now dwell safely under his own vine and under his own fig-tree, none daring to make him afraid. And while we record with satisfaction such a change in the face of things in the community which gave birth to men like Watt and Spence, with many others who have taken a high place in the walks of both literature and the arts, and whose names may yet adorn the page of our scientific annals, the unreserved tribute of our gratitude is, unquestionably, in the highest sense due to our SCHOOLS and our SCHOOLMASTERS,—a distinguished succession of whom have, during the last century, though, it must be admitted, occasionally under a patronage far from encouraging, contributed their zealous labours to the advancement of the town's welfare.

Most ardently is it hoped that a liberal and enlightened policy, on the part of those entrusted with our public seminaries, will more and more evidence the wisdom, not to say the beneficial results to the community, of such a generous and fostering care bestowed on the education of the youth of Greenock, as, in the words of James Watt himself, in founding the Greenock Scientific Library, will "render our townsmen as eminent for their knowledge as they are for their spirit of enterprise."

CHAPTER III.

THE YOUNG MECHANICIAN AND HIS TOOLS—DEVELOPMENT OF THE ARTIST-LIFE—FIRST EFFORTS—HIS MECHANICAL MODELS—HOME MISFORTUNES—IS SENT TO GLASGOW, AND TO LONDON—ARRIVES A SECOND TIME IN GLASGOW—NEW CHAPTER IN HIS LIFE—IS APPOINTED MATHEMATICAL INSTRUMENT MAKER TO THE UNIVERSITY—FALLS IN WITH AN OLD FRIEND—INCIDENTS AND EVENTS OF THE COLLEGE WORKSHOP.

WHATEVER may be the relish which begins to be felt by youths who have reached the fifth or sixth form, for the beauties and style of the old Roman authors, there is assuredly but one opinion among them in regard to the " Rudiments" and the " Prosody Rules,"—that they are a drudgery and a bore, and worthy, in the profoundest degree, of universal execration. Young Watt was probably in this respect like most other boys of his own age and standing : and though he could in riper years smooth the asperities of toil and increasing harassment by a page of Cicero ; or throw the enchantment of youthful feeling over the downward path of age, by a Satire of Juvenal, or an Elegy of Catullus, still, in those redoubtable days of the Tyro's Dictionary and Select Extracts, we can more easily picture the thoughtful youth in the congenial solitude he so much loved, poising by night his glass, to observe the planet traverse its field ; or, at home, pursuing those boyish speculations to which he neither thought of nor needed any " royal road :"—delicious moments those, that were already feeding from nature's secret rills the rootlets and delicate stem of that genius, that in manhood was to put forth so many and such massive boughs of beauty and strength.

But James Watt was not now, nor at any former time, a dreamer. This was effectually prevented by his innate love and liking for handi-work. His thoughtfulness was only the elaborating of what, to satisfy him, must have figure and form, parts and standing,—but, above all, a use. It has been shown very successfully, by a modern popular writer on Art,[1] how the first outgoings of artist-being show them-selves in the most scrupulous " copyings of nature." Infantine though this artist-life be, it is not, however, without an *idea*, anterior to pro-duction. But the happiness that lurks in this idea is, to be able to produce " exactly after nature." The representation of the *ideal* is an after and artificial growth. Invention has not yet supervened; imitation, but correct imitation, satisfies, for the present at least, all his inward cravings.

To trace the young mechanical taste, so full of intelligence, as one would trace the artist-life or the naturalist-life, to its more secret springs. To Wordsworth's " Peter Bell," doubtless, as to all his congeners,—

> " A primrose by the river's brim
> A yellow primrose is to him,
> And it is nothing more,"—

but not so to the naturalist or the poet, to whose mind the mention of spring's pale harbinger calls up sensations of delight, and recogni-tions of beauty, inappreciable to the vulgar eye. Similar to these are the sensations of such a mind as Watt's, on the presentation of the simplest piece of mechanical contrivance—a common pulley, for ex-ample, the capstan or windlass, or the simplest form of the ship-pump. Beauty of contrivance, happy adaptation to an end designed, are, doubtless, more or less distinctly component parts of the pleasure felt

---

[1] Modern Painters. Third Edition, 1846. Preface to Second Edition, p. xxviii.

in contemplating the object. But, in Watt, the feeling goes a step further, and in him the mechanical taste is only satiated, when the little operative succeeds in *constructing*, with his own hands, the correct miniature model of the beautiful device.

Such were Watt's earliest studies in the practical mechanics,—the making and fashioning of such miniature pulleys or blocks, pumps and capstans, with their levers or bars,—all objects illustrative of the mechanical powers, and attractive in the highest degree to a young mind so sensitive and ingenious.

The reader is already aware of the general nature of the father's business at Greenock,—the worthy master-wright, merchant, bailie and treasurer of the town,—and of its miscellaneous character. A glance here at his work-benches will give us a more accurate idea of the kind of work going forward. In addition to most of the minor details of carpentry, such as the outfit and supply of the shipping demanded, we observe the carving of ships' figure-heads, the making of gun-carriages, of blocks, pumps, capstans, dead-eyes, &c. &c. The "touching" of ships' compasses also is done here, and the adjusting and repairing of such nautical instruments as are yet in use. We notice further, among other things interesting to us, a piece of mechanical work which was the construction of the same enterprising and ingenious man,—the first *Crane* made at Greenock, for the convenience of "the Virginia tobacco ships" then frequenting the harbour.

A scene of useful labour such as this was a fitting school for the genius of him who afterwards was to become the leading mechanician of his age. At such benches, and amongst so many engaging elements of mechanical contrivance, it would not be difficult to figure in imagination the precocious boy, in his twelfth or thirteenth year, busy with chisels and tools, ardent in the construction of his beautiful model-works and machines. Fortunately, however, there is very positive proof that such, at this time, were his favourite pursuits and occupations.   A late master shipwright and blockmaker of Greenock,[1] who, along with his father, had served an apprenticeship in the workshops referred to, mentioned to the author among other interesting particulars relative to young Watt, that he remembered having been sent, when a boy, to clear out an attic room in his employer's house, where he found a quantity of such ingenious models as have been described, and which Mr. Watt, senior, told him had been, some years before, made by James, who was then in business in Glasgow.   Among these models he remembered, in particular, a miniature *Crane*, and a *Barrel-organ*.[2]

[1] The late Mr. John Rodger. Mr. Rodger was born in 1754, and was, at the time of his communications to me—21st May 1827—in his seventy-third year. He died October 1827. On the occasion referred to, he produced a portion of his father's articles of indenture with Mr. Watt. The indenture was for five years, and was discharged 22d September 1734. His father's name was James Rodger.

[2] One is tempted in passing, to notice this, from its connexion, somewhat singular phenomenon,— the Barrel-organ. Watt is known to have constructed several musical instruments in the earlier part of his life, particularly an organ, of some dimensions and power, while he was in Glasgow; which, it is said, produced "the most remarkable harmonic effects, so as to delight even professional musicians." It is difficult to account for this partiality, or rather success, in the philosopher, as a maker of musical instruments,—especially if it can be successfully maintained that "he could not distinguish one note from another, and was wholly insensible to the charms of music." [*Eloge Historique de James Watt*, par M. Arago. Paris, 1839, p. 12.] Undoubtedly, successive feats of such a nature, accomplished in this delightful department of the fine arts, are made infinitely surprising when one is at the same time assured, that the musical artist was no musician. It is certainly a very possible thing that the inventor of the lyre himself was in this unfortunate case,

and that Mercury had no more sense of music than the shapeless animal which he first drew from its melodious shell; though it is not easy, in such a case, to conceive why he should have invented the lyre rather than a seething-pot, or anything else, if his ear did not detect sweet harmony in its strings. One is reluctant to rob the fine genius of the philosopher of all merit in *his* musical constructions, beyond what mere imitation in a much more ordinary workman might successfully accomplish and claim. One feels unwilling to admit an entire insensibility to *harmony* in a being whose whole nervous temperament—wherein lie the vibrating chords of musical sympathy—was so finely and delicately strung as Watt's. The question is certainly to some extent an open one,—how far a deaf man, for example, or even one without any "ear," might frame and arrange an intricate musical instrument, and, unaided, turn its lignean pipes to such admirable harmony as to charm the most accomplished professors of the art. To pronounce, *ex cathedra*, in a case of such a nature, requires, we suspect, a soul that is itself exquisitely alive to the delicious pain of harmonious sounds. "Non ex quovis ligno fit Mercurius." One is far more inclined to believe the amiable philosopher [to have been more or less thus gifted; especially as it would be easy to demonstrate, from the harmony which exists between all the passivities of taste, and delicate sensibility to the impressions

20

Having completed his attendance at the grammar-school, young Watt was, for a year or more, industriously occupied about his father's premises, either as an amateur, or in the way of intentionally acquiring an accurate knowledge of the various nautical and scientific instruments left with his father for adjustment. At all events, he had here a small forge erected for his particular use; the purpose of which, no doubt, was the constructing, or, in any case, repairing and setting of such instruments as came to his hand, with, probably, other experiments in a branch of art in which he took peculiar delight, and for which the niceness and delicacy of his manipulation remarkably fitted him. It is probably to this period that his fabrication, for one of his friends, of a "*punch-ladle*," out of a large silver coin, is to be referred.

Such, however, was not destined to be the sphere of James' life-labour; nor, indeed, was he to continue long under the immediate guidance or counsel of his father. There was ere long to take place the first of those rude but timely severances which usually powerfully affect a sensitive disposition, and give impulse and motion to forces which, till then, had been only statical in the mind. In the sudden death of his mother, James suffered a severe loss—the rupture of that earliest tie which bound a gentle spirit to home and its grateful protection and shade.[1]

We are not able to say, with much certainty, whether it is to this date, or one somewhat later, that those reverses of fortune are to be referred which overtook his father, who was at this time a councillor of the town. That Mr. Watt, subsequently to this period of his life, met with such commercial losses as told heavily upon a fortune, till

---

of the senses, inseparable altogether from a fine understanding and lively imagination,—that the susceptibility to music, and that generally in some positive degree, though it be only *passive*, and not creative, is an almost unvarying accompaniment of marked genius, whose first and essential attribute is—delicate and *discriminating* perception.

[1] She died in 1753, at the early age of fifty-two. Her death was sudden. She is said to have had a singular dream, in which " she heard a voice requiring her to prepare for appearing within three days before the judgment-seat of Christ;" and that within three days she died.

then in all respects adequate to the maintenance of an easy respectability, is undoubted. An anecdote of him, communicated by the informant above mentioned, has reference to these losses, but is still more valuable as illustrative of the prudence and singular benevolence of character of this estimable man :—When boatswains of ships came to his place of business to have stores made up, the old gentleman was in the habit of throwing in an extra parcel of " sail-needles and twine," with the characteristic remark,—" See, take that too ; I once lost a ship for want of such articles on board." Whatever the nature or extent of the losses referred to, it is certain that they in no way tended to affect or diminish the confidence and respect entertained towards him by his townsmen, as four years later than this [1757] he was raised to the dignity of magistrate, and continued for nearly twenty years more connected with municipal office.

However the death of his mother or his father's circumstances may have influenced the decision in regard to James, the young mechanician was, in the same year, 1753, or the one following, sent to reside with his maternal relations in Glasgow, at the age of seventeen or eighteen ; and, in the year 1755, went to London, with the view of perfecting himself in the profession which, it would appear, the inclination of the time, as well as the circumstances in which he had been brought up, dictated as the most expedient. Ill health, however, compelled him to make his stay in London of short duration, and he soon returned to Scotland ; at all events, he was again in Greenock in 1756.[1] In the course of this year he finally settled in

[1] I find the following entered in the public accounts of his father, who was treasurer of the town of Greenock in this year :—" September 11, 1756, paid Hugh Campbell and James Watt, junior, charges at Glasgow sundrie days, settling accounts of cellars, 15s." The accounts which the junior James Watt was here employed to settle, were certain dues leviable by the town of Greenock from the merchants in Glasgow, for cellarage of tobacco in the Royal Close Warehouses. These warehouses were held in lease by the community, and consequently were under the management of Mr. Watt's father, as town-treasurer.

Glasgow for the prosecution of his business as a mathematical instrument-maker.

This event closes that portion of James Watt's history which is
properly denominated his early life and education, in regard to which
it is but justice to add, on his own authority, that he received no
other education or instruction, either school or university, after this
period;[1] all his subsequent advances in knowledge, as already stated,
having been the result of his own unaided industry and labour.   And
yet, the reader who has followed the narrative of his progress, up to
this point, will be the last to conclude that Watt's education was very
defective.   In this respect, indeed, he had received, perhaps, even
somewhat more than the modicum which usually is found to have
fallen to the lot of men who have distinguished themselves in science
and the arts.   The foundation, at least, of his intellectual culture was
solid and good; and when to it is added that further and independent
discipline, to which the motion and bent of his own genius prompted
him, it will be admitted that his whole training had been singularly
advantageous, and one calculated most felicitously to prepare him for
the grandeur of that work which was to him, as yet, future and
unknown.   Up to this period his several mental and manual endowments have been slowly but steadily unfolding themselves, and pro-
gressing to maturity.   The mechanical or artist life evolving itself in
obedience to a law of nature, although it has not yet shot forth into
any decided reach of originality, has already been emitting gleams,
though faint, of most brilliant promise.   Even the modelling or
re-constructing of objects and implements, which have attracted his
curious eye either by their workmanship or evident design, has not
been without its use, as he has been acquiring that facility in minute
and delicate handicraft, which he afterwards displayed in the admirable beauty and perfection of his instruments; and which, in a branch

---

[1] Robison's System of Mechanical Philosophy, 1822, vol. ii. p. vi.

of business then little known or practised in Scotland, was well fitted to attract the attention of scientific men who could appreciate and value such niceness and skill. His coming to Glasgow, however, is the commencement of a new chapter in his interesting life. It is to exhibit new phases in his intellectual development. Imitation and ingenuity are to have grafted upon them contrivance ; this, in its turn, is to be subjected to scientific reason ;—and INVENTION, now first asserting its eminence and power, and henceforth to be the great master-faculty of his genius, is to come forth, not, in any sense, as a blind and fortuitous effect of necessity or of mere happy thought,—but as the result purely, and as it were only the handmaid, of a preliminary and most rigid scientific induction.

Watt's arrival in this city, therefore, in the twenty-first year of his age, with the view of establishing himself in business as a mathematical and philosophical instrument-maker, cannot but be regarded as a notable point in his life. Clouded and unpromising as it was in the outset, it was to open up a train of events the most propitious to his genius ; and, in introducing him to the sphere best of all calculated to nourish and call forth into energy all that yet remained in his mind in a latent or only nascent state, was to prove the pivot or turning-point of all his future career.

The most remarkable and, perhaps, by him, least calculated of those events was his introduction at once to the protection and patronage of the University of Glasgow, thus briefly narrated by M. Arago in his eloquent Eloge :—" Watt . . . . returned to Glasgow, where difficulties of a sufficiently serious character awaited him. The corporations of arts and trades, [the Corporation of Hammermen,] grounding upon their ancient privileges, looked upon the young artist from London as an intruder, and obstinately denied to him the right to open even the most humble workshop. Every means of conciliation having failed, the University of Glasgow interfered, arranged and put at the disposal of young Watt a small apartment within its own buildings, allowed him to establish a shop, (boutique,) and honoured him with the title of its instrument-maker, (ingénieur)."[1]

Such, in a few words, is the history of young Watt's remarkable and extemporaneous elevation to position and notice. But, of an event which one already knows to be so fraught with great issues, every circumstance and particular is felt to be important. Every previous link in the incidents, and, consequently, in the eventful concatenation to which this period forms the introduction, cannot but be interesting. Yet, although by far the most pregnant passage in Watt's history,— inasmuch as it was the grand *transition* from what might else, possibly, have been but a modest and comparatively obscure life, into one of rare opportunity for distinction and eminence,—one cannot but regret the scantiness of the information at the disposal of the reader, or refrain from expressing an ardent wish, that materials might yet be found capable of relieving the unsatisfied feeling which this circumstance attaches to the mind. A certain degree of obscurity rests over the connexion of events at this juncture, and the reader is at a loss for information on the very important point of Watt's first introduction to the notice of the University ;—the mere opposition of the craftsmen, by itself, scarcely seeming to afford sufficient grounds for so remarkable and generous an interference on the part of that learned body in behalf of a young and, as yet, apparently unknown artist.[2] Resuming

[1] Eloge Historique, p. 9. For an elegant presentation copy of the original Paris edition of this famous work, the author was indebted, in 1839, to the courtesy of the late James Watt, Esq., of Soho.

[2] Since the foregoing and following pages were written out for the press, we have had the great satisfaction of perusing the very interesting account given by Mr. Muirhead,—in his work just issued from the press,—of Watt's happy introduction to several of the most learned professors in the University in 1754, "through the instrumentality of his mother's kinsman, Mr. George Muirhead, who had then just exchanged the professorship of Oriental Languages for that of Latin." For the details connected with this important juncture in the great mechanician's life, we refer to the pages of this elaborate and most interesting work, "The Origin and Progress of the Mechanical Inventions of James Watt, illustrated by his Correspondence with his Friends, and the Specifications of his Patents, by James Patrick Muirhead, Esq., M.A. London, 1854."

our narrative, therefore, at a period immediately subsequent to this singularly propitious juncture, and pursuing only the principles which have hitherto guided us in the use of the facts and materials at our disposal, we shall leave their details to throw what light they may on the continuity and connexion of those events which project their influence into the great future of Watt's career, as an Engineer and Mechanician.

In a former chapter occasion was taken to advert to some external influences, which might be regarded as having favoured the development and direction of Watt's genius into the channel which eventually conducted it to its greatest achievements. These were, in general, those events which, before or about the year 1760, had begun to signalize a new era in the arts and sciences, learned and polite, throughout the empire ; when a thirst for improvement and invention pervaded all ranks, scientific as well as productive, and everything that could contribute to comfort, wealth, and industrial prosperity, received an attention so marked, as to distinguish the period by a character altogether peculiar to it. At the threshold of Watt's entrance upon professional life, it cannot be uninteresting to observe the contact of the yet plastic mind with the new state of things around it.

Arrived in the city of Glasgow, then,—a locality already attracting to itself a large proportion of the wealth and enterprise of Scotland, and already becoming the great centre of commercial and manufacturing activity in the north,—Watt had, at the same time, come within the range of an intellectual and philosophical activity to which he could not long be altogether insensible. Conspicuous in those days in promoting and operating upon the great social movement to which allusion has been made, was one energetic mind in particular, one connected directly with the interests of science in that city, but whose public spirit, and, it may perhaps now with fairness be added, large benevolence, did not suffer him to limit his efforts for the benefit of his fellows to the most sedulous discharge of his professional duties. Bent on making the principles of science tell, to the largest possible extent, upon the industry and manufactures of his country,—at the same time that he devoted himself to the philosophical duties of his Chair with an enthusiasm then far from usual amid the studied decorums of academic life,—he was indefatigable in studying, on his own account, the application of science to mechanical practice, and, for this purpose, was in the habit of visiting the workshops of artisans in the city, and receiving, in return for the scientific doctrine he had to communicate, a full equivalent of experimental knowledge. The philanthropy of this energetic course did not terminate here ; for under the influence of what would appear to have been with him a kind of ruling passion in regard to the instruction and profit of others,—a characteristic, it has been remarked, of the man of pure science, more meritorious in those days because more rare than it happily is now,—he resolved, in addition to the labours of his own class, which were strictly academic and philosophical, to institute a class and lectures for *workmen*, and for those whose pursuits did not allow of their conforming to the pre-scribed routine of University studies ; to which *anti-toga* class, as he designated it, he continued, throughout a long life, terminated only at the advanced age of seventy, to lecture twice every week during the Session of College. To such a sketch of the multiform labours of this eminently practical philosopher it may be added, in reference to the more special duties of his sphere, that, as a professor and lecturer, he is said to have exhibited a surpassing elegance of manner,—to have been possessed of a style easy and graceful, a command of language unlimited, and to have performed the manifold experiments, illustra-tive of his prelections, with a skill and success that were in the highest degree admirable,—while within and beyond this sphere, nothing afforded him purer or more lively satisfaction than being instrumental in discovering and fostering merit, or in hearing that any who had been of the number of his very numerous pupils had distinguished themselves in the world.[1]

Some of our readers will already have recognised here the Founder of the Andersonian University of Glasgow, an individual whose influence as a contributor to the sciences, the arts, the conveniences of life, as well as to the effectiveness of public institutes of learning during his own times, can hardly now be disputed ; while, looking at the wide-spread benefits conferred in the present day upon a large portion of society by the institution which bears his name, to which he bequeathed his library and valuable scientific apparatus,—it may fairly be questioned whether the public spirit of its founder can be said yet to have obtained that full appreciation which it seems justly to claim.

Such a man, one would say, was eminently he under whose inspiriting influence it were to be desired that our young adventurer in the philosophical instrument business should have fallen. And had young Watt's fortune been other than it was ;—had he not been resisted by the Hammermen's corporation ;—had he received the sign-manual of their supreme approval, and opened his little shop in the " High Street" or "Salt Market," it is not difficult to fancy the ardent professor, in one of his rounds of investigation and search after talent, alighting upon this humble *atelier* of genius, and bringing forth into notice and fame one born of nature herself to be a peer in her realm, and trained in her own school to be a very priest of her mysteries.

But Watt's introduction to such an influence was not left to any hazard of this kind. Like the rich oriental web whose figures and flowers are all rolled up in embryo, before one throw of the shuttle or one stroke of the loom has been given to call forth into being its beauty, it would seem that the tissue of Watt's variegated history was

[1] See Glasgow Mechanics' Magazine, vol. iii., 1825. Chambers' Biographical Dictionary: Edinburgh, 1835.

all laid in the remote years of his infancy, requiring only the work-ings of time to bring out into view the figures, and the forms, and the incidents which lay hid in the pre-arranged warp and weft of his early days ;—that long years before, it had been ordained that these two men should meet in due time, in this city of Glasgow, as old friends,—should hold congenial intercourse, exchange thoughts and ideas, start problems, and, in the intimacy of friendship, be mutually helpful to each other.

Of James Watt's school-companions at Greenock, one of the earliest, and not the least estimable, was Andrew Anderson,[1] one of a family and name which, for several generations, had distinguished itself in the annals of the times by patriotism, piety, and learning ; and which still, in its descendants, does honour to the worth of its grandsires, by the genuineness of its virtues in the walks of private life. The two schoolfellows were about the same age, having been born in the same year ; and the mutual friendship, so early commenced, was continued, with longer or shorter interruptions, throughout life, as will appear hereafter from Mr. Watt's correspondence with his early Greenock friends. Andrew's elder brother, John, had, from a very early age, exhibited remarkable talents ; and before attaining his twenty-seventh year, in 1754, had been called to fill the Chair of Hebrew in the University of Glasgow, vacated by Professor Muirhead, who was translated to that of Latin. The Professor was about eight years his brother's and Watt's senior, having been born in 1728. It was not, however, in the department of the oriental languages that Mr. Anderson was to achieve his eminence or usefulness. His extensive philosophical acquirements, his generous and popular character, added to his known devotedness to the interests of practical science, pointed him out as a most proper person, in a community like Glasgow, to fill the Chair of Natural Philosophy,—his transference to which professorship,

---

[1] See reference to this worthy individual and early friend of Watt, *supra*, Introduction, p. iv.

accordingly, in 1757, was an event as agreeable to himself as it proved beneficial to his townsmen, and eventually to a much wider range of society.[1]

James Watt's settlement in Glasgow, in addition to the satisfaction of his being amongst his maternal relatives, could not, under the circumstances pointed to, have been otherwise than an agreeable event to both these young men—to the professor, who knew the singular ingenuity and talents of the instrument-maker and mechanician, to the latter, who delighted in the scientific resources of his friend,— and an intimacy, as interesting as it was advantageous to both at such a moment, was the result of their now easy proximity. Watt's evenings were spent frequently at the professor's house within the College ; the stores of whose private but spacious book-shelves were open to gratify the profound research of the thoughtful youth, now more than ever bent on study ; and whose thirst for speculation and science seemed only to gain intensity from the new facility with which he could minister to it,—stimulated also by the academic air, and still more by the high academic associations with which it was his privilege to feel himself surrounded.

It will have been observed that Mr. Anderson was already a professor in the University on Watt's coming to Glasgow. What amount of influence this circumstance, in conjunction with the intimacy just referred to, might have had on the important events of this section of Watt's life, can of course only be conjectured. But that Professor Anderson's friendship had the claim of very early date, and that he was in a position to be most directly helpful to the restless current of the young mechanician's thoughts during those pregnant years, cannot, with any propriety, admit of a doubt. Yet, singularly enough, a

---

[1] For the facts and dates above cited, as well as others regarding his learned relative, obligations are due to Andrew Anderson, Esquire, of Greenock, the worthy representative of the name of James Watt's early schoolfellow and friend.

chapter in Watt's history which has been justly rendered luminous by
the emblazonry of all the other great names which at the time adorned
this ancient seat of learning, has hitherto contained no reference to
this early and attached friend, whose house, conversation, library, and
valuable scientific apparatus, had been at all times free to satisfy the
strongly awakened exigencies of that inquisitive and ingenious mind.
His name alone appears to have been dropped out of the splendid
galaxy, and to have failed of any due remembrance in the records of
those years.[1]   Even had the Professor no more title to remembrance
in connexion with the great mechanician than that it was he who put
into his hands, for adjustment and repair, the famous model of the
Newcomen's Engine, which belonged to the apparatus of the Professor's class,—THE incident, after all, which, though apparently at
the moment trifling, was destined to revolutionize the commerce and
even the customs of our country, and eventually of the globe, while it
has immortalized James Watt,—his name appears fairly to merit
from Watt's biographers something more than the most incidental
mention, in recording the incipient though earnest efforts of that
great spirit, to baffle the obstacles that intervened between its embryo
thoughts and the grand vista of invention, already more than half
seen beyond.[2]

[1] Among those to whose distinguished acquaintance and conversation James Watt's connexion
with the University of Glasgow introduced him,
were Dr. Adam Smith, Dr. Black, Professor
Simson, Dr. Dick, Mr. (afterwards Professor)
Robison, and others;—the three first cotemporaries and colleagues of Mr. Anderson, the last, a
student at the University, probably attending Mr.
Anderson's lectures in 1757-8. Dr. Dick died in
1757.

[2] Mr. Chambers, in his biographical sketch of
Mr. Anderson, in a concluding footnote, having
reference to an anecdote of the Professor while in
Paris, during the memorable events of 1791, thus
expresses himself:—" For this striking anecdote
of Mr. Anderson's enthusiasm in the cause of
liberty, as well as most of the particulars of his
conduct as a professor, we are indebted to a
memoir in the *Glasgow Mechanics' Magazine*,
vol. iii. 1825, when, strange to say, *for the first
time*, was any notice of the life of this great man
presented to the public ; a striking instance of
the neglect with which mankind sometimes treat
their greatest benefactors, while they blazon the
fame and glory of those who have treated them
as slaves or tools, with the most abject adula-
tion."—*Biograph. Dict. of Eminent Scotsmen*,
1835.

Photographed from Original.

Schenck & Mc Farlane, Lith.rs Edinburgh.

MODEL OF THE NEWCOMEN'S ENGINE,

IN THE HUNTERIAN MUSEUM OF THE UNIVERSITY OF GLASGOW.

Dimensions —— Length 27 Inches. Breadth 12 do. Height 50½ do.

"IN 1765 JAMES WATT, IN WORKING TO REPAIR THIS MODEL, BELONGING TO THE NATURAL PHILOSOPHY CLASS IN THE UNIVERSITY
OF GLASGOW, MADE THE DISCOVERY OF A SEPARATE CONDENSER, WHICH HAS IDENTIFIED HIS NAME WITH THAT OF THE STEAM ENGINE."

Note appended to Model.

But to conclude this transition chapter, with its illustrations. How Watt in his little University room now speculated and experimented; how his workship became the resort of learned professors as well as students,—"a kind of academy," says M. Arago, "whither all the notabilities of Glasgow repaired, to discuss the nicest questions in art, science, and literature;"—how difficult problems were solved for the one, or profound disquisitions entered into with the other;—how German was mastered in order to read Leupold on Machines, or Italian acquired with some similar view;—how he threaded the intricate theories of Smith's Harmonics, to qualify himself to build an organ;— or how, finally, he took within his ingenious hands the little model of the Newcomen's engine, and, all the while, worked assiduously for his livelihood, at the making of his delicate and beautiful instruments, —it does not fall within the plan of these pages more minutely to detail.[1]

Those were the hours of the young artist's most serious and most varied study, all-essential, doubtless, to the future of the great Inventor. But—though standing, apparently, as it were on the very threshold of that after-fame—the die of the youth's life is not yet finally cast.

[1] The experiments in natural philosophy which occupied this period of Watt's scientific life, have been already detailed in so many biographies of Watt, as well as in every treatise on the early history of the steam-engine, that it is not deemed necessary to include them within the more limited scope of the present undertaking—which does not profess to deal with the history of the progress of Watt's several inventions. A very full exhibition of his early philosophical experiments while at Glasgow, on the nature and properties of steam, together with his first application of the principles ascertained to the improvement of the steam-engine, is given by Professor Robison, in the articles on Steam and the Steam-Engine, in his System of Mechanical Philosophy, (1822, vol. ii. pp. 4, 108, &c.,) enriched by notes and observations from the pen of the great mechanician himself. See also *Encyclopædia Britannica, in loco.*

CHAPTER IV.

STEAM AND INVENTION SEEM TO HAVE MET A FATE—SURVEYS OF THE CLYDE INTEREST
THE YOUNG WORKMAN——HE FALLS IN WITH THE ENGINEER SMEATON AT GLASGOW—
SIMILARITY IN THEIR HISTORIES—THE MATHEMATICAL INSTRUMENT-MAKER BECOMES
SURVEYOR AND CIVIL ENGINEER——ENGAGED AT THE CARRON IRON-WORKS——THE
ENGINE GOES, AND COMES TO A STAND-STILL—SURVEYS THE CLYDE AND REPORTS—
OTHER ENGINEERING UNDERTAKINGS—EMPLOYED ON HARBOUR WORKS AT GREENOCK
——ESTIMATES FOR——EMPLOYED TO BRING WATER INTO THE TOWN OF GREENOCK—
ESTIMATES, PLANS, BUSINESS HABITS—NOTICE OF BY M. ARAGO—PROPOSALS AS TO
SOHO——CHARACTER OF MR. BOULTON—FLATTERING PROPOSALS—DEATH OF HIS
FATHER——EXTREME MENTAL SUFFERING ON THE OCCASION——STILL THE BUSIEST
PERIOD OF HIS LIFE——WRITES AN INSCRIPTION FOR HIS FATHER'S TOMBSTONE.

NURTURED, so to speak, trained, and even more than qualified as
Watt, to all appearance, was for entering immediately upon the functions of the great and successful mechanist, the final decision even yet
trembled in the balance. Notwithstanding the regular employment
of a mechanical nature brought within his reach by his recent advantageous position, powerful circumstances, against which neither his
intellectual nor physical being could successfully wrestle, intervened
to obstruct that decisive impulse which his great powers ought even
now to have had, and to have retained through life. Having already
accomplished his grand discovery, the "Separate Condenser,"—having
formally registered his patent for a "Method of lessening the consumption of Steam, and consequently of Fuel, in Fire-Engines,"—
having so far perfected the engrossing idea of his thoughts, during
days of toil and nights of sleepless speculation, as to have enrolled in
Chancery his threefold specification of an effective, workable Steam-

DIONYSIUS PAPIN M.D.

MATH. PROF. ORD. AC. REG. SOC. LOND. SOCIUS.

ANNO 1689.

From the original Portrait in the Aula of the University of Marburg

Engine, a High-Pressure Engine, and a horizontal Rotatory Engine, —what is wanting, forthwith and at once, to give to his country's Arts and the world's Civilisation, the boon for which Science and Labour are alike waiting, with eager though hardly known impatience?—Money—and that encouragement which only the autocrat of capital can supply. These, however, are not forthcoming; and that modest and sensitively retiring nature, whose secret joy lies deep, fostering itself in the patient elaboration of great and intensely absorbing truths in science, wherein also it finds its solace and the truest portion of its recompense, shrinks from the more vulgar task of the man of business, in recommending, and pressing, and overcoming the self-complacent prejudices of men. Still, the mathematical instrument-maker must live,—those nobler and gentler spirits which stand nearest and dearest to him must be provided for. . . . . Failing the laboured, and to him costly, "Fire-Engine," he is not without his resources.

In the mind of Watt were lying, latent, scientific seeds—very early deposited there—which it required only the concurrence of events to cause to germinate, and to shoot forth into observation. They were, indeed, in a sense congenital with his being, and, since more than one generation, hereditary in his family. These, under the encouragement of a different train of events, would have led him from the outset of his life, rather to the profession of civil engineering, than that of the scientific industrial arts. As it was, there were, occurring in more or less immediate contact with him, circumstances which tended, very strongly, to direct his mind and energies into this new channel of professional activity.

At the period referred to, the commercial corporations of the West of Scotland, particularly those of the wealthy city of Glasgow, were making prodigious efforts to improve all their means of trade. The best mode of operating upon the channel of the Clyde above Greenock, so as to afford increased facilities for the navigation of that river—so invaluable in its since improved state to that splendid capital of manufacturing and commercial enterprise—had become an engrossing consideration in the public mind ; and the arrival in Glasgow, in 1755, of Mr. Smeaton, the celebrated Engineer, to make the necessary surveys, with a view to ascertaining how far it might be practicable to adapt its waters to the reception of vessels of a greater tonnage than had yet been accustomed to resort to the Broomielaw, naturally excited among professional men much speculation as to the probable results of so important a project.[1]

Mr. Smeaton, in a report dated 3d September of that year, proposed to have a " lock and a dam" at Marlingford, in order, as the report states, " to secure four and a half feet of water, at all times, up to the quay at Glasgow." By whomsoever this idea was first originated, whether by Mr. Smeaton or the magistrates of Glasgow, the practicability only of that measure was reported upon by the engineer. Certain it is, however, that the magistrates of that city so far adopted it as, in 1757, to prepare a Bill to be brought into Parliament, a copy of which they transmitted to the magistrates of Greenock, with the intimation that they intended to carry the project into execution.

Mr. Watt's father was then one of the bailies of Greenock, and he and his colleague, with the other members of the town-council, resolved to oppose the Bill. In November 1759, in consequence probably of additional reports by Mr. Smeaton[2]—for it appears he made more than one Survey—the scheme was revived, as may be gathered from a movement in the town-council of Greenock. That corporation em-

[1] For a view of what were anciently the capacities of this now so remarkable river—for the present conveniencies of which Glasgow has to thank science, in conjunction with the indomitable energies of her " River Trustees"—the reader is referred to page 121, *supra*.

[2] These Reports of Mr. Smeaton in reference to the River Clyde Surveys are not found in the Collection of the Engineer's Reports, published in 1812 by the Committee of the Society of Civil Engineers, 3 vols. 4to.

powered Bailie Watt to repair to Edinburgh, for the purpose of engaging Mr. Walter Steuart, advocate, to proceed to London, to act as counsel for them in opposition to the proposed " Lock-bill."

Into a matter of such a nature, in which not only his father the bailie, but also his Greenock friends generally were so deeply interested, it may easily be conceived the speculative mind of Watt would enter with some ardour. It was a subject not unfamiliar to him,—his grandfather, probably, but particularly his uncle, John Watt, having, as we have already seen, directed his attention, as a practical surveyor, to the navigation of the Clyde, and, as early as 1734, made a survey and map of the river, to which was annexed a chart of the Firth and adjacent Islands, as far as the North Channel,—a most valuable contribution to the hydrography of those days.[1] This fact might, of itself, be sufficient to induce the supposition of Watt's forming an acquaintance with the able engineer now officially employed by the city of Glasgow to report on the river improvements. But other elements might have assisted in bringing about an intimacy ; in which case, the striking similarity so discoverable in the events of their respective lives, could not fail to be suggestive, at least to one of them, and be productive of convictions that were capable of leading to important ulterior results. Both of these young men had spent their early days in precisely similar pursuits, and both had started in life as philosophical instrument-makers. Smeaton, who was only about nine years older than Watt, was already in the possession of public confidence, and reaping the fruits of an established reputation as a civil engineer ; Watt, though at the same moment giving proofs, in his less public vocation, of possessing a vigorously inventive genius, was yet far from earning the rewards which that genius merited, or which the circumstances of his position rendered desirable and even necessary.

[1] For a succinct account of John Watt's Map, see page 53, *supra*.

22

Whether the temporary pre-occupations alluded to, or his own felt ability for the profession of civil engineering, suggested the change in his views or not, certain it is that Watt's original business and speculations were suspended ; and that he more than half resolved to adopt that profession which seemed to present a more accessible pathway to both reputation and emolument.

There is nothing, so far as we are aware, which can be referred to that goes to show whether, in the new channel of his thoughts in regard to the "Clyde surveys," Watt entered into the views of the town-council of Glasgow, and of Mr. Smeaton, with reference to the river improvements, or whether he rather countenanced the opposition which his father and the town-council of Greenock had resolved to give to the projected measure. How far, on the other hand, between 1755 when the survey was made, and 1759, when the determined opposition of the people of Greenock manifested itself, his mature judgment operated on his father's mind to produce his hostility to the plan,—or how far, by possibility, his suggestions tended to modify the views of Mr. Smeaton, or to open the eyes of the magistrates of Glasgow to the practical inefficiency of the scheme, is not known ; the Bill, however, was, for one reason or another, eventually abandoned. It is not at all improbable, that it was in connexion with the opposition to this Bill, on the part of Bailie Watt and the town-council of Greenock, that John Watt's Map and Survey of the River Clyde was *published* by the Bailie's youngest son, John Watt, the younger brother of the incipient civil engineer ; its publication having taken place, as we now know, in 1760.

That Watt now took a recognised and public interest in the engineering questions of the day is placed beyond a doubt, by the fact of his soon becoming extensively employed in making surveys and estimates for most of the great public works and improvements that were then so urgently demanded, by the rapid march of commercial and manufacturing enterprise in Scotland ; and his being for several years engaged in such works as canals, docks, harbours, throughout the country ;—undertakings, in the execution of which he acquired such reputation as his scientific knowledge and inventive genius eminently entitled him to. During the same period, however, the fame which he had acquired from his successful experiments connected with Steam and Machinery, while yet employed by the University of Glasgow, led to his assistance being sought in reference to necessary mechanical improvements at the Carron Iron-Works—then under the energetic management of Dr. Roebuck—in some of the original arrangements of which Mr. Smeaton also had preceded him. Owing to their vastness, and the admirable ingenuity displayed in their machinery, these works continued to be for many years the most remarkable of their kind in Europe. In Vol. IV. of the Transactions of the Royal Society of Edinburgh, in an interesting biographical notice of Dr. Roebuck, a valuable record is left of the undaunted enterprise with which that ingenious and indefatigable philosopher prosecuted his herculean undertakings, particularly that for the manufacture of the finer qualities of iron by means of pitcoal,—a process then for the first time attempted in Scotland, and little known or practised in England.[1] The adaptation of the machinery aimed at in these great works contemplated some of the most important scientific and mechanical problems of the day. It was thus a place and occasion most suitable for the application of Mr. Watt's talents and experience ; while their active exercise tended to keep alive

[1] This Paper was communicated by Professor Jardine of Glasgow, so justly remembered for his ability and *Method* in the Chair of Logic and Rhetoric, which he long held in that University. The Biographical Notice is reprinted from the Trans. R. S. E. in the *Scots Magazine* for May and June 1799, and is followed, in the latter month, by an interesting article, containing " An Account of the Carron Foundry, from the travels in England and Scotland of M. Saint Fond ; " from which it appears that the machinery, constructed in great part by Mr. Smeaton, and altered and improved by Mr. Watt, was, even then, the most remarkable of its kind in Britain, both for its elegance, accuracy, and adaptation to the purposes to which it was applied.

those speculations which, though so auspiciously begun, had for a time been practically suspended.

We are not aware to what extent, or with what regularity, Mr. Watt was employed in the experiments and improvements going forward about this time at the Carron Iron-Works. It is certain, however, that for a series of years prior to the failure of Dr. Roebuck's magnificent undertakings, and Mr. Watt's consequent settlement at Soho, about the year 1774-75, his principal professional occupations were those connected with the business of civil-engineering, or survey-ing, as it then continued to be called. Among many other surveys and estimates furnished by him for public works in Scotland, subse-quently to his quitting his *atelier* within the College of Glasgow, he was employed, in 1769, to survey the river Clyde; and on 20th October of that year gave in a report to the magistrates of Glasgow, showing the depths of water at given points. In this report by Mr. Watt no mention is made of any such plan as *locking* the river, which Mr. Smeaton had reported practicable, though the idea was aban-doned. Although Mr. Watt's report makes no suggestion, it is most probable that he took the rational view of the matter, which was that also of the several engineers who followed him, and who suggested the " deepening of the channel," with the various means of effecting that object. It need only be added, that when it is reflected what, at no very distant period, were the extremely limited capacities for naviga-tion, of that portion of the river Clyde more particularly embraced in the soundings and surveys of Smeaton, Watt, Golborne, Rennie, and immediately subsequent engineers,—compared with the present state of its channel, offering a depth of water sufficient for the passage of the largest merchantmen, and affording means of all but uninterrupted communication to steam-vessels at almost all states of the tide,—the operations here effected cannot but be regarded as without parallel in this country, and as affording an example of one of the most

extraordinary and successful achievements in engineering, to which
the records of that now so essential branch of practical science can
point.

The only other works of Mr. Watt of this kind which it is proposed
to mention here, are two which have reference, and consequently are
interesting, to the community of Greenock. These were, the extension
of the harbour accommodation, and the conveyance of water into the
town for the supply of the inhabitants. Both of these undertakings,
although of comparatively minor importance, received a cordial and
minute attention from Mr. Watt in all their details. They were the
last acts of his civil-engineering ; and, from their having occupied him
at a moment when he was much pressed by business,—being then
engaged in his great work, the survey of the country between Inverness and Fort-William, for what is now the Caledonian Canal, as well
as already making arrangements for his removal to the new scene of
his labours in England,—ought not to be without their just appreciation among his townsmen.

On 24th November 1772, it was reported at a meeting of the
Town-Council of Greenock, that a letter had been received by the
magistrates from Lord Cathcart, in which his lordship desired that a
plan might be made of the ground required to be feued for a new
quay ;[1] and the same, with proposals, given in to his Lordship.
The magistrates informed the meeting, that they had got a land-
surveyor from Glasgow to measure the ground, and that the
plan would be made out that afternoon.[2] The surveyor from
Glasgow is indicated by the following letter addressed by " James
Watt, junior," to Bailie Gammell, his old schoolfellow, which we
give entire :—

[1] The east branch of the Custom-house Quay.

[2] The minute of the meeting is signed by James

Donald, James Gammell, James Scott, Andrew
Donald, James Wilson, Archibald Crawford, John
Campbell, and James Watt.

"GLASGOW, *December* 9, 1773.

"SIR,—I only returned from a survey of the Forth two days ago, and have been so much indisposed since, that I could not consider your subject. I am to be at Port-Glasgow to-morrow with our magistrates, where I hope to have the pleasure of seeing you, as I understand you are to dine there with them. I refer most of what I have to say till that time, and hope you will come provided with the necessary queries, and the plan of the harbour. In the meantime I send you the dimensions of the breast-walls, which I find I intended to be fifteen feet high; that is, I supposed them to be founded as low as the ordinary spring-tides, low water;—you will at Port-Glasgow see the contract for their pier, which I propose for a model for yours. The breast should be founded seven feet thick, and should, by two intakes in the first two courses, be taken in off the outside to six feet thick, from which it should batter to four feet thick at tops, the greatest part of the batter should be off the outside, thus :—[Here a drawing is given of the section.]

"Thickness at bottom, seven feet, .	.	7 0
Thickness at top, .	.	4 0
The two searcements at bottom, .	.	1 0
The inside bottom,	.	0 6
The outside do., .	.	1 6
		7 0

On second thoughts, as it will not much increase the expense, I believe it will be best to give it no inside batter, but to make the top thickness four feet six inches, and make the inside perpendicular, which will strengthen it against the earth that presses it outwards. I would build in treshes of old ships'-oak to fix the sliders for bearing off ships' sides, as proposed in Port-Glasgow new quay; but these particulars and others necessary I will explain to-morrow, and furnish articles of

Glasgow Dec 9th 1773

Sir

I only returned from a survey of the Forth two days ago, & have been so much indisposed since that I could not consider your subject —

I am to be at Pd Glasgow to morrow with our Magistrates where I hope to have the pleasure of seeing you as I understand you are to deal then with them — I referr most of what I have to say till that time & hope you will come provided with the necessary Queries & the Plan of the Harbour — In the mean time I send you the dimensions of the Breast walls, which I find I intended to be 15 feet high, that is I supposed them to be founded as low as the ordinary Spring tides low water — you will at Pd Glasw see the contract for their pier which I propose for a model for yours —

The Breast should be founded 7 feet thick, & should by 2 intakes in the first 2 courses, be taken in off the outside to 6 feet thick from which it should Batter to four feet thick at top

the

who greatest part of the Batter should be off
the outside thus

6inch 2 feet 6inch

	Feet – inches
Thickness at bottom seven feet	7 „ 0
Thickness at top ———————	4 „ 0
the two scarcements at bottom —	1 „ 0
the inside batter ———————	0 „ 6
the outside do ———————	1 „ 6
	7 „ 0

on second thoughts, as it will not much increase
the expence I believe it will be best to give it no
inside batter but to make the top thickness 4 feet
6 inch & make the inside perpendicular, which will
strengthen it against the earth that presses it
out wards — I would build in, tushes of old ship
oak to fix the sliders for bearing off ships sides
as proposed at port Glasgow new quay but these
particulars & others necessary I will explain to morrow
& furnish articles of contract ——

Such a wall will contain 12 yards of masonry of

feet thick in the running yard, and should cost
as follows ——

For the Hewen stones in the facing
  average length 2½ feet — 105 cube feet d   £ 1 « 15 « ——

For the Capping, long stones quite across
the wall 13½ feet at 5d ——————————   « 5 « 7½

For the Rubble stones & leading ——————
  5½ yds of 2 feet thick at 4/3d pr ——————   « 6 « 10½

Building Hewen stone & Rubble
  12⅓ yards of 2 feet thick at 1/2d pr
  that is 42/ pr wood ———————————   « 14 « 4 ¾

            Total expence of Stonework }   £ 3 « 1 « 10 ¾
            per running yard ——————— }

casting the foundation & drainage ———

Excuse haste, I have not time to copy this & will be
oblige to you for copy when we meet

        I remain with regard
            Dear Sir
              Your Obedient servt
                James Watt

Basilio scampa Gennuil

Governor

contract. Such a wall will contain twelve yards of masonry, of two feet thick in the running yard, and should cost as follows :—

" For the hewn stone in the facing, average length $2\frac{1}{2}$ feet, 105 cube feet, at 4d., ...	£1 15 0
For the capping long stones quite across the wall, $13\frac{1}{2}$ feet, at 5d., ...	0 5 $7\frac{1}{2}$
For the rabble stones and leading, $5\frac{1}{2}$ yards of 2 feet thick, at 1s. 3d., ...	0 6 $10\frac{1}{2}$
Building hewn stone and rabble, $12\frac{1}{3}$ yards of 2 feet thick, at 1s. 2d., that is, 42s. a rood, . .	0 14 $4\frac{3}{4}$
Total expense of stone-work per running yard, casting the foundation, and drainage, .	£3 1 $10\frac{3}{4}$

" Excuse haste. I have not time to copy this, and will be obliged to you for copy when we meet.—I remain, with regard, &c. &c.,

" JAMES WATT."

The work was accomplished in conformity with Mr. Watt's plans and specifications.

The other undertaking to which reference has been made, was commenced in the same year, 1773, also during the magistracy of Mr. Gammell. In pursuance of an Act of Parliament which had been applied for and obtained, the magistrates and trustees who had been appointed acquired titles from John Stewart Shaw, Esquire, afterwards Sir John Shaw Stewart, to two pieces of ground, lying at the base of the " Whin-hill," for the formation of two reservoirs or dams ; and another smaller piece, on the north side of the present Well Park, for a cistern. Plans and drawings of these several works were made by Mr. Watt. They are still extant, and exhibit not only a thoroughly business-like exactitude, but also great neatness and accuracy in the drawing and general execution. It is gratifying to be enabled to illustrate to some extent this " neat-handedness," for which Mr. Watt was so remarkable. Fac-similes of some of the documents here referred to, will be found to be not the least interesting of the illustrations of the volume. The first is a plan of the two Reservoirs, upon a scale of 22 yards to the inch, with calculations of their admeasurements. The second draught gives the length of the water-course, from the burn of Iverton (Overton) to the reservoirs, and from the Fairy Bridge to the Square, 734 yards; the third, the water-course from Ingleston Spring to the Fairy Bridge, 850 yards.[1]

The following letter on the subject may be regarded as an example of Mr. Watt's minuteness and scrupulous accuracy in similar matters of business :—

" GLASGOW, *August* 13, 1773.

" To BAILIE JAMES DONALD, Greenock.

" SIR,—Yesterday I received a letter from Mr. Cumming, London, about the pipes. As he was uncertain what quantities we would want, he had laid off for us, when he was in the north, 1100 yards 4-inch, and only 1000 yards 3-inch pipes. There was at that time plenty at the shore, but some ships have been loaded since, and he cannot be sure that our full quantity can be had ready bored, but has wrote to have these done with all possible despatch.

" ANSWER TO QUERIES.

" 1*st*. He thinks that they could not undertake to deliver them in Clyde.

" 2*d*. About 30 yards of 4 and 3-inch bore, mixed, will be a load, which is 50 cube feet.

" 3*d*. Speymouth is a good natural harbour; but if the vessels

---

[1] I do not recollect to have heard of the locality here called the " Fairy Bridge," before perusing these documents. It seems to have dropped out of the topography of Greenock. In the feu-contract for the ground required for these works, it is, by a clerical error apparently, written " Ferry Bridge." The lower reservoir was bounded, according to Mr. Watt, by the west wall of Fairy Bridge. It must have been situated near the head of the new street now called Lynedoch Street.

Glasgow Aug 13th 1773

Sir

Yesterday I received letter from Mr Cuming about London the pipes — as he was uncertain what quantitys we would want, he had laid off for us when he was in the north 1100 yards 4 inch & only 1000 yds 3 inch pipes, there was at that time plenty at the shore, but some ships have been loaded since & he cannot be sure that our full quantity can be had ready bored, but has wrote to have them done with all possible dispatch —

answers to Queries

1st He thinks that they could not undertake to deliver them in clyde

2d about 30 yards of 4 & 3 inch bore mixed will be a load, which is 50 cube feet

3 Speymouth is a good natural harbour, but if the vessels draw above nine feet water, some part of their cargo must be floated to them Vessels of 200 tuns have loaded there

4. They generaly contract for freight pr load of timber free of charges — they paid pr Load port charges at London & Speymouth for a small vessel before their trade was established.

5. The pipes run from 12 to 14 foot long but some few run to 16 foot — The New river Co require the 3 inch pipes to be 9 inch diameter at the

big

end, but for the 4 inch pipes they require 11 inch
diameter at the Big end — Mr Cumming generaly
makes them an inch more rather than have
reflections — their timber is straight & tapers
little I intend to be with you next week, to
set the dams agoing.

       I remain
          Sir
          Your Obedient Servt
            James Watt

The quantity of pipes ordered is 1100 yards 4 inch
& 2000 yards 3 inch ——

         To

Bailie James Donald

        Greenock

draw above 9 feet water, some part of their cargo must be floated to them.   Vessels of 200 tons have loaded there.

" *4th*. They generally contract for freight per load of timber free of charges.   They paid one shilling per load port charges at London and Speymouth, for a small vessel, before their trade was established.

" *5th*. The pipes run from 12 to 14 foot long, but some few run to 16 foot.   The New River Company require 3-inch pipes to be 9 inch diameter at the big end ; but, for the 4-inch pipes, may require 11 inch diameter at the big end.   Mr. Cumming generally makes them an inch more, rather than have reflections.   Their timber is straight and tapers little.   I intend to be with you next week to set the dams agoing.—I remain, &c.,   JAMES WATT.

" The quantity of pipes ordered is 1100 yards 4-inch, and 2000 yards 3-inch."

The dams were accordingly forthwith commenced ; and, on 29th March 1774, were reported to be finished.   The cistern also was constructed under the eye of Mr. Watt.   The whole works were executed in a most thorough manner.   The dams or reservoirs remain very nearly in the same condition in which they were originally constructed, with the exception of the lower one, which was deepened, and a little enlarged, by the labour of a number of artisans and workmen, thrown out of employment in 1817, by the stagnation of trade consequent on the peace after the Battle of Waterloo.   The *cistern* was in a state of such entireness and solidity as rendered its demolition a work of extreme difficulty, when, as late as the summer of 1852, its removal became necessary, under the operations connected with the conversion of the Well Park into public pleasure-grounds.[1]

[1] For the plans and estimates Mr. Watt was paid, according to an observed entry, 26th March 1774, the sum of £26, 15s.

23

From the minutes of the trustees, 11th October 1774, it would appear that Mr. Watt was in England ; and, from those of 13th December, it seems to have been even thought that, owing to his pressing engagements at the time, it would be necessary to employ another surveyor, to ascertain the proper "levels" for the pipes. So much personal interest, however, did Mr. Watt take in the execution of this work, that although his father—who, as a councillor, was at this time a member of the board of trustees—was fully capable of ascertaining and marking off the levels, he himself hastened, at great inconvenience, to Greenock, and with the assistance of the old gentleman, his father, and a lad to carry the stakes, laid down the levels with his own hand ;—thus completing, to his satisfaction, an undertaking which was at the time as beneficial, as the remembrance of his connexion with the work is now gratifying to his townsmen.

These works, as before remarked, formed the last of Watt's civil-engineering undertakings. When it is reflected that, in the difficult and responsible profession in which he had been during these several years engaged, we see neither the certificated pupil of a polytechnic school, nor the accredited associate of a privileged and professional body,—but one who, unsupported in his proper calling, and pressed by the necessity of finding the means of livelihood almost, had but recently quitted his workbench and delicate tools, to enter, *impromptu*, the lists, with the Brindleys, the Smeatons, the Golbornes, and the Rennies of his age,—we cannot regard the display of such versatility in adapting himself to circumstances and commanding success in them, but as a signal instance of that breadth of mental power, —that many-sidedness of parts,—that self-possessed intellectual audacity which everywhere makes Watt's genius wonderful. But there is more in it that is worthy of observation than this. In the fact just narrated above—all the more deserving of notice that it was on the very eve of his new destiny—we remark a happy illustration of those qualities which so ennobled the character of this great man, and to which the eloquent Academician has so gracefully attracted attention, —" that serenity of disposition, that moderation of desires, that genuine modesty," unconscious of and indifferent to its own greatness, which have ever marked the presence of true genius and worth. We see, in fact, pursues M. Arago, " the creator of an engine destined to form an epoch in the annals of the world, undergoing without murmur the undiscerning neglect of capitalists,—during eight years lowering the lofty powers of his genius to the getting up of plans—to paltry level-lings—to wearisome calculations of excavatings, and embankings, and courses of masonry."[1]

The termination of such engagements introduces us to a new phase in his life, and a new cycle in the history of world-inventions, con-sequent upon the arrangements formed with Mr. Boulton of Soho. Although these necessarily withdrew our countryman and townsman from the immediate sphere of his most important education, and what we must hold to have been the birthplace and cradle of his mechanical ingenuity, we cannot but rejoice in their accomplishment. Happy in finding that that rare and most precious talent, after a brief period of suspense, and of anxiety as to its fate, has at length resumed its first-created channel,—we must be content to know that it will now pursue its course, aided by every circumstance that can give it alike scope, efficiency, power, in its display. Into that new sphere of arduous yet brilliantly successful labour, it does not belong to the plan of these memorials minutely and chronologically to follow their subject, still less, to chronicle, even though the means were available, the steady progress in discovery and invention of that genius whose infant though herculean efforts we have been enabled to record. Happily the

[1] " Nous verrions le créateur d'une machine destinée à faire époque dans les annales du monde, subir, sans murmurer, les stupides dédains des capitalistes, et plier, pendant huit années, son génie supérieur à des levés de plans, à des niv-ellements minutieux, à des fastidieux calculs de déblais, de remblais, à des toisés du maçonnerie." —*Eloge Historique*, p. 46.

general result of that invention and that discovery are familiar to every observer.[1]

So successful, however, had Mr. Watt been in his own country as a surveyor or civil-engineer, that his reputation in this department of practical science would seem, even after a number of years, to have instigated the desire, on the part of his old friends, to secure his permanent services in Scotland, in connexion with the great national work, the Caledonian Canal, to the survey of which he had, in 1773, contributed. The following letter, addressed to his father-in-law, Mr. M'Gregor of Glasgow, refers to the subject of the proposal, with which, however, it is unnecessary to say that, if at all admitting of being even seriously entertained, it was found impossible to comply :—

"BIRMINGHAM, *October* 30, 1784.

"DEAR SIR,—I have the pleasure of receiving your kind letter of the 22d. In relation to my survey of the ground between Inverness and Fort-William, it is not so perfect as I could wish it to be, both in point of language and in other respects ; and if it is proposed to be printed, I could wish to be permitted to revise it, that I may at least correct inaccuracies in language,—for, as to the matters of fact, it is too long ago since the survey for me to do it. I am afraid that the expense in the estimate is less than it can be done for.

"As Mr. Boulton is absent, I cannot give any answer to your kind propositions about the engineership of the great canal. The place is

[1] Of the value, in Mr. Watt's own estimation, of the relations induced by the partnership at Soho, and of the judicious and high-principled friendship which he so long enjoyed in Mr. Boulton, the following graceful testimony occurs in his Notes on the Steam-Engine :—" As a memorial due to that friendship, I avail myself of this, probably a last public opportunity, of stating, that to his friendly encouragement, to his partiality for scientific improvements, and his ready application of them to the processes of art ; to his intimate knowledge of business and manufactures, and to his extended views and liberal spirit of enterprise, must in a great measure be ascribed whatever success may have attended my exertions."—*Robison's Mech. Phil.*, 1822, vol. ii. p. 144.

honourable, and I am much obliged to those friends who have named me for it ;—yet I cannot tell that it would be right for me to accept it, at least for a continuance, and that, for two reasons,—my mind being almost wholly turned towards the steam-engine, almost all the minutiæ and necessary matters of fact relative to the canal business are gone from me, so that all that remains to me is the power of judging when the facts are present, and that is certainly now more mature than when I left you. Secondly, the contriving of engines and the other necessary attentions to a business which is now very extensive, take up all the time that bad health will permit me to work ; and it is possible that, setting aside the damage which the distraction of my attention might do the partnership, my own share of the loss in the engine business might exceed my gains by the canal direction. In other respects, you may be certain, that the being enabled to spend some part of my time among my friends must prove highly agreeable to me. The matter, therefore, shall have serious consideration. . . . .

" Our rotative engines, which we have now rendered very complete, are certainly very applicable to the driving of cotton mills, in every case where the conveniency of placing the mill in a town, or ready-built manufactory, will compensate for the expense of coals and of our premium. Our premium we have fixed at £5 per annum for every horse power the machine is equal to, and the coals are about ten pound weight for each horse. . . . . We find that we must, in spite of every peaceable disposition, go to law with some people, who encroach upon our patent rights ; and as our very being depends on the success of that suit, we must bestow every attention on it, which necessarily takes up much of our time,—and we think of beginning it this term, that is, within a month, if the advice of our counsel prove favourable, otherwise we had better bear with some inconvenience than lose all. Yet, if we do not vindicate our rights, we run a risk of losing all that way. I wrote to Mr. Hamilton some time ago, concerning the present system of taxation, which is exclusively levelled at trade and manufactures. I expect that a formidable opposition will be made to all the new taxes, and many of the old ones will be done away. I think it the duty of every man who lives by trade to attend to the subject, and I know few more capable than yourself. I hope, therefore, you will commit to paper such facts and arguments as you think may be useful; and if you transmit a copy to me, you will oblige me. Our business is going on successfully, and could we only depend on its durability, we need look for no better, and probably will never find another equally good; but, at the same time, it requires an uncommon share of our personal attentions. Annie desires her love to you, her sisters, and brothers, in which I join sincerely. We are all well, and the little ones are very thriving. Jamie is returned from Wales, and is just fitting out for Geneva, on his studies. I mean that he should pass a year there at least. With compliments to all friends, I remain, dear Sir, yours affectionately,

"J. WATT."[1]

Watt, at the period of his leaving Scotland, was about thirty-eight or thirty-nine years of age; still, therefore, in the prime and vigour of life. His father, who was at this time, though in his seventy-fifth year, a councillor of the town of Greenock, survived his son's estab-

[1] For the letter from which the above paragraphs are extracts, I am indebted to the kindness of Mr. Robert Napier, Engineer, Glasgow; of whose valuable collection, at West Shandon, Gareloch, of the curiosities of literature as well as art, the original forms a not uninteresting item. The entire letter is, in many particulars, very instructive, and may be regarded as in a high degree characteristic of Mr. Watt.

Mr. Napier's Gallery at West Shandon possesses an object of great interest to the admirers of Watt, in an original portrait of the great mechanician, and which Mr. Napier has very kindly permitted to be copied on stone for the present volume. It is that painted by Partridge, after Sir W. Beechey's, an excellent work of art, and an admirable likeness. It was presented to Dr. Barr, the physician who attended Mr. Watt in his last illness. By him it was bequeathed to the late Dr. Smith, bookseller, of Glasgow, [afterwards of Crutherland,] purchased by Dr. Fleming, one of the professors of the University, and presented by him to Mr. Napier.

lishment at Birmingham several years, and had the happiness of seeing more than the commencement of his public usefulness and fame,—unalloyed, probably, by any very minute knowledge of many of the painful harassments to which the new outset in life subjected him. The tranquil prolongation of the old man's life, on the other hand, was a subject of quiet satisfaction to the son. Family trial, however,—which, it would seem, in the sovereign appointments of Providence, could not be, at any period of Mr. Watt's life, far distant, —was again at hand, and, in the death of his father, a new shock was given to the delicate framework of that spirit that so often already had quivered under the infliction of very near and peculiar bereavements. To the sensitive and affectionate nature of Watt, dispensations of this afflictive kind were occasions of a mental suffering so acute, that nothing but that firm reliance on the divine Wisdom and Goodness, which was at all times one of the most prominent features in this great man's philosophy, could have enabled him successfully to surmount their prostrating effects. Many circumstances over which he had no control conspired to render this year a sad and melancholy one, in a memory too keenly retentive, for its own comfort, of that which caused either prolonged chagrin or pain. About the beginning of the year in which his father's death took place, we find him " returned from planning and superintending the erection of his steam-engines, during a long sojourn in Cornwall, where he had been much harassed by attempts to pirate his improvements. Through the greater part of the subsequent period, he was laboriously engaged in making out drawings and descriptions for the long specifications of his three great patents for mechanical improvements and inventions, taken out in the years 1781, 1782, and 1784; besides giving the constant attention necessary to the concerns of a nascent manufactory, and himself writing volumes of letters on business, which alone would have furnished full employment even to an industrious intellect." To this period, moreover, is to be referred the correspondence relating to his splendid discovery of the Theory of the Composition of Water. It was "unquestionably the busiest, as well as the most anxious, portion of his life, and fraught with the most important results." So many and such conflicting occupations, from which no escape seemed to be possible, were distressing in an intense degree, to one who always shrank instinctively from what has been so happily styled "the velocity of affairs." They could not but be painfully ruffling to a spirit whose earthly paradise lay in the calm of domestic seclusion, its learned recreations, its study and books. "To those," writes his amiable son, referring to this period, "who may wish to form a just appreciation of the circumstances in which the 'Correspondence' took place, and of the merit that attaches to my father for the discovery it records, I beg to state, in the words of the great master of the English tongue, that 'it was written not in the soft obscurities of retirement, or under the shelter of academick bowers; but amidst inconvenience and distraction, in sickness and in sorrow.'"

In such sorrow, it was not the least bitter ingredient, perhaps, that he was unable by his presence to minister to the last wishes of his revered parent,—who, from the solitariness in which the vicissitudes of life had left him, stood in need of, in those last moments, and was felt in a peculiar manner to claim, all the solicitude which an affectionate and dutiful son could so well have bestowed. The constrained and unavoidable absence from his father's deathbed greatly affected his mind. Glimpses like this into the personal and domestic history of this great man, enable us not only to form our estimate more correctly of his character as a whole, but also to appreciate more duly the vigour of those mental powers which render his scientific life one so signal and so wonderful. It is a filial hand that has momentarily withdrawn the curtain, and revealed to us the son, the husband, the father, during the greater part of this well-remembered time of trial,

" suffering under the most acute sick-headaches, sitting by the fireside for hours together, his head leaning on his elbow, scarcely able to give utterance to his thoughts." Some of his own private and familiar letters at this period, shew the depressed state of his feelings and his health. Writing to his brother-in-law, Mr. Hamilton, 3d January 1783, he says :—" My spirits have been so much affected by one thing and another, and my headaches have been so frequent and of such long continuance, that there have scarcely been two days in the week this long time, that I have been tolerably well ; and even at those times, my head stupid and confused. This, united to the necessity of writing such letters of business as required immediate answers, and contriving many things which were to be contrived, has made me put off from day to day everything I could. As you know the keenness of my sensibility, you can conceive how much these various accidents have affected me. . . . This is the first day of a clear head I have had this fortnight ; I dare not strain it too much. . . ." And again, writing to the same, 18th February, he says :—" As to my own health, it is as usual ; headaches frequent, listlessness, confusion of head, and inactivity constant, or nearly so."[1]

His father died at a good old age, having attained to his eighty-fifth year. By those to whom he was personally known, he has been described as a man of ingenuous character, benevolent, and remarkable for sagacity and prudence in all the engagements of life. In his domestic relations he was simple, sociable, and kind ; in business, scrupulously upright ; and in all his public capacities, exact, candid, sincere. Before his death he suffered a slight decay of his mental faculties, yet not such as to indispose or incapacitate him for taking an interest in all that was going on around him. On the occasion of bringing the supply of water into the town, as already noticed, he

[1] Correspondence of the late James Watt on his Discovery of the Theory of Composition of Water ; edited by James Patrick Muirhead, Esq., F.R.S.E., 1846, pp. xiii, 8, 16.

walked over the ground, assisting his son in planting the stakes which were to mark the levels on the adjoining hills.

He lies buried in the West Churchyard of Greenock, by the side of his venerable father, the "Professor of the Mathematicks." The particular locality is marked by the tombstone containing the inscription already given in a former portion of our work relating to the grandfather. In 1808 the grandson caused a stone to be placed over the grave of his own father, the Bailie, and transmitted from Heathfield, to his old friend and correspondent, the late Mr. James Walkinshaw, of Greenock, the inscription he wished to be cut upon it. In this inscription it will be observed that Mr. Watt omits any notice of two predeceased brothers and a sister of his own, who died in infancy,[1] mentioning only John, his immediately younger brother,— the *Editor*, it will be remembered, of the map and survey of the River Clyde,—who perished at sea, and in whose death it is natural the surviving brother would feel the liveliest sympathy. It is gratifying to be enabled to introduce here the letter of Mr. Watt, giving specific directions in regard to the stone, as also the inscription ; both of them, as will be seen, affording graceful evidence of filial piety and right feeling :—

"HEATHFIELD, *Jan.* 27, 1808.

"MR. JAMES WALKINSHAW, Greenock.

"DEAR SIR,—I send you annexed the inscription intended for my

---

[1] It will be recollected that the tombstone which covers the remains of the venerable grandfather, the Professor of the Mathematicks, contains an obituary, bearing evidence of having been drawn up by his own hand, of such of his family as had died previous to 1735; which specifies not only the dates of the respective deaths of his children, but also the *years*, *months*, and *days*, which each of them had lived. His son, the Bailie, exemplifying the strong family predilection for exactness and minute computation, laid the ground for a similar obituary of his family also, in the manner in which he recorded the deaths of his children in the register of the Old West Church. These registers relate to a son, " Robert Watt, who died 27th April 1730, aged 2 months, 17 days ;" " Margaret Watt, who died 16th December 1732, aged 1 year, 20 days ;" and " Thomas Watt," no doubt named after his grandfather, " who died 30th September 1734, aged 15 months, 16 days."

Mr James Walkinshaw,
Greenock ——

Heathfield Jany 27th 1808

Dear Sir

I send you annexed the inscription intended for my fathers gravestone, which I shall be obliged to you to get neatly executed in the same form as written. I mentioned having the two stones rebated upon one another thus but on consideration it will be better to make them plain joint thus When the weather becomes milder, I wish also to have the letters cleaned & repaired upon my Grandfathers stone

. . . .

- -

- I shall thank you to get the workman to lose no time in getting it finished, otherwise it is possible a stone may be laid upon me before I have laid one on my father.

I shall be glad to hear from you of the receipt of this letter mean while Mrs Watt joins me in best compts & good wishes to you & miss Walkinshaw, with remembrances to other friends, and I remain

        Dear Sir
            Your obliged
                humble servt
                    James Watt

father's gravestone, which I shall be obliged to you to get neatly executed in the same form as written. I mentioned having the two stones ribated upon one another, thus—[giving a diagram]—but, on consideration, it will be better to make them plain joint, thus—[diagram.] When the weather becomes milder, I wish also to have the letters cleaned and repaired upon my grandfather's stone.[1]

"I should have sent you this sooner, but was indisposed with one bad cold after another since I came home; and also found a good deal of business behind. I shall thank you to get the workmen to lose no time in getting it finished, otherwise it is possible a stone may be laid upon me before I have laid one on my father.

"I shall be glad to hear from you of the receipt of this letter; meanwhile, Mrs. Watt joins me in best compliments and good wishes to you and Miss Walkinshaw, with remembrances to other friends,—and I remain, dear Sir, your obliged humble servant,

"JAMES WATT.

---

[1] In regard to the reference here made to the cleaning and repairing of the letters upon his grandfather's tombstone: It will be recollected that two instances of discrepancy between the dates upon this stone, and those contained in the Records of the Kirk-Session, were adverted to in our memorials of the grandfather, Thomas Watt —one of these occurring in the year of the death, the other in the age, of his wife, Margaret Sherrer. As there is no reason to doubt the perfect accuracy of the Session record, and as the tombstone, laid down in 1701, would be much obliterated during the period which intervened between that year and 1808, when the letters were "cleaned and repaired," it is not to be wondered at, that, in the hands of a person who might not have access to, or have consulted the record, as seems to have been the case in this instance, but should trust to his reading of the stone, mistakes should be committed. I assume confidently, that *an error has been committed* in retracing the figures under the authority of the above letter from Mr. Watt; for, the death of Thomas Watt, and that of Margaret Sherrer, are separated from each other, in the record, by eleven pages only, showing indubitably that twenty-one years could not have elapsed between these events. The date upon the stone, therefore, which is erroneously 1755, ought clearly to be 1735, the year after her husband, the good mathematician's death. The birth of their illustrious grandson in 1736, stands recorded in the same volume, at the distance only of eight pages farther on. The errors which have been pointed out show with what care the restoration of inscriptions, when defaced, ought to be gone about, as gross blunders may otherwise be committed; and it is matter of regret that the inscription just recited has undergone a very considerable obliteration since it was copied by me upwards of twenty years ago.

" Remember me to my cousin Anna.   I could not go to see Mrs. Wilson, but saw Mrs. Birnie."

The following is the inscription as it now appears in the West Churchyard of Greenock :—

In memory of
JAMES WATT,
Merchant in Greenock,
A benevolent and ingenious man,
and a zealous promoter of the
improvements of the Town,
Who died 1782, aged 84,

of
AGNES MUIRHEID,
his Spouse,
Who died 1755, aged 52 ;

and of
JOHN WATT,
their Son,
Who perished at Sea, 1763, aged 23.

To his revered Parents,
and to his Brother—James Watt
has placed this memorial.

These stones, which cover the mortal remains of the immediate ancestors of Watt, are rapidly suffering decay in the form of the letters and figures.   Being laid flat, and consequently frequently trodden upon by those resorting to the churchyard,—for here, too, repose the ashes of one consecrated in the popular memory, whose rustic graces of person and mind inspired some of the tenderest strains of our national poesy—the " Highland Mary " of Burns,—

the inscriptions cannot fail, in the course of a few years, to be considerably injured, if not altogether effaced. Recently great improvements have been effected in this ancient burial-place surrounding what are now the ruins of the oldest Kirk that remains in the town. The surface has been in some degree levelled, trees and flowering shrubs have been planted, the curb-stones, many of which were buried beneath the soil, have been raised ;—

> " The long flat stones
> With nettles skirted, and with moss o'ergrown,
> That tell in homely phrase who lie below,"

have been brought into their horizontal, and the oblique restored to their perpendicular positions,—operations in which, it is gratifying to be able to add, the WATT tombstones have been particularly attended to ; and it is hoped that what has been done will tend in some degree to their conservation.[1]

---

[1] These improvements were carried out under the superintendence of Mr. Murray, late of the Royal Botanic Garden, Glasgow, under the tasteful directions of John Gray, Esq., to whose zealous exertions in regard to this and similar public benefits, the community stands most deeply indebted.

CHAPTER V.

CORRESPONDENCE WITH HIS OLD FRIENDS AT GREENOCK——RETIREMENT FROM THE
PARTNERSHIP AT SOHO——DEATH OF MR. BOULTON——DEATH OF HIS SON GREGORY——
HIS OCCASIONAL VISITS TO SCOTLAND——ZEAL FOR THE PROGRESS OF MECHANICAL
SCIENCE——RESOLVES TO FOUND A SCIENTIFIC LIBRARY AT GREENOCK——PATRIOTIC
OBJECTS IN THIS DESIGN——TO TRANSPLANT A SCIENTIFIC KNOWLEDGE OF THE
MECHANICAL ARTS TO HIS NATIVE TOWN.

IN the death of the estimable Bailie, the town of Greenock lost the
last of those links which during two generations had perpetuated
among its families the distinguished name of WATT.   There still
remained, however, not a few elements which served, for some years
longer, to keep alive the connexion, and to maintain in some degree
the interest which that connexion was fitted to afford.   On the part
of the eminent son, an intimacy between his own and his father's old
friends continued to exist; and occasional visits were exchanged, and
a correspondence kept up by him, till within a short period of his
death.   It is matter of regret that so few of those private letters, so
very small a portion of a correspondence which is known to have been
sufficiently voluminous, seems to have survived.   Such fragments,
however, as we have been fortunate enough to collect are here reve-
rently preserved.   They belong altogether to the later portion of Mr.
Watt's life, to that period, consequently, when the ardour of invention
had all but subsided, and the engrossing cares of business had given
place to the grave and more leisurely occupations of the sage.[1]   He
had passed considerably his seventieth year.   Care had silvered his

[1] Mr. Watt retired from business in favour of his sons and Mr. Boulton, junior, in 1800.

head, and time greatly thinned the ranks of those friends who, through a long course of anxious and busied years, had been the associates alike of his private and his philosophic life. In this isolating process, which always tells more or less painfully on the advanced years of a kindly and sociable nature, the severest blow of all which had fallen upon him, and which doubtless was felt to be irreparable, although contemplated with that mental calm and chastened resignation which formed a marked characteristic of this great mind, in presence of the supreme dispensations of Providence,—was the heavy bereavement sustained a few years before in the death of his son Gregory, at the early age of twenty-seven, and when he had hardly done more than given the most brilliant earnests of the finest genius, and the most graceful and manly accomplishments. However philosophically borne, this stroke manifestly communicated a somewhat sombre tone to the rest of the father's life, though it might not have entirely obliterated the character of his ordinarily cheerful disposition.

One of Mr. Watt's principal friends and correspondents at Greenock was the late Mr. James Walkinshaw. He was a retired merchant, and in every way fitted for the agency of friendship with which Mr. Watt intrusted him. In some respects he was a notable personage. He was endowed with many excellent qualities; and, from his dress and habits, might, not inaptly, be taken for a fair type of the good old gentleman of a former generation. His gait and appearance in public will be as long remembered by his townsmen, as the recollection of his quaint remarks, terse humour, and urbanity of manners will be cherished in the circle of those friends who were privileged with his intimacy. In the letters addressed to him by Mr. Watt there is evidence of one strong trait in his character,—a certain morbid antipathy to "rendering accounts," which possessed his mind. Having what he considered a competency, he was little careful to increase his store by " plaguing himself with business." All his time, accordingly, was at the disposal of his friends ; and, within the circle of a simple and uniform routine of amusement, his highest gratification consisted in ministering, by offices of kindness, to those to whom such cheerful interest and attention were an object, as well as in all the exercises of a general and genial benevolence. His regard for his old friend, Mr. Watt, amounted almost to veneration. A singular, but very graceful, proof of the attachment, and even affection, which subsisted between the two friends, is afforded by the fact of Mr. Watt having, at his death, desired a favourite waistcoat worn by him to be sent to Mr. Walkinshaw ; which piece of dress the latter was wont, with allowable pride, to show upon his person. Mr. Walkinshaw was remarkable for his orderly, neat, and gentlemanly appearance. He was unmarried, and lived with an excellent and respected sister, much about his own age, Miss Walkinshaw, to whom Mr. Watt in his correspondence frequently alludes. The reader has already perused Mr. Watt's letter to this gentleman regarding the tombstone and inscription for his father's grave at Greenock. The following makes reference to the same subject, and expresses his distress on occasion of the death of his esteemed partner, Mr. Boulton :—

"GLENARBACK, *Aug.* 22, 1809.

"DEAR SIR,—I have been in this country about a fortnight. My stay is uncertain ; circumstances may make it short, and it is probable I may not come to Greenock this time. I shall also be glad to know whether my father's tombstone has been placed as I directed ; how my cousin A—— does, and if you can give me any information concerning Mrs. W——, her daughter and family, with intelligence concerning any of my other friends in your place. I shall stay here about a week, after which I go to visit my friend Mr. Muirhead, on the Water of Endrick ; but letters directed for me at Miss M'Gregor's, No. 9, Cochran Street, Glasgow, will be forwarded to me,—and it will give me pleasure to hear of your and Miss Walkinshaw's welfare, not forgetting my much esteemed friend Mrs. Shaw, and her family.[1]

"I am at present very much distressed by having yesterday received the account of the death of my very worthy friend, Mr. Boulton, senior, who has been long painfully afflicted, but is now relieved from his sufferings. There are few better men existing, and none who have been of more use to society. He had attained the venerable age of eighty-one; but several of the last years of his life have been embittered by a very painful and incurable malady.

"I left my son, and other friends, at Birmingham, well; and Mrs. Watt and I enjoy as good health as our time of life admits; though she has had the misfortune to lose the sight of one of her eyes, yet it has been without pain.

"Mrs. Watt joins me in best wishes to you and Miss Walkinshaw, and with kind remembrances to other friends.—I remain, dear Sir, your obedient servant, JAMES WATT."

Having incidentally alluded to GREGORY WATT, we cannot omit the occasion of paying a passing tribute to the memory of one so eminent. The scattered notices which current literature[2] furnishes of this noble youth, amply justify the references to his worth which are found in the pages of several of his father's panegyrists. In the present more unpretending contribution to the name he bore, our simplest, and, perhaps, not least appropriate, tribute to the virtues and talent of this great-grandson of the old Professor of the Mathematicks may be allowed to be, that he was, in all respects, VIR PATRE, AVO, MAJORIBUS SUIS, DIGNISSIMUS.[3] His name frequently occurs in the records of the early friendships of Thomas Campbell, who was one of his most inti-

[1] See reference to those old friends, the minister's family, *supra*, p. 100.
[2] See Brougham's *Lives of Men of Letters and Science*, 1845; *Watt*, p. 383; *Davy*, p. 450.

Encyc. Brit. Art. *Davy*, p. 637. Beatie's *Life of Thomas Campbell*, 1849, vol. i. pp. 82, 109, 110, 112, 113, 115, 119, &c.
[3] Cic. *Philip*, iii. 10.

mate College associates at Glasgow ; and although, according to the poet, of a spirit and temper the most widely different from his own, is always mentioned in terms of the most affectionate admiration and eulogy.   A single allusion to his " generous, liberal, and open-hearted" friend, in the bard's own words, gives an idea of " this splendid strip- ling," whose " unparalleled talent for eloquence," and general literary attainments, formed the boast of the youth of those days at the northern University :—" With melodious elocution," continues the poet, " great acuteness in argument, and rich unfailing fluency of dic- tion, Gregory Watt seemed born to become a great orator ; and, I have no doubt, would have shone in Parliament, had he not been carried off by consumption, in his five-and-twentieth year.   He was literally the most beautiful youth I ever saw.   When he was only twenty-two, an eminent English artist—Howard, I think—made his head the model of a picture of Adam."[1]   No wonder if the father of such a son, even while, with a noble resignation, " expressing his con- fident hopes that Gregory had changed this mortal state for a far happier existence," and " as if anxious to avoid all suspicion of his giving way to excessive sorrow," should still have been conscious, though not, it would seem, of passionate grief, yet of something akin to a permanent and settled regret at his earthly loss ![2]

But to return.   A letter to the same correspondent illustrates gracefully some features of Mr. Watt's character often remarked upon,—his eminent benignity of heart, his considerate remembrance of relatives and friends, as well as the scrupulous exactitude he displayed in all affairs of business, however trifling their import or amount :—

" HEATHFIELD, *Feb.* 14, 1811.

" MY DEAR SIR,—I blame myself much for not answering your very

[1] *Life and Letters of Thomas Campbell,* by William Beatie, M.D., 1849, vol. i. p. 82.

[2] Lord Brougham's *Lives of Men of Letters and Science,* 1845, p. 384.

kind letter of July 4th, sooner. I was in the act of setting out for Wales when I received it. I made a month's stay there, and many things occurred to make me neglect it since, till the annual time of settling my accounts brought it before me. Permit me to hope that you will forgive my omission, which has been more caused by the failure of recollection, than by any want of a due sense of my obligations to you on this and other occasions.

"I found, on questioning your friend, Mr. S——, that he had not that genius for mechanics he had flattered himself to have; and as there was no likelihood of his obtaining as good a salary here as he enjoyed in Greenock, I thought I could not do him more kindness than by advising him to endeavour to get into some merchant's counting-house, either in Liverpool, or in Scotland—in consequence of which he went from hence to Liverpool, since which I have not heard of him.

"I am to thank you for your very great care and attention to my poor cousin A——; and observe your account of her funeral charge, which is very moderate, and which I am very sorry my neglect has kept you so long out of. If you will favour me with a copy of my account-current with you to this date, I shall send you an order upon Mr. Archibald Hamilton, junior, who will pay it you. Till I received his account the other day, I thought you would have drawn upon him, as I requested you, but nothing is charged in that account.

"In respect to the seat in the kirk, please to sell it for what you can get, and send me a form of a proper assignation, which I will sign and return.

"I have heard nothing of Mrs. B. since you wrote. I hope she arrived safe, and with her husband is doing well. I shall be glad to hear how her mother is, and if she has enough to support her. If that should not be the case, please to inform me what help may be wanted from me; meanwhile, please to remember me to her.

" I have had but indifferent health in the latter part of summer and fall, and have had some very bad colds in the winter, and am now very much better, perhaps as well as I ought to expect to be, and do not go much out.

" Mrs. Watt seems to have quite recovered her broken arm ; her sight continues much as it was, at least not materially worse ; and, though she has had some colds and rheumatism this winter, she is now tolerably well—we are old folks, and cannot expect to be quite so. Thank God, we enjoy, on the whole, better health than most people of our age.

" I beg you will remember me kindly to any enquiring friends at Greenock, and also to our good friends at Paisley, Mr. Love and Bailie Barclay, when you see or write to them.

" Mrs. Watt joins me in very best wishes to you and Miss Walkinshaw, and you will oblige me very much by writing to me soon. Do not imitate the bad example I have set you.—I remain, my dear Sir, yours sincerely,   JAMES WATT."

Another letter to the same friend accompanied one or two copies of an engraving of his portrait :—

" HEATHFIELD, *Oct.* 29, 1816.

" MY DEAR SIR,—I send you, by Miss M'Gregor, three copies of Cadel and Davies' engraving of my portrait,—one for yourself, one for Mr. Andrew Anderson, and one for Mr. M'Goun, which I beg may be presented to them with my best respects. They are not very like ; and the picture from which they were taken was done when I was much younger than I now am. They are, however, the best which have been done, and as such, I hope you will accept them.

" I shall be glad to hear from you of your welfare, and that of my other friends, to all of whom I request to be remembered, especially to my cousin, Mrs. W., of whom I shall be glad to hear, and of her daughter and family.   Please remember me also to Mr. Love and Bailie Barclay.

"Miss M'Gregor will inform you of Mrs. Watt's and my health, which, though not perfect, is perhaps better than we have a right to expect at our age.

"Mrs. Watt joins me in best wishes to you, Miss Walkinshaw, and other friends, and I remain, my dear Sir, your sincere friend,

"JAMES WATT."

One of Mr. Watt's last visits to his friends in Scotland took place in the year 1815.   Interested as he was known to be in all matters relating to the improvement of the mechanical arts, and ever accessible to applications for opinion or counsel in such subjects, his advice was frequently solicited, and as promptly placed at the disposal of the inquirer, in regard to all kinds of devices, whether these were of real, or, as was more generally the case, of merely fondly imagined utility. Even in cases of this nature, were there but some fair display of invention or ingenuity to recommend them, Mr. Watt never seemed to think of any condescension being exercised on his part, or of the subject of reference being unworthy of at least some particular notice, —a notice which was always expressed in terms of equal frankness and candour, and, wherever it was possible, in a manner favourable to the applicant, and accompanied with valuable hints for its alteration or improvement.

It was on the occasion of this visit, and during his sojourn in Glasgow, that an intelligent and ingenious individual addressed an application to the philosopher, in regard to the merits of a clock or machine of intricate and peculiar construction, which it was proposed to erect at the Custom-house of Greenock.   The writer of the communication in question was the late Mr. Colin Buchanan, master of the mathematical school of Greenock,—a man in numerous respects well deserving

of the remembrance of his townsmen, and of whom a slight notice
ought not to be here out of place.[1]   To great benevolence of disposition, a feature very prominent in the character of the old gentleman,
Mr. Buchanan added many superior qualifications for his office.   He
was among the last of what might be called " the teachers of the old
school" of Greenock.   And yet, even as such, he may now be admitted to have been far in advance of his times, both in the theory and
practice of what is now so deservedly prominent and increasingly
important a science or art,—that of tuition.   There was much about
the man and his whole *modus operandi*, to attract the observation of
one so attentive as Mr. Watt.   His class-rooms were in one point of
view, in fact, a kind of incipient school of design, where, on particular
days, not only were the principles of mechanics popularly communicated, but admirable instructions were given in the various branches
of drawing, etching, ornamental design, &c.   In these departments of
useful mechanical art,—branches of school instruction in those days
not much attended to in Scotland, and, even now, far less cultivated
with us than they deserve to be, or than they are with our Continental neighbours, particularly in France,—he was indefatigably
zealous, always on the alert to discover talent, and to foster invention
and skill in the youth brought within his influence.[2]   And in these
efforts, it should be added, he was remarkably successful ; more than
one of his old pupils having since risen to high places as artists, whose
names, appended to the etchings and engravings of some of our

[1] His son, Dr. Robert Buchanan, late Master
of the Mathematical School, and now Rector of
the Academy, more than inherits his father's
scientific tastes and endowments, as well as his
spirit and success as an instructor of youth.

[2] It is long since the WATT CLUB had engraved
for itself the die of a beautifully executed Medal-
lion of JAMES WATT, the object being, to have
at its disposal a MEDAL which it might award
under specified regulations, for the encouragement of native talent, particularly of ingenuity in
various branches of the mechanical arts. It were
greatly to be desired that this excellent purpose
were resumed by the Club, it being difficult to
conceive any more legitimate way in which it
might exercise its functions, or make its influence
felt usefully in the most important section of this
community.

scientific works, are familiar to those interested in such illustrations, particularly in the departments of Natural History and Practical Mechanics.[1]

The machine adverted to, which was minutely described in the letter to Mr. Watt, was the invention, it is understood, either of Mr. Buchanan himself, or of one of his pupils. It was intended to indicate the hour of the day or night, the direction of the wind, and the state of the tide. Its moving power was to be the wind. Mr. Watt's reply to the communication, manifesting the great engineer's usual extent and accuracy of knowledge, was to the following effect, and, as usual, decisive :—

"GLASGOW, *Oct.* 18, 1815.

" SIR,—In reply to your letter of the 12th, my age and the state of

---

[1] These remarks on the procedure and views of this excellent and sagacious teacher are intended in the spirit of sincere eulogium. In these days the high importance in a national point of view of such instructions as those referred to in the text, *and that in our common schools*, cannot be too often or too earnestly pressed upon public attention. In full remembrance of the great results that were promised from Mechanic's Institutions at their founding some years ago, it is difficult to resist the conviction that they have failed of their object. If they may not be said to have entirely done so, they by no means meet the exigencies of the day, in respect of that kind and degree of knowledge, *and of taste*, required in the British Workman, if he is to compete successfully with his neighbours of another tongue. The great Industrial Exhibitions have, in this very particular, revealed some humbling facts, proving beyond all contradiction that in not a few even of those arts, on our superiority in which we have been accustomed to plume ourselves, we have been really surpassed! Nothing, it is believed, will secure amongst us the attainment of that exquisite taste and skill in execution which characterize our Continental rivals in many im-portant branches of the useful arts, but a recurrence to some such plan of instruction as that noticed; nothing but our making up our minds without loss of time to take a lesson in this matter from our French neighbours, and make it a part of the education of our *common schools*, to give instructions not only in the elements of Science, but, what is quite as essential,—being so necessary to the education of the Eye, alike of the master and the workman,—lessons for practical purposes in the various kinds of Drawing, Ornamental Design, Colour, &c.

An earnest appreciation of the value of some such course of proceeding ought, IN EVERY MANUFACTURING COMMUNITY, to be a special and supreme requirement in the consideration of all corporations charged with the direction of Public Instruction in the present day ; and it is devoutly to be hoped, that in our own community, supplemented as it is far beyond other provincial towns with the highest educational appliances, in its academy and libraries, matters of the nature referred to, so directly affecting its wealth and population, will not be lost sight of in its school programmes.

my health do not permit me to enter fully into the subject of your letter. The contrivance you mention does not seem to me entirely new. Clocks have been made which have been wound by the action of the tide, by running water, by the rise and fall of the barometer, and, I believe, by the wind; and watches which have been wound up by the motion of the person who carried them,—but all these methods have, for some reason or other, been found more curious than useful. I have seen more than one excellent clock, which has drawn upon a piece of vellum, changed annually, the rise and fall of the barometer; and there is somewhere, I believe, in some of the early volumes of the Memoirs of the French Academy, descriptions of clocks to keep register of the directions and force of the wind, and various other meteorological matters. I conceive that an ingenious mechanic would not find great difficulty in executing the machine you mention; but it would occupy much time and attention, and would be expensive, and I doubt whether its utility would be commensurate to these circumstances.

"If, however, you should think your ideas worthy of being followed any further, after making proper drawings, I would recommend a *model*[1] to be made of a tolerable size before you proceed further.— I remain, Sir, your obedient servant,   JAMES WATT."

The circumstance, however, of so much ingenuity being exhibited in the complicated contrivance, by one of his townsmen, did not escape the reflective observation of the great mechanician, and originated a train of events important to the community in general. Being in Greenock some days subsequent to the writing of the above letter,

---

[1] This was Watt's ultimate or rather initiatory test for *all* inventions and fondly cherished "improvements." It was that which he applied rigidly in every instance, in his own case; and it would be well if all speculators in mechanics, at the earliest possible moment, were to reduce it to practice. It would save infinite disappointment, and often profitless waste of money as well as time, and disburthen the arts of much that hardly belongs to their loftier province.

and happening, in company with his friend Mr. Walkinshaw, to enter the shop of Mr. John Heron, Watchmaker, a clever and ingenious workman, Mr. Watt's attention was attracted by a water-colour drawing of a group of shells that had been left there for exhibition. Struck by the merits of its execution, and having been informed that it was the work of a youth in humble circumstances, whose taste for drawing and design had been discovered and directed by Mr. Colin Buchanan, Mr. Watt, pursuing the reflection which had been suggested by the ingenious machine so recently submitted to him, inquired whether there were any other young men of promising talents in town, and whether native genius might not be successfully stimulated by some judiciously directed means of encouragement. The answers received to his interrogatories were so satisfactory, that a desire to be instrumental in advancing the interests of his native town, in a way which might influence beneficially its intelligence as well as its productive industry, pressed itself upon his attention and began to occupy his mind. The result of more deliberate consultations with one or two of his friends in regard to his contemplated project, was his determination to appropriate a sum of money to the founding of a Scientific Library in Greenock, with this public-spirited object in view;[1] a resolution which he communicated before leaving town to his friends, Mr. Walkinshaw, Mr. Anderson,[2] and Mr. Watt,[3] who cordially agreed

[1] Mr. Watt had, a few years previously to this, animated by the same patriotic motives and devotedness to the interests of science, founded an exhibition, or rather, annual prize, in the University of Glasgow, open to competition among students in philosophy, in actual attendance at that seminary. It was to be awarded to the best Essay on one or other of a series of subjects which were specified by himself, in connexion with practical mechanics and chemistry in their application to the arts.

[2] Andrew Anderson, Esq., Mr. Watt's old schoolfellow, already frequently alluded to, brother to the Professor of Natural Philosophy in the University of Glasgow, who was founder of the Andersonian University in that city.

[3] James Watt, Esq., of Crawfordsdyke, justly esteemed for his many private virtues, afterwards raised to the Provostship of the town of Greenock. Although not related to the family of the great engineer, he enjoyed his intimate friendship during a series of years, and long after the mechanician's death, continued to be the correspondent and esteemed friend of the late Mr. James Watt of Soho.

26

to co-operate with the donor in carrying into execution his generous scheme.

On Mr. Watt's return to England his plan was matured. The following letters on the subject detail the steps he had taken, and specify the rules and conditions he wished to be observed in instituting and giving permanency to the proposed Library. From Heathfield he writes to Mr. Anderson, 12th Jan. 1816 :—

" MY DEAR SIR,—In consequence of your obliging consent to act for me in the following business, I applied to my friend Mr. Watt of Crawfordsdyke, to join you in it, which he kindly agreed to, and mentioned the Rev. Dr. Scott as a proper co-adjutor in the choice of the books, which I approved of ; but not being personally acquainted with that gentleman, and the shortness of my stay not permitting an introduction, I begged he would mention it to him, and request his consent to my naming him as one of my trustees in it.

" As I had not then made out a draft of the conditions on which I proposed to give the money, I left it with my friend Mr. Walkinshaw to deposit in the bank, until I should have time to consider the subject. An accumulation of business, from my long absence, and other matters which a younger man would probably have soon dispatched, have made me delay doing so until the present time.

" I now request that, at your convenience, you will consult with the above-named gentlemen and Mr. Walkinshaw, and make the following proposal on my part :—

" JAMES WATT of Heathfield, in the county of Stafford, LL.D., offers to the Magistrates and Town-Council of Greenock, the sum of One Hundred Pounds sterling on the following conditions, which he hopes they will do him the favour to agree to :—

" 1st. That the said sum shall be laid out upon books for the use of the Mathematical School of Greenock, which books shall be such as treat of Natural Philosophy

And.w Anderson Esq.   Heathfield Birm.m — Jan.y 12.n 1816
Greenock

My Dear Sir

                In consequence of your obliging consent to act for
me in the following business. I applied to my friend Mr Watt of
Crawfords dyke to join you in it, which he kindly agreed to, and
mentioned the Rev.d Dr Scott as a proper coadjutor in the choice
of the books, which I approved of; but not being personally acquainted
with these Gentlemen, and the shortness of my stay not permitting an
introduction, I begged he would mention it to him and request his
consent to my naming him as one of my Trustees in it.

As I had not then made out a draft of the conditions, on which
I proposed to give the money, I left it with my friend Mr Watkinshaw
to deposit in the Bank, until I should have time to consider the
subject. An accumulation of business from my long absence and
other matters, which a younger man, would probably have soon dispatched,
have occasioned me delay doing so until the present time.

I now request that at your convenience you will consult with
the above named Gentlemen & Mr Watkinshaw, and make the
following proposal on my part. ————

     ("James Watt of Heathfield in the county of Stafford LL.D.
offers to the Magistrates & Town council of Greenock the
sum of £100 Ster. on the following conditions, which he hopes
they will do him the favour to agree to

" 1st   That the said Sum shall be laid out upon books for the use
" of the Mathematical School of Greenock, which books shall
" be such as treat of Natural Philosophy & Mathematicks &
" more especially upon Geometry, mechanicks, Astronomy,
" navigation, the motion resistance and other properties of Fluid
" Statickes, and the science & art of ship building.

2d That a catalogue shall be made of the said books, signed by the
" Guardians thereof hereby appointed & the books shall be mark
" and numbered in some durable manner, as belonging to the
" Mathematical schools & they shall be kept in some proper
" place under the care of the master of the said: School

3° That if any of the said books shall be lost or destroyed, the
" Magistrates & Town Council shall engage for themselves as
" their Successors, or in office, that the same shall be replaced at
" the publick expence of the said Town.

4th That a small annual subscription be exacted from each
" Scholar using the said books, in order to add to their number
" and to make up for their wear and tear

5th That the Revd Dr Scott, one of the ministers of Greenock,
" Messrs Andrew Anderson, James Watt of Crawfords dyke
" and James Walkinshaw, along with the master of the said
" School for the time being, and any two other gentlemen as
" shall be named for that purpose by the sd Magistrates, Sh
" be the purchasers and Guardians of the said books; and
" whenever the 6 Guardians first above named, shall by death
                                                                    resigna

signation or disability shall be reduced to two, the said shall be lawful for the remaining two to chuse two others in their place and at all times hereafter when such like vacancies shall occur they shall be supplied by their proper persons chosen by the Governors or Trustees. and in like manner the said Magistrates shall from time to time supply any deficiencies which shall occur in the Guardians to be appointed by them. (see next page for article 6'ty)

6. That an act or Instrument shall be entered in the Town books agreeing to the above terms and confirming the same an attested copy thereof shall be transmitted to the said James Watt of Heathfield. ——————

(My intention in this donation is to form the beginning of a Scientific library for the instruction of the Cause of Governing & I hope it will prompt others to add to it, and to render my Townsmen renowned for their knowledge, as they are for & Spirit of Enterprize —— Thus being my views they induce me to hope for your & the other Gentlemen I have named assisting me in it, And that the Magistrates and Council will honour my proposal with their Countenance and acceptance

I send inclosed Mr Watkinshaws receipt, upon the production of which he will pay the money & any interest the Bank may have allowed for the same

Mrs Watt joins me in offering our Compts & best wishes to you, Mrs Anderson & family, begging to be kindly remembered to your Brothers & other friends, and I remain with sincere regard & esteem

My Dear Sir   Your obliged friend & Servant
                                         James Watt

To follow article 5 on preceding page. 6th And at any time or times hereafter it shall be competent to the said Magistrates, with the advice and consent of the major part of the said Guardians, for the time being, to make such additional rules and regulations for relative to the use or preservation of the said Books as shall to them seem meet & proper.—

Andrew Anderson Esqr

Merchant

Greenock N.B.

Post paid

only sheets

and Mathematics, and more especially upon Geometry, Mechanics, Astronomy, Navigation, the Motion, Resistance, and other properties of Fluids, and the science and art of Navigation.

" 2d. That a Catalogue shall be made of the said books, signed by the guardians thereof hereby appointed, and the books shall be marked and numbered in some durable manner as belonging to the Mathematical School, and they shall be kept in some proper place under the care of the master of the said school.

" 3d. That if any of the said books shall be lost or destroyed, the Magistrates and Town-Council shall engage for themselves and their successors in office, that the same shall be replaced at the public expense of the said town.

" 4th. That a small annual subscription be exacted from each scholar using the said books, in order to add to their number, and so make up for tear and wear.

" 5th. That the Rev. Dr. Scott, one of the ministers of Greenock, Messrs. Andrew Anderson, James Watt of Crawfordsdyke, and James Walkinshaw, along with the master of said school for the time being, and any two other gentlemen who shall be named for that purpose by the said Magistrates, shall be the purchasers and guardians of the said books, and whenever the four guardians first above-named, by death, resignation, or disability, shall be reduced to two, then it shall be lawful for the remaining two to choose two others in their place; and at all times hereafter when similar vacancies shall occur, they shall be supplied by other proper persons chosen by the surviving trustees; and in like manner, the said Magistrates shall, from time to time, supply any deficiency which shall occur in the guardians to be appointed by them.

" 6th. That any time or times hereafter, it shall be competent to the said Magistrates, with the advice and consent of the major part of the said guardians for the time being, to make such additional rules and regulations relative to the use and preservation of the said books, as shall to them seem meet and proper.

" 7th. That an act of sederunt shall be entered in the Town's Books, agreeing to the above terms, and confirming the same; and an attested copy thereof shall be transmitted to the said James Watt of Heathfield.

" My intention, in this donation, is to form the beginning of a scientific library, for the instruction of the youth of Greenock ; and I hope it will prompt others to add to it, and to render my townsmen as eminent for their knowledge, as they are for their spirit of enterprise.   These being my views, they induce me to hope for your, and

the other gentlemen I have named, assisting me in it, and that the
Magistrates and Council will honour my proposal with their countenance and acceptance.

"I send inclosed Mr. Walkinshaw's receipt, upon the production of
which he will pay the money, and any interest the bank may have
allowed for the same.

"Mrs. Watt joins me in offering our compliments and best wishes
to you, Mrs. Anderson, and family, begging to be kindly remembered
to your brother and other friends.—And I remain, with sincere
regard and esteem, my dear Sir, your obliged friend and servant,

"JAMES WATT."

To Mr. Watt of Crawfordsdyke, he writes on following day :—

"MY DEAR SIR,—I ought before now to have written to you concerning my proffered donation to the Library of the Mathematical
School of Greenock, but on my return here I found an accumulation
of business awaiting me, which at my time of life it has been difficult
to get through.   I have, however, at last digested my proposals to the
Magistrates on that head, and have transmitted them to my friend,
Mr. Andrew Anderson, who will shew them to you ; and I request
you will assist him in the application to the Magistrates, and that you
will second my wishes in taking upon you the trust I have therein
assigned you.

"You will see that in consequence of what passed in our conversation upon the subject, I have also named the Rev. Dr. Scott as a
guardian ; but as I am not personally known to him, I must request
you to use your endeavours to excuse my not applying to him directly,
and to prevail upon him to accept the proposed office, both as an
obligation he will confer upon me, and on account of the benefit which
the public may derive from his knowledge of the proper books.   To
the Master of the Mathematical School, I request it may be said, that

Jas. Watt Esqr.
Cranfordsdyke

Heathfield Birm.m Jany 13th 1816

My Dear Sir

I ought before now to have written to you
concerning my proposed Donation to the library of the Math.c School
of Greenock; but on my return home I found an accumulation of
business awaiting me which at my time of life it has been
difficult to get through. I have however at last digested my proposal
to the magistrates on this head, & have transmitted them to my
friend Mr And.w Anderson who will shew them to you, and I
request you will assist him in the application to the Magistrates
I trust you will second my wishes in taking upon you the trust
I have therein assigned you.

You will see that in consequence of what passed in our
conversation upon the subject that I have also named the
Revd Dr Scott as a guardian, but as I am not personally
known to him, I must request you to use your endeavours to
excuse my not applying to him directly & to prevail upon him
to accept the proposed office, both as an obligation he will confer
upon me, and a benefit the public may derive from his
knowledge of the proper books. To the Master of the Math Schoo
it may be said that I have named him as a person
I have heard spoken of as well qualified for his office & have

therefore

therefore have supposed he will willingly further any thing which
may tend to the improvement of his pupils

To my friend Mr Jas. Watkins have I shall be obliged
to you to say that I have sent his receipt for the money to Mr
Anderson, and that I have named him as a Guardian not on
account of his knowledge of the proper books, but as a person
who will faithfully execute the trust reposed in him to the
utmost extent of his power hoping he will excuse my
writing to him at present as I have written fully to you and
Mr Anderson, I shall write to himself soon

Asking your excuse for the liberties I have taken in troubling
you with so many commissions & begging you will accept
and present to your family Mrs Watts & my best compts, wishing
you all many happy new years, I remain with much esteem

My Dear Sir

Your obliged humble servant,

James Watt

James Watt Esqr
Crawfords dyke
near Greenock N.B.

Post Paid?

I have named him as a person I have heard spoken of as well qualified for his office, and have, therefore, supposed he will willingly further anything which may tend to the improvement of his pupils.

"To my friend, Mr. James Walkinshaw, I shall be obliged to you to say that I have sent his receipt for the money to Mr. Anderson, and that I have named him as a guardian, not on account of his knowledge of the proper books, but as a person who will faithfully execute the trust reposed in him, to the utmost extent of his power, —hoping he will excuse my writing to him at present, as I have written fully to you and Mr. Anderson, and shall write to himself soon.

"Asking your excuse for the liberty I have taken in troubling you with so many commissions, and begging you will accept and present to your family Mrs. Watt's and my best compliments,—wishing you all many happy New-Years, I remain, my dear Sir, your obliged humble servant, JAMES WATT."

And to Mr. Walkinshaw on the 17th :—

"MY DEAR SIR,—On the 13th instant I wrote to Mr. Andrew Anderson, and sent him the proposals I wish to be made to the Magistrates concerning my donation of money to purchase books for the Mathematical School, in which I have taken the liberty to nominate you a guardian along with Dr. Scott, Mr. Anderson, and Mr. Watt of Crawfordsdyke, and which I hope you will accept. At the same time I send your receipt to Mr. Anderson ; so that if the Magistrates accept my proposals, he may be enabled to pay them the money, which you will please to pay to him on his delivering to you the receipt. As Mr. Anderson and Mr. Watt will shew you the letters I wrote to them on the 13th, I shall now say no more on this subject at present.

"We have had a stormy winter, without much frost or snow. Mrs. Watt has had a good deal of illness, but is now better. I have got through pretty well, (as well, indeed, as I could hope to be in winter,) and as it is now looking towards spring, hope to escape any severe cold.

"Mrs. Watt and Miss M'Gregor join me in best wishes to you and Miss Walkinshaw, requesting to hear from you soon, and I remain, my dear Sir, yours sincerely,   JAMES WATT."

On the 7th February 1816, the letter to Mr. Anderson was laid before the Town-Council by Mr. Quintin Leitch, then chief-magistrate, when a minute of acceptance was recorded in the following terms :—

"And the object Dr. Watt has in view, marking distinctly a kind remembrance of his native town, a benevolence of heart, and an unceasing regard for the progress of science, the Council with pleasure agree to accept the proposed deposit, and to follow out the plan of the donor."

As soon as the necessary preliminaries were arranged, a considerable portion of the donation was at once expended in the purchase of books ; and these, in conformity with the desire of the donor, were deposited in the Mathematical School of Greenock.

Something of the particular nature of Mr. Watt's intentions in regard to "the scientific and commercial distinction of his native town," may be gathered from the character of the works which he designed for his foundation, and which embraced generally both the theory and practice of those arts and departments of industry which were most prosecuted at that time, and in which improvement was equally attainable and to be desired.[1]   A very general spirit of inven-

[1] The following is the original List of Works proposed by Mr. Watt himself :—
Hutchinson's Naval Architecture, (Merchant Ships.)
Shipwright's Vade Mecum.
Venturi on the Motion of Fluids.
Clare on Fluids.

Elementary Illustrations of Laplace's Mechanics.
Smeaton on Wind and Water Mills.
Desagulier's Experimental Philosophy.
Legendre's Geometry—Translation.
Desagulier's Conic Sections.
Gravesande's Introduction to Newton's Mathematical Elements of Natural Philosophy.

tion had begun to manifest itself here and elsewhere. It was in great measure the spirit and the character of the times. Numberless and protracted failures, however, far too generally marked the first rude essays made to attain the objects aimed at. In the infancy of those mechanical arts which belong peculiarly to our modern times, this might be admitted to be in a great degree, perhaps, inevitable. But there was more than merely the delay and temporary frustration of cherished schemes, in consequence of immature plans or unperfected experiment, evils to which the designs of the most apt and capable are ever more or less subject. Blunders in practice of the most obvious and palpable description were far from rare ; and in too many instances guess-work and blind experimenting were all that were relied upon for ultimate success.[1] To an eye like that of Watt, the real cause of both these evils could not but be quite apparent. In the estimation of the philosopher whose own rule of procedure was so purely scientific, and based on a mental process so rigidly inductive, offences of this last nature hardly admitted of pardon or even of palliation. The truth is, however, few workmen were *qualified* to do engine-work at this time, unless they came down directly from Soho itself,—the "millwrights" of those days having little practical experience in the nice adjustments of the Steam, or Fire-engine, as it was then called. Being even at that time a "new power," the know-

Buchanan on the Economy of Fuel.
Gregory's Mechanics.
Tredgold on the Strength of Cast Iron.
Lanz and Bétancourt's Analytical Essay on the Construction of Machines.
Kelly's Spherics and Nautical Astronomy.
Keith's Theory and Practice of Plane and Spherical Trigonometry.
M'Laurin's Algebra.
M'Laurin's Fluxions.
Lacroix on the Differential and Integral Calculus —Translated.
Attwood on Rectilinear Motion and Rotation.

[1] An illustration of the guess-work in experimenting to which reference is made, might be afforded by an account of the first efforts to arrange the machinery of the *Comet*—the first successful steamboat—so as to make *motion* in her case a bare *fait-accompli*. Many other examples could be cited, which were immediately anterior to the period under consideration, and of which Mr. Watt could not be ignorant. Allusion is made to these matters not in any invidious spirit, but simply as exemplifying the actual state of practical and scientific knowledge at the time referred to.

ledge of or acquaintance with its construction, even in its *old* form as employed by such engineers as Mr. Smeaton and others, for mining and similar purposes, was limited to a very few practical millwrights beyond the precincts of the great works at Birmingham, of which Boulton and Watt were the skilful and successful directors. The desire, therefore, on the part of the great engineer to *transplant* the knowledge of so valuable and important a branch of industry to the incipient workshops of his native place, and to bring within the reach of his townsmen the means of acquiring a theoretical acquaintance with its details, cannot but be regarded as indicative of a feeling the most patriotic and generous. It was manifest that a thorough intimacy on their part with the fundamental laws of mechanics, and with their practical application in the different departments of ingenuity, could not but contribute at once to a more useful expenditure of labour, and to more generally successful and beneficial results,—such were some of the ends proposed in founding the library referred to.

That Mr. Watt's own rule of practice as a natural philosopher was such as has just been described, is incontrovertible, being evidenced by the whole history of his own Invention and wonderful Improvements. And that anything like scientific *maladresse*, in the case of professedly practical men around him, should have been contemplated by him with a certain degree of impatience, is far from surprising. In regard to the most valuable gift which the arts of life have ever received from the hands of the philosopher, it has been well remarked, that while the mariner's compass, the telescope, gunpowder, and other most useful servants to human weakness and ingenuity, were in a great measure the productions of chance,—at all events, so little connected with the records of scientific inquiry and research, as to have left few traces in history either of their inventors, or of the process by which the results were attained,—the STEAM-ENGINE, even in its very beginnings, was the result of reflection, ingenuity, and mind ;—every improvement it has received, and every important alteration in its construction which has been made, having been equally the consequence of philosophical study and design.[1]

Considerations of this nature may tend to place in their legitimate light the real motives of our great townsman in establishing the philosophical and scientific library of Greenock, and ought to enhance in our estimation the value of the gift.   In another chapter, which it is proposed to devote to a sketch of the rise and progress of Steam Navigation and the art of Naval Architecture in the Clyde, it will be seen how important a contribution to the science and even wealth of the community such an institution was capable of being made.   Meantime, let it suffice to draw attention to the additional view which the motives just illustrated afford, of the wisdom, the true magnanimity of this illustrious person, whose spirit and character, whether as a philosopher, or as a citizen and a man, cannot but gain in the estimation of posterity from every fresh examination of his principles or his private worth.

[1] Robison's System of Mechanical Philosophy, 1822, vol. ii. p. 46.

CHAPTER VI.

GREENOCK AND THE CLYDE PRIOR TO INTRODUCTION OF STEAM POWER——BEGINNING OF
THE NEW ERA——ORIGIN OF STEAM NAVIGATION IN THE CLYDE——ITS EARLIEST HIS-
TORY——THE FLY-BOATS——RENNIE'S WHEEL-BOAT——EFFORTS TO RENDER STEAM POWER
AVAILABLE——WANT OF KNOWLEDGE OF MECHANICS GENERALLY PREVALENT——HENRY
BELL'S FIRST STEAMBOAT——DIFFICULTIES——THEY ARE OVERCOME——ORIGIN OF FOUND-
RIES AT GREENOCK——OTHER STEAMBOATS BUILT——MR. WATT SENDS MODEL ENGINES
FROM SOHO——THE GREAT MECHANICIAN ON BOARD A STEAMBOAT——PROGRESS OF
STEAM NAVAL ARCHITECTURE AT GREENOCK——INTRODUCTION OF IRON STEAMBOATS
AND SCREW-PROPELLER——GREAT CHANGES THE RESULT——STATISTICS OF STEAMSHIP
BUILDING ON THE CLYDE——ITS VALUE AS A BRANCH OF INDUSTRY.

THE town of Greenock, at the period to which the notices of last
chapter refer, was already a place of some standing and consideration
compared with many of the seaports of the time. It had long been,
according to the testimony of the chronicler of the period, " the place
of best account on all this coast, being the principal harbour to all the
Glasgow merchants, a good roadstead, and a well-built town."[1]   Its
trade, which for several years had been in a flourishing condition, had
greatly increased ; and while good fortune had attended the foreign
adventures, and enterprise at home had opened up channels for the
employment of the growing population, many of its merchants and
craftsmen had large sums at their credit in their banker's hands.
Already the ship-builders of the town had won for themselves the
repute of being masters in their craft, and were engaged to a large
extent in the supply of ships required by other and perhaps less

---

[1] Sibbald MSS. by " Mr. William Dunlop,   in Hamilton of Wishaw's " Descriptions of Lan-
Principal of the University of Glasgow ;" printed   ark and Renfrew."—Maitland Club.

favoured trading localities. Glasgow was not then what she has of late years become, a seaport as well as a manufacturing city. Beyond the name of her ancient University, that great emporium of wealth was, in those days, famous for its muslins, as Paisley for its shawls, rather than for those wonderful structures in marine and other machinery, which now, in common with this neighbourhood, occupy so busy a suburban population. Though she had her rich Virginia merchants, she had neither the ships nor the actual trade. The river, which the genius of Watt contributed at a later period to make passable for burthened vessels, not only presented barriers of sand to the transit of ships, but was too narrow to admit of even the smallest craft being built or launched. Nor was the greatest haven of the empire then what it is now, with its miles of docks and crowded masts. In the commencement of last century the population of Liverpool consisted of four thousand two hundred and forty souls,—having in 1710, the period under consideration, eighty-four ships, averaging less than seventy tons each, belonging to the port.[1] In 1763, two years before James Watt first handled the wondrous little engine in the College of Glasgow, the population of that city was only twenty-eight thousand three hundred.[2] It was that great man's mind and invention applied to this insignificant, and till then almost unknown machine, that, within the space of forty years from the time of its application to the cotton manufacture, was to raise the population of the former of these places to 380,000, and of the latter to 360,138 souls![3]

We have already seen that Mr. Watt had been far from uninterested in the accomplishment of just such a result for the place of his birth, in his anxious desire to supply for the benefit of the operative population the means of an accurate acquaintance with the scientific elements of their respective crafts. Even now he could not but discern many

[1] Aiken's History of Manchester.
[2] *Encyc. Brit.* Art. *Cotton Manufacture.*
[3] Census, 1851.

tokens of a great transmutation. The railed-off beach which had
been wont to give to the deep its tiny vessel was beginning to extend
its bounds. The hereditary smithy was becoming a forge, even a
foundry ; the shoeing of horses giving place, it might be said, to the
creation of a portentous *iron* " horse-power" that would soon change
all other things.[1] But even Watt did not foresee to what an extent
that beach was, ere many years, to be covered with spacious dockyards, made conspicuous by the stateliest erections of naval architecture ; and he of all other men perhaps, could the prediction have
been made, would have been the most sceptical as to its being ever
realized, that the largest and most splendid of such structures,
impelled by the new and as yet almost infantine machinery, should,
ere the lapse of many years from that time, be bearing round the
globe a practical exhibition of that genius whose persevering labour
had given to mankind the power of all but annihilating distance as
well as time, and adding to all the conveniences and luxuries of life.
The subject of the present chapter is interesting in many respects,
and in many ways suggestive. No apology is deemed necessary for
the local character of the details ; the only regret really felt being,
that the data for such a sketch as the present are not to a far greater
extent available.

Although the magnificent ocean steamships, both in wood and iron,
which weekly project themselves from the building-yards of the Clyde,
can hardly be said to be anywhere rivalled, in strength, symmetry of
mould, power and capacity for speed,—qualities which an admirer of
excellency in such exhibitions of art may be pardoned dwelling upon
with complacency,—still scarcely a century has elapsed since the *first*

---

[1] It is a fact not generally perhaps known that
no farther back than the grandfathers of some of
our most celebrated engine-makers, the shoeing
of horses was a principal part of the hereditary
employment of their hammers and anvils.

square-rigged vessel was launched from these shores. This vessel, which was called the *Greenock*, was brig-rigged, and built about 1760 by " Peter Love, Shipbuilder," or by his son, on a piece of land now considerably within the range of houses in the east part of the town. The building-yard was on the upper side of the road leading to Craw-fordsdyke ; consequently the launch had to cross the road before reaching the sea. To go a step farther back than this period, in order to glance at the " Clyde ships" of an older time, would almost take us out of the chronology of commerce altogether. Pleading, however, for the reader's indulgence,—in gratification of hitherto suppressed antiquarian predilections,—we shall venture for a moment to take this glance, and then resume our narrative.

The records of the Scottish Parliament afford ample proofs of the loyalty of the Lairds of Greenock. They seem to have taken an active part in the transactions, civil and military, which were conse-quent upon the dispute between the unfortunate royal house of Stuart and the Parliament ; for, besides taking the command of a troop of horse, called " Greenock's Troop," and lending to the Government a sum of money for the special purpose of suppressing the rebellion in Ireland, Johnne Schaw, the Superior of the Barony, seems to have taken some interest in fitting out an armament by sea.

In 1641 a body of Scots troops having been sent to Ireland to put down the insurrection which broke out in that country—that insur-rection, which, according to Hume, was followed by the massacre of the English Protestants by the Irish Catholics—it became necessary from time to time to send the troops supplies of provisions. On the 19th of July 1643, an Act of the Scottish Parliament was passed for outfitting, or, as it is termed, "outreiking" two ships, one of them the James of Saltcoats, commanded by Captain James Brown, and the other the Providence of Irvine, commanded by Captain James Blair, " with men and victualls, and artailliarie, great and small, and with

poulder and lunt, and all other warlyk furnitoure and provisioun, and
to mak their adresse to the Sea ;" and in special " to cleire the west
and north-west, betwixt Scotland and Ireland, of certain friggottis
which infested these coasts," and which are represented in the act as
" spoyleing, robbing and burning of the shippes and goods perteining
to his majesty's good subjects of the Kingdom of Scotland, travelling
toward Ireland with victual for supplie of the Scottish armie, thairwith
committed upon them be certain friggotis manned with Dunkirks and
Irish rebels, who lye in wait for them upon the north and west pairts
of this kingdom." The orders which the captains received are very
pithy, and somewhat more stringent and decisive, we should imagine,
than some Admiralty despatches of the present day. They are told
" if they shall have occasion of rancountering these friggotis, they
shall not be deficient thairin for any fears or danger whatsumever ;
and if they shall enter in combat that they shall fight till the death,
never rendering thair shippes, but shall mantaine and defend till they
be aither burnt or sunk."

Some idea may be formed of the equipment of the ships, from the
circumstance of an order having been given upon the Lord General
for six minion brass guns with two field-pieces for their use ; six guns
from the Marquis of Argyle, and two from the Earl of Eglinton were
" borrowit" for the same purpose, and bond given for their restitution.
How altered, in this respect alone, are the capabilities of the times !
To such a degree, indeed, is this the case, that although during our
forty years' peace the greatest number of all the guns belonging to
this port have found their way to the furnaces of the foundries, and,
by this time, may have been beat into ploughshares and pruning-
hooks, little difficulty, at present, would be felt here in " outreiking" a
seventy-four gun ship, within twenty-four hours, with all the essential
parts of her " artailliarie."

In March 1647 another Act was passed for " outreik" of other two ships and a pinnace, to guard the Coast. The following entry is found in the Records, 6th July 1649 :—" Remit in favors of the Laird of Greenock's boatmen." The boat here alluded to was very probably the " pinnace" ordered to be fitted out, and the remit now made, referred in all likelihood to the payment of the wages of the men on board of her. On 6th August of the same year, an entry occurs as follows :—" Commission to Captain Robert Hall, and the friggate of Greenock,"—very likely the first mention upon record of a war vessel belonging to and fitted out from, the Harbour of Greenock. In the month of June of the following year, Charles II., on the invitation of his Scottish subjects, arrived in the Cromarty Frith, from Breda, under an escort of Dutch ships of war. As the intended arrival of the king was, of course, known to his friends in the North, in particular the Marquis of Argyle, then in the chief direction of affairs, and as an armed vessel might be useful to the King on the East Coast, to strengthen the position which the royal army afterwards took up and fortified, between Edinburgh and Leith, to await the advance of Cromwell's army,—the Marquis had given orders to Captain Hall to sail round to Leith, and for his exoneration, had procured the following, which is entered in the Parliamentary Record, 29th May 1650 :— " Act approveing the warrant given to the Marquis of Argyle, to bring Captain Hall's ship to Leith Harbour." The Battle of Dunbar took place on 3d September following, in which, as is well known, the Scottish army was totally defeated ; and the probability is, that the *Friggate*, if she ever arrived at Leith, fell into the hands of the conqueror ; at all events, no further traces of Captain Hall and the " Friggate of Greenock" can be obtained.[1]

[1] An account of the Friggate of Glasgow, the *George*, is given by John M'Ure, *alias* Campbell, in his History of Glasgow, published in first half of last century. He recounts, that " in the beginning of the year 1644, war broke out betwixt Britain and Holland, and acts of hostility falling out betwixt both nations,—the Dutch having seized and caped some of our ships to our great loss,—for Remead whereof some of our Merchants did nominate and appoint Captain Robert M'Allan,

But to return to times of peace and civilisation.   It will serve even as a strong contrast to the present condition of our mercantile marine, to show the number of vessels built and registered at Greenock some seventy-five or eighty years ago.   In the year ending 27th February 1776, the number so built and registered was 18, of the aggregate burthen of 1073 tons.   The largest of these vessels was 77 tons. The total number of vessels, including first registrations and transferences, was 133, of the aggregate burthen of 9770 tons.   Of these, 100 were under 100 tons burthen ; the remaining 33 were from 100 to 200 tons register, with the exception of two, the *Fanny* and the *Royal Exchange*, which were of 220 tons each ; and the *Thames* and *Isabella*, which were 250 tons each.   The vessels of larger tonnage were chiefly built in the colonies, and were owned in Glasgow, though frequenting the Harbour of Greenock.   The 18, first mentioned, were built by the following ship-carpenters :—6 by Mr. Scott ; 3 by Mr. Turner ; 3 by Mr. Crawford ; 1 by Mr. Telfer ; 4 by Mr. M‘Arthur ; and 1 by Mr. Smith.

From this time the growing requirements of the " foreign trade" at Greenock were found to demand vessels of a greatly increased tonnage, and a most advantageous impulse was given to shipbuilding on the spot,—the greater cheapness of the vessels furnished by our North

commander of the Friggate, the *George* of Glasgow, and set to sea in pursuit of his Majesty's Enemies, conform to a Commission of Letter of Mark, dated the 28th day of *June*, 1665, granted to the said Captain *Robert M‘Allan*, by the High and Mighty Prince *Charles*, Duke of *Lennox* and *Richmond*, Heritable Lord High Admiral of the Kingdom of *Scotland*, as having warrant and commission from our dread Sovereign Lord the King's Majesty, for granting thereof by his commission, under his Majesty's Great Seal of the said kingdom, dated the 12th day of *June*, then lastly past, and thereby declare that the foresaid good Ship or Friggate, whereof the said Captain *Robert M‘Allan* is commander, is sixty tuns or thereby of burden, and carries on board five piece of Ordnance, thirty-two muskets or Firelocks, twelve Half Picks, eighteen Pol axes, thirty Swords, three Barrels of Powder, and with Victuals, and other necessary Provision for six months' stay at Sea; and that all the Officers, Mariners, and Sailors thereof amounting to three-score persons."

The George with her " ammunition and out-rigging, and other pertinents," belonged to Wm. Anderson, the Provost of Glasgow, and other Burgesses of that City.—She brought in several prizes to Port-Glasgow; but the peace being concluded, " the caping trade ceased."

American Colonies not being found a sufficient compensation for their want of durability, when put in comparison with the more costly ships constructed by our own carpenters.

Even these, however, of the vastly increased size of from 300 to 500 tons burden, were, in the progress of events, destined to give way before the irresistible exigencies of STEAM Navigation. The adaptation of this great power to the purposes of sea-communication, attended as it has been by such results and achievements as have been witnessed within the last few years, may be justly regarded as one of the most wonderful triumphs of human ingenuity. If the mere suggestion of the practicability of such an application of Steam were to be held as entitling the individual to the grand merit of this discovery, there are, undoubtedly, in this and other countries, many names in whose favour the claim might, with justice, be decided. Even among the large number who were eager and sanguine experimenters in this new field, there were those who deserve the highest praise,—the failure of whose efforts was, in a great measure perhaps, attributable rather to the then state of the subaltern arts, and their consequent incapacity to execute their plans, than to anything really visionary in the views of their resolute projectors. We smile now at the thought of a Steamboat Cylinder and Boilers attempted to be made in the shop of a Brazier ; —or the curious and intricate piecings of a Steam Engine forged under the rough blows of an Anchor-smith's hammer, or, still more, constructed under the delicate operations of a Mathematical Instrument-maker's tools. And yet such was very much the character of the *dernier-ressort* of non-professional experimenters, in their often laudable efforts, in the earliest stages of the mighty and impending change.

Without occupying attention here with any of the numerous experiments, from 1782 to 1786,—which, besides their being unattended by any definite results, were, in general, of a description too vague to allow of any very distinct conception being formed of their character,

28

—the first direct efforts towards an accomplishment of the design of Steam-navigation were those made in Scotland by Patrick Miller, Esq. of Dalswinton, in Dumfries-shire, commencing in 1785, and continuing till 1790, when, unfortunately, he abandoned them for other scientific speculations. In 1787 Mr. Miller published an account of several of these ingenious experiments, which he had made with single, double, and even triple boats, propelled by means of paddle-wheels, driven by manual and other power. "I have reason," says Mr. Miller in this account, "to believe, that the power of the *Steam Engine* may be applied to work the wheels, so as to give them a quicker motion, and, consequently, to increase that of the ship. In the course of this summer I intend to make the experiment." Aided by Mr. Taylor, tutor in Mr. Miller's family, and a friend of the former, a Mr. Symington, a professed engineer, or more properly, "Millwright," and at this time much occupied with experiments on the Steam Engine, very imperfectly known as yet in Scotland,—more than one trial was made, with moderate success, first, on Dalswinton Lake, with a double boat, having a paddle-wheel in the centre, and afterwards, on a larger and more ponderous scale, on the Forth and Clyde Canal, in a heavy canal barge furnished with an Engine which had been, with some effort, put together at Carron Iron-Works. Although the astonishing speed of from six to seven miles an hour was said to have been attained on this last occasion, the scheme was shortly afterwards abandoned by Mr. Miller,—his several experiments, unfortunately, as is far from being unfrequent in cases of a similar nature, having tended much more to add to the acquired experience of his times, than to his personal advantage, or the increase of his fortune.

In the experiments prosecuted by Mr. Miller, the well-known Mr. Cullen of Edinburgh, afterwards Lord Cullen,[1] seems to have taken a

---

[1] Mr. Cullen was son of the celebrated Dr. William Cullen of Edinburgh. He was admitted Advocate in 1764. Promoted to the Bench on the death of James Erskine of Alva, he took his

very lively interest. Besides writing an account of their various
success, in some of the Edinburgh newspapers of the day, he would
appear to have addressed an application, on the part probably of Mr.
Miller, to Messrs. Boulton and Watt at Soho, the object of which was
to engage these celebrated engineers to a share in Mr. Miller's undertaking. It cannot but interest our readers to peruse a letter from
Mr. Watt himself, apparently in reply to such a communication. It
is dated, Birmingham, April 24, 1790, and is as follows :—

"DEAR SIR,—We have heard of Mr. Miller's ingenious experiments
on double ships from Sir John Dalrymple, and also some vague
accounts of the experiments with the Steam-Engine, from which we
could gather nothing conclusive, except that the vessel did move with
a considerable velocity.

"From what we heard of Mr. Symington's engines, we are disposed
to consider them as attempts to evade our exclusive privilege ; but as
we thought them so defective in mechanical contrivance, as not to be
likely to do us immediate injury, we thought it best to leave them to
be judged by Dame Nature first, before we brought them into an
earthly court.

"We are much obliged to Mr. Miller for his favourable opinion of
us, and of our engines, which we hope experience will more and more
justify. We are also fully sensible of his kind attentions in offering
to associate us in his scheme ; but the time of life we have both
arrived at, and the multiplicity of business we are already engaged in,
must plead our excuse from entering into any new concern whatsoever,
as partners,—but as Engineers and Engine-makers, we are ready to
serve him to the best of our abilities, at our customary prices of

seat by the title of Lord Cullen, on 18th November 1796 ; and succeeded Lord Swinton as a
Lord of Justiciary, 29th June 1799. He was the
author of several excellent papers in the *Mirror*
and *Lounger*. His Lordship died at Edinburgh,
on the 28th November 1810.—Brunton's *Senators
of the College of Justice*. Edinburgh, 1832.

ECONOMIC HISTORY CLASS LIBRARY
UNIVERSITY OF GLASGOW.

Rotative-Engines, and to assist in anything we can to bring the scheme to perfection.

"We conceive there may be considerable difficulty in making a steam-engine to work regularly in the open sea, on account of the undulatory motion of the vessel affecting the engine by the *vis inertiæ* of the matter ; however, this we should endeavour to obviate as far as we can.

"It may not be improper to mention, that Earl Stanhope has lately taken a patent for moving vessels by steam, but we believe not by wheels. His Lordship has also applied to us for engines, but we believe we are not likely to agree with him, as he lays too much stress upon his own ingenuity.

"We cannot conclude without observing that, were we disposed to enter into any new concern, there is no person we should prefer to Mr. Miller as an associate,—being fully apprised of his worth and honour, and admirers of the ingenuity and industry with which he has pursued this scheme.

"Permit me now, Sir, to return you my thanks for your obliging attention to me, and the trouble you have taken in this affair, and to ask the favour of you to present Boulton and Watt's respectful compliments to Mr. Miller.—Dear Sir, your obliged humble servant,

"JAMES WATT.

"ROBERT CULLEN, Esq., Edinburgh."

How little could JAMES WATT even foresee,—what doubtless happened within the experience of some even of the Soho apprentices,—the engines of Robert Napier bearing themselves weekly, in all the august majesty of power—and without a falter—over, and through, the most tremendous "undulations" of a winter Atlantic ! It is to be remembered, however, that this letter was written twenty-two years before even the first successful experiment "in the open sea," by Henry Bell, in 1812.

At Paris as well as London, other attempts, practically to solve the grand problem, were made, subsequently to those by Mr. Miller. It was reserved neither for the Seine nor the Thames, however, to work out the first successful experiment in European steam navigation ;— let us glance at its first efforts in the hands of the speculative and ingenious artificers of the Clyde.

There are some still living who can remember what were called the *Fly-Boats*, which formed the principal means of communication on the Clyde, between Greenock and Glasgow, towards the close of last century. A short preliminary description of these primitive structures, and of their spirited builders and owners, is here necessary, as they were unquestionably the pioneers, and indeed for a time the rivals, of the first steamboat made available for passenger conveyance in the British waters.

The Fly-Boats were constructed by Mr. William Nicol of Greenock, —a well-known and excellent builder of ships' boats, for a long course of years, at this place.[1] They were about 28 feet keel, from $7\frac{1}{2}$ to 8 feet beam, about 8 tons burden, and wherry-rigged. A slight deck or awning was erected abaft the main-mast, so as to cover in the passengers, who sat in the after part of the boat on longitudinal benches. Some of them, on a still more improved principle, it was conceived, had a contrivance by which part of the deck or awning might be lifted up on hinges, to permit of the passengers, in fine weather, enjoying at once the scenery and the voyage. A kind of platform or plank ran along the edge of the deck, outside, to admit of the people belonging to the boat passing from forward to the stern where the steersman sat, without incommoding the passengers ; and in fair weather, those among the latter who were particularly favoured,

[1] Mr. Nicol was wont to estimate the extent of his boat-building, on a scale as large as its method of computation was singular. He built during the active years of his business 7868 boats, extending, in lineal measurement, to upwards of thirty miles.

and had no dread of falling overboard, were allowed to sit upon the
raised deck, placing their feet for security upon the before-mentioned
plank. The boats generally started from Greenock with a flowing
tide if possible. If the wind happened to be favourable, a passage of
four or five hours to Glasgow, was considered a very great achieve-
ment. If, however, wind and tide were adverse, which was frequently
enough the case, no little labour was required, with sails and oars, to
make any advance whatever ; and both passengers and crew, in such
untoward circumstances, were often right glad, on getting as far up
as Dunglass, to rest there for five or six hours till the next tide should
favour their further progress,—exchanging, meanwhile, their irksome
confinement for a ramble in the neighbouring woods, which in those
days were extensive, and, in their season, afforded excellent nutting.

Such, no farther back than even our younger days, were the accommodations and conveniences of the famous *Fly-Boats*, on that splendid
river whose surface is now skimmed by the hundred arrow-like and
flitting forms of our modern steamboat, vying, in point of luxury,
elegance, and comfort, with the arrangements of our costliest drawing-
rooms, and rivalled only in swiftness by the more favoured speed of
our railway trains.

Despicable as those antiquated remains of travelling unquestionably
were, the Fly-boats—so named from their superior swiftness—were
considered a great improvement upon the small " packet-boats" that
had been previously in use. One of their first projectors and owners
was one Andrew Rennie, " officially" the town-drummer of Greenock,
but a man of a busy and speculative mind, and possessed, withal, of
considerable tact and ingenuity. Dissatisfied with the actual attainments, and conceiving that it was practicable, in some degree, to
improve upon both the construction and management of the boats,
Rennie proposed to his partners to have one built on a different model,
and to be propelled by *wheels*. The idea was scouted at as altogether

visionary; and Mr. Nicol having hinted that the scheme "would not do," Rennie, at his own expense, got a boat constructed by another builder, somewhat broader than the old model, to which he affixed two paddle-wheels, one on either side, to be worked by manual labour, and intended to supersede the use of oars. This boat, which went by the appellation of "Rennie's wheel-boat," after making several trips to the Broomielaw at Glasgow, was sold,—the labour of the oar being found, after all, less toilsome than that of the wheel.

The unsuccessful experiment of Rennie's wheel-boat, however, did not deter another individual, destined to become more celebrated, from embarking in a somewhat similar scheme. This was Henry Bell. Mr. Bell applied to Mr. Nicol to build for him a boat, about fifteen feet keel, with a "well," or opening, in the "run," in which he placed a wheel, which also was to be worked by manual power. Finding this single wheel not to answer the purpose intended, he got Mr. Nicol to plank up the well, and tried his boat with two wheels, one on either side. The experiment convinced him that this last was much the best method of distributing the propelling power to the greatest advantage. The inadequacy of manual labour, however, to the end to be accomplished was too obvious to escape observation; and although he did not at once put into execution his subsequent and most successful plan of adapting the *Steam-Engine* to supply the deficiency in power of which his last experiment had assured him, it continued to occupy, during several years, his attention and thoughts.

Although Mr. Bell, in his correspondence with the son of Mr. Miller of Dalswinton, regarding their respective claims to the merit of the invention of the "Steamboat," has not availed himself of the fact of this connexion between his early experiments with the hand-wrought wheels, and his last and successful one with the steam-engine, an argument might, probably, have, with fairness, been adduced by him, from this circumstance, in favour of his claim.

On the other hand, it cannot but be felt that Mr. Bell has overstated his claim in regard to priority in the application of the steam-engine as a propelling power. For although he was indisputably the first in this country who permanently *succeeded* in adapting steam to the propulsion of vessels in the open waters, for purposes of actual traffic, it cannot be overlooked that Mr. Symington's boat—which we recollect to have seen, with its *brick* funnel, after having been laid aside on the Forth and Clyde Canal—had been fitted with a steam-engine, and employed on several occasions, six or seven years before the building of Mr. Bell's first steamboat, in towing vessels on the canal.

Mr. Bell, however, it will be observed, has made a step in advance, in having satisfied himself, that, if only an adequate moving power may be obtained, the *paddle-wheel* can best be made to answer the purpose of propelling in the water. He has also ascertained that two paddle-wheels are better than one.

While Bell is experimenting and speculating at Greenock, Mr. Fulton, from America, in concert with the American chancellor, Mr. Livingstone, is planning and contriving all conceivable kinds of direct moving or propelling powers at Paris. He has tried the leaves, (or duck-foot oars, invented by the Pastor of Bern.) He has also "experimented with wheels, oars, paddles, and flyers similar to those of a smoke-jack, and found *oars* to be the best." Thus he writes from "Paris the 20th of September 1802,"—the year in which his first experimental boat was built, which, however, unhappily broke in two as soon as it felt the weight and pressure of the machinery, and sank to the bottom of the Seine,—the year also before his second experiment, the ill success of which brought him to Scotland, to see and to make inquiries regarding Mr. Symington's boat, and to communicate with Mr. Bell.[1] A letter written by Mr. Fulton about this time is

[1] A full account of Mr. Fulton's communications with Mr. Bell, on the subject of the "Steamboat," was published by the latter in the *Caledonian Mercury* in 1816.

interesting, and may be given at length, simply altering the orthography, as it has not hitherto been quoted in this country.

"The expense of a patent in France is 300 livres for three years, 800 do. for ten years, and 1500 do. for fifteen years. There can be no difficulty in obtaining a patent for the mode of propelling a boat, which you have shown me. But if the author of the model wishes to be assured of the merits of his invention, before he goes to the expense of a patent, I advise him to make the model of a boat in which he can place a clock-spring which will give about eight revolutions. He can then combine the movements so as to try oars, paddles, and the leaves which he proposes. If he finds that the leaves drive the boat a greater distance in the same time than either oars or paddles, they consequently are a better application of power. About eight years ago the Earl of Stanhope tried an experiment on similar leaves, in Greenland Dock, London, but without success. I have also tried experiments on similar leaves, wheels, oars, paddles, and flyars, similar to those of a smoke jack, and found oars to be the best. The velocity with which a boat moves is in proportion as the sum of the surfaces of the oars, paddles, leaves, or other machine, is to the bow of the boat presented to the water ; and in proportion to the power with which such machinery is put in motion. Hence if the sum of the surfaces of the oars is equal to sum of the surfaces of the leaves, and they pass through similar curves in the same time, the effect must be the same. But oars have this advantage,—they return through air to make a second stroke, and hence create very little resistance ; whereas the leaves return through water, and add considerably to the resistance, which is increased as the velocity of the boat is augmented. No kind of machinery can create power ; all that can be done is to apply the manual, or other power, to the best advantage.

"If the author of the model is fond of mechanics, he will be much amused, and not lose his time by trying the experiments in the manner

29

I propose, and this perhaps is the most prudent measure before a patent is taken.—I am, &c., yours, Rob^T Fulton."[1]

Having failed, in the interval of his experiments, in attracting attention to the feasibility of his views in regard to the Steamboat, Mr. Bell resolved at length to enter upon the speculation at his own risk.

Nothing in the history of those wonderful inventions and improvements in machinery, which characterized the latter half of last century, is so striking as the number of instances in which we are indebted for these to men of the humblest attainments in point of education, and who could make little, or rather no pretension, to any preliminary professional knowledge, or even to any acquaintance with the leading principles of Mechanics as a Science. To the long list of the Hargreaves, the Kays, the Arkwrights, the Highs, who claimed more or less of the merit of inventing and improving the machinery of the Cotton Manufacture, and who, whatever their ingenuity, belonged admittedly to this class,—is to be added the name of Henry Bell, in connection with the first perfectly successful adaptation of the Steam Engine to Navigation. To an intellect like that of Watt, poised between lofty scientific speculation, on the one hand, and painstaking, practical ingenuity on the other, efforts such as those which frequently marked the progress alluded to, could not fail to present themselves as exhibitions, in a great measure, of mere blind and groping adventure. Nevertheless, to ascribe to meritorious individuals whose works have not only enriched the capitalist, but infinitely benefited mankind, —to attribute to them, in the absence of science in their case, no higher motive than that of vanity, or no other animating principle

---

[1] The above letter of Mr. Fulton is from an interesting volume of Fac-similes of Public and other Documents, possessing both curiosity and value, connected with the history of the American Republic—for which I am indebted to the kindness of John Gray, Esq., Secretary of the Watt Club.

than that of an ignorant and preponderating conceitedness of their own powers, would be as ungenerous as it would most probably be unwise. These men must have been possessed of some ruling quality, of perseverance, resoluteness,—indeed, it is difficult to say of what compound of mental or moral forces,—some property, at all events, to which the generality of their fellows are, habitually, either indifferent or insensible, which in them, therefore, was praiseworthy, rendering their labours deserving of our gratitude, and their names of our remembrance. A vigorous and patient imagination has been the source of many of those inventions which have exercised the greatest amount of material influence over the world. More valuable machines, it has been asserted, have been invented by the labouring artisan, the shepherd, the dreamy monk, the potter, the wool-carder, the mariner, the weaver, or the ignorant blacksmith, than by the learned or the philosopher,—and the workshop has given birth to more masterpieces in practical art than the academy. M. Lamartine, in his Memoir of Jacquard, would account for this. Ordinarily, says he, the mechanician can do nothing without geometry and mathematics. These sciences are the figures by which he calculates, and the terms by which he expresses his thoughts. But sciences, which are the necessary instruments of common minds, are the servants of genius. When genius finds them not ready at hand, it passes them over, or invents others for its own use.[1] While this is true, to an extent, there is, in the statement, just enough of paradox to make it, in its unqualified shape, hazardous. The danger is to the many who mistake aimless ingenuity for genius, who turn away from science, and dispense with the labour of acquiring a knowledge of her immutable laws, as being only a hindrance to their powers, and an obstacle to the development of their fancied merits. Arkwright and Bell attained to some degree of success despite their want of this scientific knowledge,—the means of

[1] Jacquard, the Silk Weaver of Lyons. Paris, 1854.

acquiring which were not available to every artisan as they are in our day. On the other hand, what unknown multitudes have failed and consumed a valuable existence upon experiments which an acquaintance with the very rudiments of physical science would have demonstrated to be futile, utterly worthless : and as the converse of this, which is perhaps still more universally true than any other case,—how many of our artisans are there, whose lives are spent in very contact with the most wonderful, yet not unimprovable machines, whose minds, however, unsharpened by scientific reading or observation, are, with all their advantages, really capable of nothing higher or more useful than the mechanical intelligence that dictates the oiling of the wheels !

Henry Bell, though he could, at that time, with no propriety be considered an Engineer, either theoretical or practical, had indomitable perseverance and some ingenuity. He had resolved to prosecute his steamboat scheme as a personal venture ; and addressing himself to the since so celebrated steamship builders, Messrs. John and Charles Wood of Port-Glasgow, the keel of the FIRST STEAMBOAT was laid down in their building-yard some time in October 1811,—and the *Comet* was launched in June 1812. Her dimensions were 40 feet, keel ; 10 feet, 6 inches, beam ; and 25 tons burthen. The greater part of the engine-work was made at Greenock by the firm of Anderson, Campbell, & Co., who were smiths or hammermen in this town and Port-Glasgow, —the same company which afterwards became Anderson and Caird, and is now the famous engineering firm of Caird & Co. at Greenock. The boiler was made by the same parties in Port-Glasgow ; the cylinder was cast in Glasgow.[1]

---

[1] It is interesting to trace the development of a branch of business which has become one of the most essential and important in this country,— that of Founding, Engine-making, or Engineering. In some instances, in this immediate neighbourhood, as before noticed, it sprang from the simple smithy or shoeing-forge. In other cases, the premises of the brassfounder or hammerman enlarged rapidly into works which embraced the new demands for machinery and castings. The first foundry, if it might be so called, in Greenock, was in the north-west corner of what

Bell having received his machinery, which was of a sufficiently rude description, set about its arrangement on board of his little vessel, aided by one or two working millwrights, who were but imperfectly acquainted with the fitting and adjustment of such an engine. It was tried in different ways, both longitudinally and transversely. That much difficulty was experienced in the novel and anxious task cannot excite surprise. During the continuance of Boulton and Watt's term of patent, practical knowledge of the steam engine was confined, in great measure, to their engine-works at Soho, and to such ingenious workmen as they were in the habit of sending out to superintend the erection of Engines made by themselves. Referring to this period, Professor Robison remarks :—" Our engineers by profession are, in general, miserably deficient in that accurate knowledge of mechanics and of chemistry which is necessary for understanding this machine ; and we have not heard of one in this kingdom who can be put on a par with the present patentees in this respect."[1] If such was the case with engineers of that time by profession, it cannot be wondered at that Henry Bell, who could make little claim to any such distinction, should have made many vain attempts to *faire marcher* the intricate structure. The thing, however, was at length achieved to his great satisfaction. The engine began to move and perform its desired

is now called Cathcart Square, and was necessarily on a very small scale. It was carried on under the firm of Brownlee and Campbell. The ordinary work executed here was such, generally, as was required for ships, including also the casting of grate-fronts, bars, &c. The only furnace employed was the old-fashioned bellows or air furnace. The next was on a larger scale, established by an English company about the year 1790. They set down their works in the east end of the town, adjoining the Cartsburn Water, for the sake of a cupola furnace which they first erected. This work had all the improvements then known ; but not proving successful, it was abandoned in 1793 or 1794, and purchased for £1300 by Brownlee and Campbell. It was carried on by these parties till 1808, and by Mr. Brownlee alone till 1825, when the whole was transferred to Messrs. John Scott and Sons for £5000, who erected the new and now very extensive works of Messrs. Scott, Sinclair, & Co. In 1808 Mr. Campbell joined Mr. Anderson in the new works in Crawfordsdyke, which occupied to a limited extent, under the firm of Anderson & Caird, the site of what are now the wide-spread engineering premises of Messrs. Caird & Co.

[1] Robison's system of Mechanical Philosophy. 1822. Vol. ii. p. 148.

revolutions. It was a vertical one, and of about three horse-power.[1]

Having satisfied himself, in his first experiments with Mr. Nicol's boat, that two paddle-wheels were better than one, Mr. Bell's first trial of the *Comet* was with *four*, instead of two. This not being found successful, she was eventually fitted with two wheels, with floats of about twenty inches square ; and after numerous trial trips between Greenock and Port-Glasgow, the completion of the FIRST STEAMBOAT was thus announced in the *Greenock Advertiser*, of 15th August 1812 :—

"STEAM PASSAGE-BOAT, THE COMET, between Glasgow, Greenock, and Helensburgh, for passengers only.

"The Subscriber having, at much expense, fitted up a handsome Vessel to ply upon the River Clyde, between Glasgow and Greenock,—to sail by the power of Wind, Air, and Steam,—he intends that the Vessel shall leave the Broomielaw on Tuesdays, Thursdays, and Saturdays, about mid-day, or at such hour thereafter as may answer from the state of the tide, and to leave Greenock on Mondays, Wednesdays, and Fridays, in the morning, to suit the tide.

"The elegance, comfort, safety, and speed of this Vessel require only to be proved, to meet the approbation of the public; and the Proprietor is determined to do everything in his power to merit public encouragement.

"The terms are, for the present, fixed at 4s. for the best Cabin, and 3s. the second, but beyond these rates nothing is to be allowed to servants or any other person employed about the Vessel.

"The Subscriber continues his Establishment at Helensburgh Baths, the same as for years past ; and on the Comet's arrival at Greenock, a vessel will be in readiness to convey any Passengers that intend visiting Helensburgh.

"Passengers by the Comet will receive information of the hours of sailing, by

[1] For many of the particulars in regard to the *Comet* and Henry Bell, I am indebted to the obliging communications of Mr. Anderson of High Holm,—whose father was the original partner of the firm previously alluded to,—of Mr. John Wood, and Mr. Reid of Port-Glasgow. Reference to the incidental meeting with these gentlemen, in February 1852, recalls a trifling incident, which, however, may give the non-professional reader no very inaccurate idea of the dimensions of the engine of Henry Bell's steamboat. Speaking of the difficulty of getting the cylinder cast at that early period,—lifting a hat from the table, one of the gentlemen said, "the *Comet's* cylinder would not be much larger than that !"

applying at Mr. Thomas Stewart's, Bookseller, Square; and at Mrs. Blackly's, East Quayhead, Greenock, or at Mr. Houston's Office, Broomielaw.

"HENRY BELL.

"HELENSBURGH BATHS, *5th August* 1812."

It is not wonderful that the *Comet*, under the combined powers of "Wind, Air, and Steam," not to mention the elegance of her accommodations, soon beat the "Fly-boats" out of the river. We well remember her "accommodations," as well as her "superior speed," having had, more than once, a long passage in her to and from Glasgow. Her cabin,—not saloon, as now-a-days, was scarcely an improvement upon those of the "Highland Packets," which indeed it closely resembled,—low-roofed, of course, having a deal table in the centre, with benches, or "lockers," of the same material, on each side, for the dozen or more passengers to sit upon;—contrast inconceivably great to the rosewood and velvet couches of our modern *papillons*, or river martins,—as unlike their homely prototype as the gay winged creature is to the unsightly chrysalis from which it has emerged.

The success of Henry Bell's *Comet*, scouted at as the project had at first generally been, began to attract attention to the value of the enterprise. In 1813 another steamboat was started. She was of somewhat larger proportions than the *Comet*, and of greater horse-power. This vessel also, the *Glasgow*, was built by Mr. Wood. She was succeeded by a third, by the same builder, the *Morning Star*, in 1814, for Mr. John Robertson, Engineer, Gorbals. The next steam-boat built by Mr. Wood was the *Elizabeth*, 58 feet deck, and 8 horse-power, for Mr. John Thomson, Smith, of Gorbals. She was followed by the *Caledonia*, of 32 horse-power, and about 200 tons burthen. This vessel was purchased by Mr. James Watt, Junior, of Soho, for purposes of scientific experiment. Her comparatively rude machinery was replaced by two engines of 14 horse-power each, manufactured at Soho; and the observations made upon her performances suggested many useful improvements in the structure and arrangements of marine engines. The *Glasgow* was contracted for by a company, of which Messrs. J. and D. M'Goun of Greenock, and Messrs. Lilly and Johnstone of Glasgow were the principal partners. The patterns for her castings, as well as the greater part of the smith-work and machinery, were executed by Anderson, Campbell, & Co. of Greenock, and the fitting of the engine on board was superintended by Henry Bell. We have before us a large collection of the business letters of Henry Bell about this period, which are curious, and in many ways instructive, particularly in regard to the crude and jejune state of engineering in those its earlier stages, and in a neighbourhood in which it has since attained to such a distinguished eminence, aided by capital that seems almost without limit in its sources. The engine of the *Glasgow* proved a failure, involving Mr. Bell in much litigation and embarrassment. After plying on the Clyde for some time, at a rate of speed which did not come up to the expectations formed of her, the engine was replaced by one constructed by Mr. James Cook, Engineer, of Tradeston, Glasgow.

The first steamboats built at Greenock were two little vessels which at the time attracted much attention. They were built in 1815 or 1816 by Mr. James Munn, for a company in Greenock, Glasgow, and other places. They were the *Princess Charlotte* and *Prince of Orange*. Their peculiarity consisted in their having each *two* steam-engines of 4 horse-power each, and these, moreover, contracted for and made by Boulton and Watt at Soho, and fitted up on board by Soho workmen. These were the first specimens of marine steam-engines from so celebrated a quarter, seen in the Clyde. Their beauty of construction, symmetry, and smoothness of motion were regarded by our engineers as a kind of marvel, and excited universal admiration. It may easily be believed that particular pains had been bestowed on their execution. It was in this same year [1816] that

Mr. Watt founded the "Scientific Library of Greenock;" and in his patriotic and generous design of transplanting a knowledge of this invaluable branch of the arts to the dockyards and workshops of his native town, he might have had in view to illustrate, by those four beautiful little machines, what might be done by care *and scientific exactness* brought to bear on all their details.

The spirit of enterprise being awakened, that of emulation naturally followed; and one steamboat rapidly succeeded another, on those beautiful waters, so admirably fitted by nature for such incipient achievements. Each successive construction rivalled its predecessor both in beauty and speed. Still much remained to be effected both in the management and economy of these new and increasingly important undertakings. Beyond the illustrations already afforded of Mr. Watt's concern for the benefit and advance of his townsmen in the mechanical industries, he is understood not to have either very directly or personally occupied himself with the earliest efforts of steam-navigation in this country,—not only his distance from the scene of operations, but his retirement, many years previously, from the active business of Soho, having removed him from their immediate contact, unless on occasion of his brief periodical visits to Scotland. It is interesting, however, to observe the Great Mechanician himself, actually on board of one of these creations of his own ingenuity and invention. During his last visit to Greenock in 1816, Mr. Watt, in company with his friend Mr. Walkinshaw,—whom the author some years afterwards heard relate the circumstance,—made a voyage in a steamboat as far as Rothesay and back to Greenock,—an excursion which, in those days, occupied the greater portion of a whole day. Mr. Watt entered into conversation with the engineer of the boat, pointing out to him the method of "backing" the engine. With a foot-rule he demonstrated to him what was meant. Not succeeding, however, he at last, under the impulse of the ruling passion, threw off his overcoat, and, putting his hand to the engine himself, shewed the practical application of his lecture. Previously to this the "back-stroke" of the steamboat-engine was either unknown or not generally acted on. The practice was to stop the engine entirely a considerable time before the vessel reached the point of mooring, in order to allow for the gradual and natural diminution of her speed.

The *Comet*, after plying on the Clyde, and subsequently on the Frith of Forth, was lost on one of the Highland shores. She had been lengthened in the interval of her first starting, at Helensburgh. The operation was clumsily performed, and, on her going ashore on the occasion referred to, the old part speedily separated from the new, and she became a total wreck. Mr. Bell himself happened to be on board on the occasion of this catastrophe. Fortunately no lives were lost. The original draught or "lines" of the *Comet* were, several years ago, presented by her builder, Mr. Wood, to Mr. Robert Napier, Engineer, of Glasgow, in whose possession they are understood now to be. As a curiosity which has become of some interest and value, we give a fac-simile drawing of this primitive specimen of steam naval architecture, from an original which was possessed by Mr. Bell, and bears his holograph.

As British Steam Navigation had its origin in the Clyde, at Greenock and Port-Glasgow, these places continued to retain unimpaired their acquired precedence in this pre-eminent and all-important branch of British industry. For the enterprise which made steamboats available for purposes of deep-sea navigation, as well as for the supply of most of the early post-office stations, which soon became so serviceable at all points of the British coast, this country is indebted to Mr. David Napier. The establishment, in 1818, of his steamboat communication, by means of the *Rob Roy*, of about 90 tons burthen, and 30 horse-power, to ply between Greenock and Belfast, led the way for other and continually extending lines of traffic. Mr. Wood of Port-Glasgow

Schenck & Macfarlane Lithog.rs Edinr

THE FIRST STEAM BOAT, THE COMET, BUILT BY

HENRY BELL, 1811 *H Bell*

WHO BROUGHT STEAM NAVIGATION INTO PRACTICE IN EUROPE.

soon after built the *Talbot* of 120 tons, which was placed on the station between Holyhead and Dublin. This was immediately followed by that enterprise which brought upon the station between Greenock and Liverpool an as yet unwitnessed class of steamers. Beginning with the *Robert Bruce* of 150 tons, with two engines by Mr. Napier of 30 horse-power each, this Scottish proprietary at Glasgow and Liverpool has continued, year by year since then, to launch steamships of increasing beauty and power, a class of vessels altogether unrivalled, and which, in their representatives upon the Liverpool, Halifax, and New York Mail Station—whose splendid line of ships emanates from the same intelligent and spirited men—might be considered to have reached the highest perfection of which the art of steam naval architecture is capable, did not the almost daily production of something, in both mould and machinery, superior to its predecessor, contradict such a belief. Of this magnificent fleet of steamships, the entire number, with the exception of one or two fine specimens from the building-yards of Messrs. Wood, has been constructed at Greenock by Mr. Steele, from whose dockyard the first of this leviathan class of vessels, intended for the conveyance of large numbers of passengers as well as goods, was launched in 1826. This was the *United Kingdom*, 160 feet in length, $26\frac{1}{2}$ feet beam, with engines of 200 horse-power, by Mr. Napier. This large vessel was considered a prodigious step in advance, in her size, power, speed, and the whole style of her furnishings and appointments. She started from Greenock on her first trip on 29th July 1826, with a hundred and fifty passengers on board, and circumnavigated the whole of the North and part of the West coast of Scotland, on her way to Leith, performing the distance, 789 miles, in what was considered the incredibly short space of sixty-five hours, deducting stoppages. The cost of her construction was said to have been £40,000. So great had been the increase of steam-vessels up to this time, that in this year, 1826, there were already upwards of seventy belonging to the Clyde, and upwards of fifty belonging to the Mersey, a great proportion of the entire number having been supplied by the dockyards of the former river.

The rapid and extraordinary demand, however, for steamers of a large size, for purposes of river as well as coasting navigation, hastened, in this country, the greatest revolution in this modern commercial art of which it had as yet been the subject. It consisted, on the one hand, in the adaptation of wrought-iron to the construction of the hulls of steam-vessels, and, on the other, in the application of the Archimedes screw, as a propelling power in room of the paddle-wheel. This great change has, of late years, well-nigh transferred the building of steamboats from the hands of the shipwright to those of the hammerman and engineer. Though the introduction of these two great modifications in the construction and economy of steam-vessels was long vigorously contested by practical men, and only adopted in our naval as well as our mercantile marine after many years had thoroughly tested the value of the experiments made, both the new material and the new propeller threaten now to become all but universal for steam-vessels of the most prodigious size and power. One of the first attempts in this new kind of shipbuilding was made at Birkenhead by Mr. Laird, formerly of Greenock, in 1832. At the present day by far the largest proportion of steam-vessels launched in the Clyde are of iron. From a valuable paper read by Dr. Strang of Glasgow, before the Statistical Section of the British Association in 1852, it appears, that of 247 steam-vessels built in the Clyde during the seven years anterior to 1853, 14 were of wooden hull, and 233 of iron! Of these, 141 were of paddle-wheel, and 106 of screw. The aggregate burthen of the wooden steamers amounted to 18,331 tons; that of the iron to 129,273. The engine horse-power in wooden hulls was 6739; that in iron hulls, 31,593. Of the whole wooden steam-vessels constructed in the Clyde, or in progress at the various building-yards in 1852, amounting in all to 73, only 4 were of wood; while the proportion of screws to paddle-wheels was as 43 to 30.

Within the last few years Glasgow has entered largely upon the construction of steam-vessels. From obvious reasons connected with the narrowness of the channel of the river, the absence of timber yards, &c., these constructions have been limited to iron. For contrary reasons, Greenock, though by no means limited to the erection of wooden hulls, has continued to be the principal seat of building in the class of large steamships in wood required for ocean navigation. During the seven years above specified, accordingly, while Glasgow and its neighbourhood launched 122 iron steamboats, having an aggregate burthen of 70,441 tons, and only one wooden hull of 200 tons,—Greenock, and Port-Glasgow in its neighbourhood, launched 13 large wooden steamships of an aggregate burthen of upwards of 18,131 tons, in addition to 53 of iron, of 29,071 tons. As a specimen of one of the latter magnificent vessels recently constructed at the iron steamship building-works of Messrs. Caird & Co. here,—and, at the same time, as illustrative of the prodigious revolution achieved in this important art since the appearance in these waters of the little *Comet* in 1812,— a draught of the exquisite lines of the *Atrato*, obligingly furnished by Mr. James T. Caird of that enterprising firm, is here presented. The *Atrato* was contracted for, built, supplied with machinery and other equipments by the same great establishment, for the West India Royal Mail Steam Packet Co., on which important line this superb vessel is altogether unrivalled in speed. The statistical tables of Dr. Strang illustrate the progress referred to in a very striking manner. From the year in which the *Comet* started, down till 1820, only one or two river steamers were launched every year. In the next five years, from 1821 till 1825, there were 16; from 1826 till 1830, there were 22; from 1831 till 1835, there were 41; from 1836 till 1840, there were 53 ; from 1841 till 1845, the number had diminished to 35 ; but from 1846 till 1850, it had mounted up to 132 ; and in the three years, 1851-53, the number was as high as 206. The number of tons from 1821 to 1850, was 103,270 ; but from 1850 to 1853, it increased to 141,713. This is a rate of increase to which neither the Thames nor the Mersey presents a parallel. At one period, about two years ago, there were 32 shipbuilders on the Clyde, who were constructing or had contracted for 266 steam and sailing vessels, with an aggregate of 168,000 tons, and marine engines of 29,000 horse-power. The value of the whole was about five millions of money.

Of the immense capital embarked in similar undertakings emanating from the Clyde, as well as of the progressive change in both the theory and practice regarding the size, proportions, power, &c., best adapted for ocean steamships, an estimate may be formed from a glance at the following table of vessels, in wood and iron, built for the proprietary of the British and North American Royal Mail Steamships. The table is confined to their steamships on the New York, the Central American, and Levantine lines.

Year.	Ship.	Material.	Builders.	Length.	Breadth.	Tonnage.	Power.	Propeller.	Engine Makers.
1840	*Britannia.*	Wood.	R. Duncan & Co.	203	31	1155	440	Paddle.	Robert Napier.
,,	*Acadia.*	do.	John Wood.	202	30	1135	440	do.	do.
,,	*Caledonia.*	do.	Ch. Wood.	202	31	1138	440	do.	do.
,,	*Columbia.*	do.	R. Steele & Co.	205	31	1175	440	do.	do.
1842	*Hibernia.*	do.	do.	217	33	1421	500	do.	do.
1844	*Cambria.*	do.	do.	217	33	1423	500	do.	do.
1847	*America.*	do.	do.	249	35	1826	650	do.	do.
,,	*Niagara.*	do.	do.	249	35	1824	650	do.	do.
1848	*Europa.*	do.	John Wood.	249	35	1834	660	do.	do.
,,	*Canada.*	do.	R. Steele & Co.	249	35	1831	660	do.	do.
1850	*Asia.*	do.	do.	265	37	2226	750	do.	do.
,,	*Africa.*	do.	do.	265	37	2226	750	do.	do.
1851	*La Plata.*	do.	do.	284	37	2402	830	do.	do.
1852	*Arabia.*	do.	do.	284	37	2393	830	do.	do.
1855	*Persia.*	Iron.	R. Napier & Sons.	375	46	3590	850	do.	do.
1852	*Australian.*	Iron.	Denny & Brothers.	226	33	1401	300	Screw.	Tulloch & Denny.
,,	*Sydney.*	do.	do.	226	33	1401	300	do.	do.
,,	*Andes.*	do.	do.	236	33	1440	300	do.	do.
,,	*Alps.*	do.	do.	236	33	1440	300	do.	do.
1854	*Emeu.*	do.	Robert Napier.	268	34	1695	400	do.	Robert Napier.
,,	*Jura.*	do.	J. & G. Thomson.	313	35	2240	440	do.	J. & G. Thomson.
1855	*Etna.*	do.	Caird & Co.	304	36	2215	440	do.	Caird & Co.
1853	*Balbec.*	Iron.	Denny & Brothers.	206	29	838	150	Screw.	Tulloch & Denny.
,,	*Taurus.*	do.	do.	210	29	1126	180	do.	do.
,,	*Melita.*	do.	Alex. Denny.	232	29	1060	180	do.	do.
,,	*Teneriffe.*	do.	Denny & Brothers.	210	29	1126	180	do.	do.
,,	*Karnak.*	do.	do.	210	29	1126	150	do.	do.
1854	*Delta.*	do.	Barclay & Curle.	208	27	644	120	do.	A. & J. Inglis.
1855	*Lebanon.*	do.	J. & G. Thomson.	252	30	1383	280	do.	J. & G. Thomson.

With reference to the importance and the value in an industrial point of view of such a branch of trade to the Clyde, it may be stated, that while the earliest of the first class of these splendid ocean steamers started at a cost of from £40,000 to £50,000 for each ship, the last of the same class sent afloat, owing to their increased size and power, as well as the luxury and elegance of their arrangements, reach the sum of £110,000 to £120,000. The most recent of this splendid line, the *Persia*, the largest steamship afloat, built by Messrs. R. Napier & Sons, has achieved a rate of speed hitherto unparalleled. One of the voyages just accomplished by this magnificent vessel, gives the following as the passage " out" and " home," respectively :—Liverpool to New York, (adding difference of time,) 10 days, 1 hour, 1 min.; New York to Liverpool, (deducting difference of time,) 9 days, 5 hours, 46 min. !

Thus, in the present chapter, an attempt has been made to lay before the reader some of the minor, yet most characteristic details, not elsewhere to be met with, connected with the origin and progress of Steam Navigation in the cradle of WATT's own practical genius and invention,—than which details, nothing, surely, can be more significant of the value of that genius and that invention, to the capitalist, to the country, and to the World !

CHAPTER VII.

ON the 25th of August 1819, James Watt tranquilly expired, at his residence, Heathfield, in the county of Stafford, near Birmingham, in the eighty-fourth year of his age. To attempt here any new and laboured panegyric of the great Inventor, Philosopher, and Benefactor to his country, would be difficult as it would be superfluous. Much, however, as has been already written in such a strain, though graced with all the elegance which imagination and the most polished accuracy in taste and style could supply, we confess to a certain unsatisfied feeling still, in regard to the subject in some of its views. In the popular mind,—and even the man of letters has by no means been free from the influence,—the prevailing consciousness which hitherto has seemed naturally to associate itself with the name and personality,—for we will not speak here of the *idea* of Watt,—is that either of the great Mechanist, or, more usually still, that of his WORK and its WONDERS, the changes it has wrought, and the facilities it affords. As if the thunder of the steam-engine in its ponderous march, the din and endless rattle of its million spindles, or its shriek in the ever advancing and disappearing monster of the rail, uncon-

31

sciously arrested attention, and, by the very clamour and uproar made, absorbed and engrossed it all,—the thought of the Man has been lost, or at least obscured, in the marvel of his Machines. This, on the one hand, may be attributable, in some degree, to the great deficiency of information which has hitherto existed in regard to many of the events of the Philosopher's life and personal history;—on the other, wholly to disengage and abstract the mind from those more present and material objects of reflection, in view of this great man, is neither perhaps altogether possible nor to be desired. Whatever the immediate cause, it is felt that they have rather too universally been made the subject of notice and of eloquent declamation, to the exclusion of any more sober and distinct consideration of the structure and powers of the massive and majestic MIND, of which those prodigies were but the emanations, and the prolific phenomena.

In the STATUES of Watt which our national, and many of our provincial public buildings enshrine, the chisel of Chantrey has no less happily displayed its own marvellous powers of personification, than immortalized the lineaments of a man whose appearance and advent was one of the most remarkable events of modern times, and whose invention has formed an era in the history of the world. Even without any further revelations touching the life and history of their subject, than we have long possessed, we have here something which hardly any effort of ancient sculpture that has descended to our day at all rivals, in the intellectual power of which it is suggestive. We place ourselves in view of the all but breathing representation of the now familiar features and form, and feel as if in the presence of the very embodiment of genius and of lofty abstract speculation :—the massive head, bowed by the study of years,—the brow, broad, full, elevated, throne of intellect, of imagination, of benevolence,—the temples, perceptibly depressed, as if from the tension of habitual thought,—the soft, over-shadowed eye, that seems to communicate and hold converse with the depth of soul within, rather than with the objects of sense and the external world,—the mouth, unopen, rather than compressed, the seat of moody meditation, rather than morose reserve, of self-reliance, rather than self-complacency, of gentle benignity, rather than distance from the commoner sympathies of men, —the whole countenance radiant of calm and majesty, to which the unimpassioned marble lends as much of the severity that engages and attracts, as of the severe grandeur of repose which impresses and overawes the mind.

We ask nothing more from the artist. The chisel has surpassed its usual power and skill. The pencil too has handed down to us, in warmer tints, though not more impressively, the same imposing resemblance. But

> " Outward forms, the loftiest, still receive
> Their finer influence from the life within."

What we desiderate is, some competent guide to those interior depths, whose existence is betrayed or revealed by the forms which meet the eye,—some key by which we may read the cypher of those grave but noble lineaments,—some analysis of the inner being,—some truthful portraiture of those strong mental and moral powers whose workings have left so deep an impress on the marble itself. We ask nothing more from rhetoric. Eloquence and imagination have spent themselves in celebrating the last great gift of science to humanity. Even vaticination has uttered its last prediction, and returned from wandering to the outermost limits of the habitable globe, having foretold all of wonder, of progress, of civilisation, that the inventions of Watt are destined to accomplish for the great family of man. From any further consideration of all these, therefore,—of the effluences which have so long attracted the popular gaze, in connexion with the Man,—we would have attention turned to the Man himself. We would claim regard to the MIND, from which all these wonders sprang ;—to the hidden workshop within, in which they were conceived ;—to the living laboratory, whence, after being held in solution while undergoing all the needful tests of the spiritual alchemy, issued, in new forms, thought after thought of tried and accredited value.   We would look now to the mental analyst rather than the academician,—not so much to the biographer as the psychologist,—less to the political economist than the mental historian.   In the exhibition, or rather betrayal of so many and such rare intellectual endowments,—for some of them we arrive at only by inference, in our present state of information,—we seem to have offered to us a subject worthy of minuter study than it has yet received, and that promises to reward a much more careful elaboration than has yet been bestowed on it.   Science, we conceive, as well as our popular arts, demand something of this kind.   Our age and country demand *another* " Eloge" of WATT, whose point of departure shall be the MAN, rather than his WORKS, the MIND and its intellectual manifestations, rather than, exclusively, its CREATIONS and their wonderful effects.

Watt's character thus contemplated,—that is, from an intellectual as well as scientific point of view,—presents a large group of remarkable and striking combinations of gifts and endowments.   We look in vain among the number of men who distinguished themselves either in mechanical invention or philosophical discovery during his time, to find any parallel.   A cursory glance over the crowd of busy speculative spirits who gave such astonishing animation to the arts and manufactures of their day, reveals the moodily meditative, intensely industrious, social, often lively and cheerful, always benevolent WATT, prominent amongst and above them all.   Each period of his life as it advances and develops itself, exhibits peculiar and interesting phases. To watch and examine these as they successively unfold themselves, offers a charm similar to that which is felt in observing a like process in nature,—arising, in the case of the great mechanician, from the entire absence of anything reflective on his part in regard to this happy development,—a certain modest unconsciousness of anything peculiar in his life,—traits which, negative though they are, exhibit the true greatness of his mind and genius, and shed an engaging and attractive grace over his whole character.

We could desire to see Watt, with this object kept in view, traced throughout his long busy life,—from suffering infancy to youth, from youth to manhood, from manhood to old age,—that manhood during which INVENTION, like a second nature, seemed to rule and sway his intellectual being,—that old age, when his faculties only slackened their pace because they were weary, without the painful exhibition of either intellectual decline or decay.

It is of this late period of Watt's life that we have hitherto possessed the most full and interesting details. From the noise of the hammer, the iron turning-lathe and the file, they enable us to follow the old man to his retirement, his study, his books, or the genial circle of his learned and admiring friends. Of this retired, yet far from unsocial life, what pleasing reminiscences have been recorded by some of the most distinguished and illustrious of his cotemporaries in our own and neighbouring countries, whose hospitality and friendship he deemed it a privilege to reciprocate. They represent to us one for whom what we call the Sciences,—marked off one from another, and bounded by defined limits as if to suit the capacity and grasp of more ordinary intelligences,—were only units in that great whole of human knowledge, in which he seemed to wander familiarly as in his proper domain, to comprehend by a kind of intuition, to expound and illustrate as their chosen and authorized interpreter. Nor need this seem extravagant, when it is considered how singularly Watt was gifted with the prerequisites for such varied and remarkable attainments ;—in how eminent a degree he possessed those two prime constituents of the scientific mind—Imagination and Memory,—imagination, so essential an instrument in all physical research,—memory, no less requisite to the successful prosecution and application of the pure and the mixed mathematics. In sciences of which such pursuits and studies formed the basis, his induction was necessarily rapid, as the processes and results were never forgotten. Add to such qualities a mental and physical industry which hardly knew repose,—despite a both physical and mental depression which clouded the greater portion of his years, —with a passion for literature in all its departments, speculative, philosophical, imaginative, classical, limited only by the leisure he could snatch from continuous and pressing avocations,—and it is not difficult to account for either the breadth and accuracy of his scientific knowledge, or the extent and almost universality of his ordinary information.

Multiplied and concurrent as the testimonies on these various points fortunately are, we could desire to know much more of the Philosopher as the Husband, the Father, the Master, and the Citizen,—in the gentle privacy of the domestic hearth, the kindly intercourse of his boys, the easy negligence of form among his workmen and subordinates. In our admiration too of a mind so exalted in its powers, of a spirit so gifted and amiable, of a nature endowed with such inbred benignity and candour and truthfulness, of a temperament so gentle, so morally serene,—we could desire to know more of the state of those affections which are more purely spiritual in their nature and origin,—his disposition towards those supreme truths of Revelation, which alone really elevate and purify the soul, and which, for ends inscrutable to us, often hid from the wisest, and revealed unto babes, are so far from being inconsistent with the highest " philosophy," that they alone confer upon it the character which makes it " divine."

Interested as one cannot fail to be in the WHOLE history of such a mind, even to its latest recorded intercourse with family and friends, it is impossible not to desire to follow it, with earnest regard, towards the outmost margin of life,—towards those moments when the reality of things unseen, dawning on the departing spirit, renders augustly solemn the last hour of existence, if not to the indurate and unreflecting, certainly to one to whom the unfathomable mysteries of the soul, its relation to its Maker, and its future destiny, have been subjects of earnest and sincere and familiar meditation. In the absence of much information of a very positive kind in regard to such points of character and life, we instinctively revert, in a case like this, to the principles and maxims of an infantine and early training. Remembering the piety portrayed in the ancestors of this great man, one cannot but cling to the hope that his many virtues reposed on a substratum of more than merely moral excellence. Misfortune, of whatever kind it be, it has with much truth been remarked, has a profound effect on the Scottish character. That of Watt, which had not been untried with even severe affliction, bore throughout his life many and deep traces of some hidden influence which might be referred to such a cause, and which gave to his character something more than the grave and earnest type of his nationality. That he distinctly and gratefully recognised an all-wise and overruling Providence, to whose Divine goodness he owed the many blessings and comforts which he and those most dear to him enjoyed, is abundantly evidenced by his familiar correspondence. Let us hope that in those subdued dispositions and tempers, those kindly and chastened feelings which so conspicuously marked far more than his later years, we are to trace, in a spiritual sense and degree, more than merely " the memory of suffering," which has been called " the root and support of benevolence," —something even of those salutary effects which flow from the " chastenings of love," administered by a Hand that is invisible and divine, and whose beneficial results are manifested by the fruits they bear. Let us cherish the hope that the calm which rested on the spirit of the pilgrim as he approached the confines of the dark valley, and which enabled him to be, himself, the gentle and affectionate supporter of his sorrowing family, and the friends who surrounded his couch, was one which caught its radiance from a far higher sphere than that of the purest human philosophy,—even from a simple and child-like reliance on the infinite merits of Him whose name is—The Wonderful.[1]

WATT lies buried in the parish church of Heathfield, at Handsworth, where a Gothic chapel, enshrining a marble statue by Chantrey, was shortly afterwards erected to his memory, by the then only surviving son, Mr. James Watt of Aston Hall. Over the remains of this last representative of the illustrious name, the grave has also since closed.[2]

Before his death, however, he had the satisfaction—besides witnessing the erection of the colossal statue in Carrara marble, by the hand of Chantrey, in Westminster Abbey, tribute of the nation's gratitude to the genius and worth of his distinguished father—of presenting to the University of Glasgow a similar, though not colossal statue, by the same great sculptor, gracefully commemorative of his father's early connexion with that learned body,—and of promoting the erection of the elegant and capacious edifice at Greenock, which now,

---

[1] Mr. Watt's academic titles were as follows:—

MEMBER OF THE ROYAL SOCIETY OF EDINBURGH, 1784.

MEMBER OF THE ROYAL SOCIETY OF LONDON, 1785.

MEMBER OF THE BATAVIAN SOCIETY, 1787.

DOCTOR OF LAWS, FROM UNIVERSITY OF GLASGOW, 1806.

CORRESPONDENT OF THE INSTITUTE OF FRANCE, 1808.

ASSOCIATE OF THE ACADEMY OF SCIENCES OF THE INSTITUTE OF FRANCE, 1814.

[2] The late Mr. James Watt was a son by his father's first marriage, with his cousin, Miss Miller, of Glasgow, whose unlooked-for death, in 1773, during Mr. Watt's absence in the North, was the occasion to him of the most poignant grief. He had a brother and two sisters. Only one of the latter, however, survived infancy. She married Mr. Miller of Glasgow. Mr. James Watt died, unmarried, in 1848.

The mother of Gregory Watt survived her husband upwards of thirteen years. She died at a very advanced age, in 1832, having had the misfortune to be preceded by her only two children.

in more ways than one, perpetuates the memory of Watt in his native town, his lively interest in its advancement, and desire for its prosperity and distinction.

The reproduction of a portion of the voluminous correspondence of the late Mr. James Watt, now before us, relative to this structure, and the promotion of objects connected with it, in furtherance of the intentions of his venerated father, would furnish evidence of a disinterested zeal for the benefit of the community, as eminently creditable to the generous feelings of the son, as to the noble character of his illustrious parent. From this correspondence it appears that, besides the Foundation for the Scientific Library, laid by Mr. Watt, in 1816, —the object of which was, " to render his townsmen as eminent for their knowledge as they were for their spirit of enterprise,"—it was his intention that his own private library, at Heathfield, should have been transferred, after his death, to the Public Library of his native town,—to the new and commodious edifice for the reception of which, the late Mr. James Watt so munificently contributed. Whether from any manifested or imagined apathy on the part of individuals, in regard to the former scientific bequest of Mr. Watt, having affected the mind of the generous and liberal promoter of his revered father's designs,—or from some other destiny for this, even in a national point of view, most valuable collection, having appeared desirable,—the town of Greenock, doubtless greatly to its loss, is not permitted to boast of the precious possession. Even were there no ground for fearing that the former alternative had some influence in the alienation of this inestimable boon, a sensitive apprehension as to so deplorable a possibility may well point the community to the attainment of such a state of things within the bosom of its population, as would render the recurrence of a similar public calamity, even though it might be of a character far less grave, simply impossible. Statistical tables, to assume no higher authority, may demonstrate to a com-

munity when it is too late, that, infinitely more than exclusive attention to its mere material interests, a liberal and fostering care bestowed
on its Public Institutions, educational, literary, and religious, would
have elevated it in wealth as well as in status. An inapt, neglected,
and, as a natural consequence, falling off population, may prove, when
too late for remedy, that the policy was a false and self-destruc-
tive one, which, even for a generation, sacrificed the training of its
youth, who were to be the future administrators of its municipal
affairs, to plans of mere economical and material extension ;—plans,
moreover, which the measures of men trained in more liberal views,
and pursuing a more enlarged and open-handed system of administration, that does not consider indifferent to it anything whatever of a
scientific, moral, or intellectual kind affecting the interests of its
immense population, might render, within less than a lifetime, worse
than nugatory and vain. Watt knew the natural capabilities of the
place of his birth. He did not seem to think it an impossibility vastly
to improve these to all the ends of successful manufacture and commerce,—so as to resist the absorbing influences of far less favoured
localities, which, in his day, were far from even foreshadowing the
rivalry, so formidable, that has since both asserted and maintained
itself. With the eye of a sagacious political economist he detected
the weak point, and sought to convert it into a point of strength.
The education and scientific culture of its youth, he knew, as every
wise administrator of national or of municipal interests now fully
recognises, to be the only real foundation and security for the internal
material prosperity of either a nation or a community ; and in the
measures which he originated, as illustrated in the preceding chapters,
and designed, there is every reason to believe, still more effectively to
supplement, no one can doubt that he contemplated for his native
town a marked advance in intelligence, in relative social position, in
population, and consequently in wealth.

Let it be admitted, that, in these patriotic designs, Mr. Watt was too far in advance of the views and economic, or, more properly speaking, economical, maxims of some of his townsmen in 1816, or rather, considerably later, to find, from them, any very hearty or very efficient co-operation. Such narrow-based maxims were then only too generally prevalent, perhaps, everywhere. In no community, however, it is believed, would the sordid and shortsighted policy meet with less sympathy, now, than in the birthplace of this great Man. To judge from the energetic steps which have more recently been taken to improve and extend not only the public literary and educational institutions of the town, but also to awaken and cultivate a spirit of taste and refinement in all classes of the community, the apathy of a former generation of rulers, in regard to such essential public interests, would seem to have given place to a more generous and more enlightened sense of patriotism. The new ACADEMY,—thanks to the indefatigable energy of the late Secretary and present Treasurer of the Watt Club, Arch. Denniston, Esquire,—promises to be a seminary of high class, adapted to most of the exigencies of modern education, and not inadequately comprehensive in its basis ; while the several libraries embraced within the building of " The Watt Monument" may be held to afford advantages for literary, but especially scientific study and reference, enjoyed to a similar extent by few, if any, provincial towns in the kingdom.

This elegant structure, in its now completed state, is appropriated to the reception of the books of the GREENOCK LIBRARY, British and Foreign ; those of the MATHEMATICAL LIBRARY, the bequest to his townsmen, of the Mathematician WILLIAM SPENCE ;[1] of the SCIENTIFIC

---

[1] Mr. Spence was born at Greenock 31st July 1777, and died at the early age of thirty-eight. He lived long enough, however, to win for himself a fair reputation in the scientific world as a mathematician ; and by the sterling worth of his character, and his varied acquirements, to secure the friendship and esteem of all who knew him. " In general knowledge," writes his biographer, Mr. Galt, " I do not scruple to say, that in the circle of an acquaintance that embraces many of

LIBRARY, founded by JAMES WATT ; and lastly, of the Marble Statue of the Great Mechanician, by Sir Francis Chantrey.[1] This arrangement was in conformity with the desire of the late Mr. Watt of Aston Hall, whose deed of gift contained a clause to the following effect :— That the building shall be " for the location and preservation of the Marble Statue proposed to be erected by the inhabitants of Greenock, in memory of my late father ; and likewise for the reception and preservation of the books purchased, and to be purchased, with the sum presented by my late father to the Magistrates and Town-Council of Greenock for the foundation of a Scientific Library ;—declaring always, that the building to be erected shall also be appropriated for the reception, preservation, and distribution of the books which now form, or may hereafter form, the general public or subscription library of Greenock ; which may either be united with the books purchased by my late father, or placed in a separate apartment of the building, as the committee of management of the said public library may judge advisable."

The Watt Scientific Library now contains a most valuable collection

the most accomplished characters of the age, I have met with no one who, with so much information, united the same colloquial powers of unfolding what he knew. . . . . There was no subject of which he did not possess a liberal portion of information ; in several he was profoundly versed ; and with an aptitude that often surprised by its alacrity, he could show himself acquainted with the outlines of all." Mr. Spence published during his life his " Essay on the Theory of the various Orders of Logarithmic Transcendents." Its preface is dated at Greenock in December 1808. This work, together with his other Mathematical Essays, were some years afterwards edited by Sir John Herschel, with a preface by the learned Editor, under the title : " Mathematical Essays, by the late William Spence, Esq., edited by John F. W. Herschel, Esq., with a Biographical Sketch of the author. London, 1819." A Marble Tablet, bearing an Inscription from the pen of his schoolfellow, Mr. Galt, was some years after his death erected to his memory by several of his friends, in the Middle Parish Church of Greenock.

[1] Since the completion of this beautiful edifice according to the original plan of the architect, Mr. Blore, by the addition of the wings, it now affords dwelling accommodation for the librarian ; also committee, and reference or consulting rooms, a parlour appropriated to the Members of the Watt Club, and a spacious hall, adapted for public lectures, or exhibitions of works of art. The building contains, besides the Statue, a Portrait of Watt, after that by Sir W. Beechy ; a small likeness of the philosopher after the Sketch by Henning, an original of the " Map of the Clyde," by John Watt, together with holograph letters and other documents of interest connected with the philosopher and his immediate progenitors.

of the best and most recent works in modern science, embracing mathematics, mechanics, optics, astronomy, chemistry, agriculture, architecture, &c.[1] It is a subject of just felicitation to the Watt Club, that its efforts for the completion and perfection of this building, with its several adjuncts, have been so far attended with success, that little now remains to render it, both externally and internally, worthy of the distinguished name it represents.

The notice of one other Testimonial connected with the memory of Watt will conclude these local memorials. In the laying out of the grounds of the new Cemetery occupying the heights to the west of the town, in compliance with a memorial addressed to the Corporation by the Watt Club, a plateau of considerable dimensions, and forming the highest portion of the rock, was voted by the Town-Council as a site for a great national, or rather cosmopolitan testimonial to the genius of Watt. The proposal, which originated in the Club, was, at first, to erect on this spot a vast structure of a lofty and imposing appearance, to be seen from every part of the surrounding neighbourhood, and that all the nations of the world should be invited to contribute the materials; that those materials should be simply blocks of stone more or less unchiselled, of every shape and colour and size, granite or marble, freestone or whinstone, piled aloft and fastened with cement; each block to be inscribed with the name of the donor, and the place or country whence it came. Different plans and forms of erection more or less in conformity with this view have been pro-

[1] Thanks are due in connexion with this important section of the Library, to Mr. John Gray, late chairman of the committee, at whose suggestion those books, which in a long course of years had gone astray, were replaced, and steps taken to add largely to the collection out of the remaining funds of the Watt Donation;—to Professor R. D. Thomson of London also, who kindly furnished lists of the most approved works in chemistry, &c.;—and to Mr. James Broun, of the Middle Temple, barrister-at-law, who cordially undertook the labour of selecting and purchasing the best editions of standard works in the various departments of physics,—a task for which his extended acquaintance with the literature of science, added to his characteristic zeal for the interests of his townsmen, eminently qualified him.

posed by the various architectural and scientific institutes which have interested themselves in the object. A drawing of one of these is subjoined, the only one which has been prepared for this volume, a Campanile, designed by the eminent architect, Mr. Mackintosh of Exeter. Some progress has already been made in the accumulation for the edifice of stones of enormous dimensions;—the only drawback to the liberality of some of the contributors being, in fact, the physical impossibility of transporting such masses to so great a height. But it is perhaps unwise to use the word impossibility in reference to the accomplishment of any work within the range of mechanics in the present day; and the most characteristic thing connected with the erection of *such* a testimonial might, in the event, not inappropriately be made to consist in the very gigantic nature of the work, and the immensely superhuman power of the machinery employed in its elevation.

Thus draw to a close these imperfect Memorials of the lineage and life of this great man. Brief as is the period occupied by their records, it embraces the Appearance, the Glory, and the Extinction of a Name which rendered illustrious the Eighteenth century beyond any which preceded it in the world's history. The name of WATT has already passed away from any living connexion with the generations of men;—yet no name can be more imperishable, associated as it is, not in his own country alone, but throughout the habitable globe, with everything that now affects the physical, the intellectual, and—in view of the great spread of Christianity, may it surely with the fullest truth be added—the spiritual wellbeing of man.

PROPOSED ELEVATION FOR THE CEMETERY HILL TESTIMONIAL.

By David Mackintosh Esqre, Architect.

ELEVATION OF THE PROPOSED
NATIONAL TESTIMONIAL TO JAMES WATT,
TO BE ERECTED ON THE CEMETERY-HILL AT GREENOCK.

THE TYPE OF THE DESIGN OF THIS MONUMENTAL TOWER IS DERIVED FROM SOME OF THE MOST ESTEEMED ITALIAN CAMPANILI, AND THE ELEVATION EMBODIES MANY OF THE BEST AND MOST STRIKING FEATURES TO BE FOUND IN THE TOWERS OF SANTA FRANCESCA ROMANA AND SANTA MARIA IN COSMEDIA AT ROME.— S. GIOVANNI EVANGELISTA AT RAVENNA, AND SANTA MARIA DEL FIORE AT FLORENCE, IN COMBINATION WITH OTHER FINE EXAMPLES.— THE TOWER IS UPWARDS OF 40 FEET SQUARE AT THE BASE, RISES AT THE LEVEL OF THE MAIN CORNICE TO A HEIGHT OF 163 FEET, AND IS SURMOUNTED BY A TURRET OR OBSERVATORY OF THE FURTHER HEIGHT OF 62 FEET, MAKING THE TOTAL ELEVATION 225 FEET ABOVE THE BASE LINE.— THE NOBLE EMINENCE ON WHICH THE TESTIMONIAL IS TO BE PLACED IS LIKEWISE AT AN ELEVATION OF 289 FEET ABOVE HIGH WATER-MARK, MAKING THE HEIGHT OF THE TOWER ALTOGETHER 514 FEET ABOVE THE LEVEL OF THE SEA, SO THAT IT WILL BE SEEN FOR MILES AROUND IN EVERY DIRECTION.— THE UPPER TURRET IS ADAPTED FOR THE RECEPTION OF AN ELECTRIC TIME BALL AND FOR NAUTICAL AND ASTRONOMICAL OBSERVATIONS. THUS THE STRUCTURE WILL PROVE EMINENTLY USEFUL TO ALL ENGAGED IN THE NAVIGATION OF THE NOBLE ESTUARY OF CLYDE.— THE VIEWS FROM THE BALCONIES AND SEVERAL FLOOR LEVELS WILL BE OF TRANSCENDANT BEAUTY AND VARIED INTEREST, AND INTERNALLY THE STRUCTURE WILL COMPRISE ROOMS ABOUT 30 FEET SQUARE, CONNECTED BY MEANS OF A CIRCULAR STAIRCASE AND OPEN GALLERY, AND HAVING ON THEIR SIDES A SERIES OF NICHES AND RECESSES SUITABLE FOR THE RECEPTION OF STATUES, BUSTS, OR OTHER MEMORIALS COMMEMORATIVE OF MEN EMINENT IN SCIENCE OR PHILOSOPHY.— IN THE ERECTION OF THIS GREAT NATIONAL TESTIMONIAL IT IS INTENDED TO INCORPORATE GIFTS OF MATERIALS FROM EVERY PART OF THE GLOBE, INASMUCH AS THERE IS NO PORTION OF THE CIVILIZED WORLD WHICH IS NOT INDEBTED TO THE GENIUS OF WATT FOR THE ENJOYMENT OF TRANSCENDANT PRIVILEGES.— THIS IDEA HAS BEEN CORDIALLY ENTERTAINED IN INFLUENTIAL QUARTERS, AND GIFTS OF STONES HAVE ALREADY ARRIVED FROM MONTREAL, THE ISLE OF MAN, GOUROCK, AND THE SENECA QUARRY IN THE STATE OF MARYLAND. MORE ARE PROMISED FROM ITALY, FRANCE, MALTA, CORNWALL, TIPPERARY, SINGAPORE, AND THE SHORES OF THE MEDITERR- -ANEAN.— A LIBERAL DONATION OF BLUE LIAS LIME HAS BEEN MADE, AND A HIGHLY VALUABLE CONTRIBUTION HAS BEEN TENDERED OF TWO THOUSAND TONS OF STONES OF LARGE SIZE AND SUPERIOR QUALITY FROM THE QUARRIES OF GIFFNOCK, WARD HILL, NITSHILL AND ARDEN.— THE GROUND IS BEING CLEARED, AND THE SITE ON THE CEMETERY-HILL PREPARED FOR THE RECEPTION OF THE FOUNDATIONS, UNDER THE DIRECTION OF MR DAVID M^CINTOSH, ARCHITECT, OF LONDON AND EXETER, WHO ERECTED THE EXTENSIVE AND BEAUTIFUL HOSPITAL FOUNDED IN THE IMMEDIATE NEIGHBOURHOOD BY SIR GABRIEL WOOD.

SEPTEMBER, 1856.

APPENDIX.

APPENDIX.

APPENDIX A.

THE LATE JAMES WATT, Esq.

THE following Gentlemen propose commemorating, by a Public Dinner in the Tontine, on Friday the 19th inst., the Anniversary of the Birth of their highly distinguished Townsman.   Dinner, 5/ each.

GREENOCK, *January* 3, 1821.

ALEX. DUNLOP.
JAMES WATT.
HUGH CRAWFORD.
CLAUD MARSHALL.
JOHN DENNISTON.
ALAN KER.
ROBERT D. KER.
QUINTIN LEITCH.
ARCH. BAINE.
JOHN SCOTT.
JAMES HUNTER.
ROBT. EWING.
GEO. ROBERTSON.
GEO. DEMPSTER.
JAMES OUGHTERSON.

JOHN ROBERTSON.
WILLIAM M‘DOWALL.
JAMES TASKER.
JOHN DAVIDSON.
T. LANG.
J. MACNAUGHT, PR. T.L.
G. J. WEIR.
JAMES KIPPEN.
A. CRAWFORD.
H. CAMERON.
DUN. FERGUSON.
WM. MACFIE.
JOHN SPEIRS, M.D.
JAS. RAMSAY, JUN.
JOHN RANKEN.

33

JOHN HUNTER.
JAMES STUART.
GEO. BLAIR.
DAVID CRAWFORD.
W. DUNLOP.
DUN. SMITH.
JOHN FAIRRIE.
NINIAN HILL.
ROGER AYTON.
ARTHUR OUGHTERSON.
A. LANG, ADVOCATE.
JAMES ROBERTSON.
GEO. MACKAY.
WALTER RITCHIE.
GEO. JOHNSTON.
JAMES REID.
WM. M'AULAY.
G. STEWART.
ALEX. THOMSON.
J. B. KIRK, M.D.
JOHN DAVIDSON.
JOHN MENNONS.
JAMES ANDERSON.
GEORGE ROBERTSON, JUN.
JOHN SCOTT, JUN.
ARCHD. WILSON.
J. PATON.
ANDW. MUIR.
JAMES MUIR.
WILLM. STEWART.
WILLM. TURNER.
JOHN HERON.
COLIN BUCHANAN.

JNO. M'GOUN.
SAMUEL GEMMILL.
WILLIAM HERON, M.D.
JAMES WALKINSHAW.
A. ANDERSON.
LT. GREIG.
WM. PARK.
ANDW. RAMSAY.
ALEX. M'LAREN.
ROBERT CARSWELL.
WM. SIMONS.
JO. DEMPSTER.
THOMAS FAIRRIE.
ROBERT LANG.
DAVID GREIG.
COLIN LAMONT.
JOHN FRASER.
GEO. WILLIAMSON.

CHAIRMAN.

JOHN DENNISTON, ESQ.

CROUPIERS.

MESSRS. BAINE AND STEWART.

STEWARDS.

MESSRS. WALKINSHAW.
　　,,　　CRAWFORD.
　　,,　　QUINTIN LEITCH.
　　,,　　ALEX. LANG.
　　,,　　JAMES WATT.
DR. SPEIRS.

APPENDIX B.

The house formerly called the *Greenock*, and now known as the *Watt Tavern*, occupies the site of an older house, which was built upon a piece of ground acquired in feu in 1699, from Sir John Schaw, by Alexander Scott, sometime mariner, afterwards merchant in Greenock. The old or original house fronted the sea, from which it was removed only by the breadth of an ordinary road, in process of time called the High Street, and afterwards, as it is at present, Dalrymple Street. The tenement in question is the last but one at the eastern termination of the south side of Dalrymple Street. William Street, from which entrance is obtained to the upper portion of the building occupied as the tavern, intersects Dalrymple Street at the last tenement of the latter street. It had a garden of some extent behind, which is now occupied entirely by buildings, on the west side of William Street, some of which still belong to the heir of the original feuar.

In 1727, Alexander Scott borrowed a sum of money from a Mrs. Helen Taylor, and granted her a bond over the property, then consisting of a tenement adapted for the accommodation of several families. Scott having found it inconvenient to repay Mrs. Taylor the sum borrowed, that lady, under the authority of a legal adjudication, took upon herself the charge of collecting the rents payable by the tenants, in liquidation of her bond. Mr. Watt's father was one of the tenants, and here had his dwelling-house. I am in possession of an account-current, dated 20th May 1734, between Mrs. Taylor and Mr. Scott, the debit side of which contains the interest due upon the bond, and the credit side the rents received by her. In this account Mr. Watt's name appears as tenant as far back as 1731.

Mr. Watt's name appears as a tenant in another account in my possession,

—made up in reference to the said debt between a Mrs. Hill, the heir of Mrs. Taylor, who died 12th May 1736,—the debit side of which contains the interest due on the bond for two years and a half, calculated up to the above date ; and the credit side is made up of the rents received in payment of the interest.   The following is an exact copy of the credit side of the account, so far as relates to the rents :—

By sundry rents received by Mrs. Hill—

James Watt, ...	£5 0 0
James Williamson, . . .	2 5 0
William Simpson, . . .	9 0 0
William Caldwell, . . .	6 0 0
Archibald M'Aulay, . .	1 15 0
Robert Crichton, ...	2 12 6

Now from these documents it clearly appears that James Watt, senior, occupied a dwelling-house in Scott's tenement, at an annual rent of £10 ; but as the account does not specify the term's possession,—whether for the term of Whitsunday, or for that of Martinmas, for which the above rents were received,—I am left to infer that they were received for the term of Martinmas, (11th November 1735,) and, if so, then it follows that this was the first term's rent of the year in which Mr. Watt's son, James, was born ; as, according to the uniform practice of occupying dwelling-houses in Scotland, the tenant in possession in November would occupy the house from 26th May 1735 to 26th May 1736, and the intervening period would thus embrace the birthday of JAMES WATT, namely 19th January 1736.   In these accounts there is original documentary evidence bearing on the interesting fact which I wish to establish.   But the proof does not rest on these alone.

As it was conjectured that a fact so nearly connected with the memory of Mr. Watt as the place of his birth, would in all probability be communicated or otherwise known to Mr. James Walkinshaw, Mr. Watt's friend and correspondent, he was applied to on the subject.   Mr. Walkinshaw at once pointed out the house partly occupied as the *Greenock Tavern*, as occupying the site of an older tenement in which Mr. Watt was born.   No attempt was made to overcome Mr. Walkinshaw's well-known disinclination to commit himself to writing on any occasion, and no written document from him was obtained to record his testimony ; but a gentlemen who took an interest in the investigation wrote me the letter which I now take leave to transcribe.

" Greenock, *February* 21, 1827.

" My dear Sir,—I distinctly remember calling upon the late Mr. James Walkinshaw, along with you—I think in the summer of 1822—when the old gentleman pointed out, in the most precise and conclusive terms, the house at present partly occupied as the *James Watt Tavern*, in William Street, as standing upon the site of that in which Mr. Watt of Soho was born. The circumstances stated by Mr. Walkinshaw in corroboration, were, in my mind, at the time, completely demonstrative of the correctness of the fact.—I am, my dear Sir, yours faithfully, John Mennons."

Being anxious to obtain as much collateral evidence as possible, on a subject interesting as well to the people of Scotland as to the inhabitants of Greenock, and particularly interesting to the members of the Watt Club, the late Mr. Walter Ritchie, who had been a magistrate of the town of Greenock, was next applied to. He likewise distinctly corroborated the information which had been previously obtained from Mr. Walkinshaw, and very readily addressed to me the following letter :—

" Greenock, *7th August* 1824.

" Dear Sir,—When I was connected with the magistracy of Greenock, the late Mr. James Watt of Birmingham, the improver of the Steam-Engine, with whom I was acquainted, came to this town. As we were walking together, when at, or nearly opposite, the shop lately possessed by Mr. Campbell, in Wilson's Land, he pointed out to me the house in which he was born. It was an old tenement, nearly opposite the said shop, having one of its gables to Dalrymple Street, and a small window in that gable. It was then an old tenement, has been rebuilt, and, I understand, is now the property of Mrs. Cambridge.—I am, dear Sir, your most obedient servant,

" Walter Ritchie."

In addition to these, a letter which I have seen, written by the late Mr. Hugh Crawford, factor for Mr. Crawford of Cartsburn, dated 19th August 1824, and addressed to William Crawford of Cartsburn, Esq., No. 5, Bellevue

Crescent, Edinburgh, contains a paragraph in the following words:—" Mr. Watt was born at the Mid-Quay-head of Greenock. He and my father were schoolfellows. His father and grandfather were born in Cartsdyke. The latter's tombstone in our churchyard, bears 'Thomas Watt, Professor of the Mathematicks in Crawfordsdyke.' The property No. 21, was their natal spot." I may here remark that the Mid-Quay-head forms the lower portion of William Street, already mentioned as intersecting Dalrymple Street, at the east end of the latter street. Mr. Crawford's letter is quite right with regard to the birthplace of James Watt, but incorrect as to the birthplace of the old mathematician;—the grandfather was born in Aberdeenshire, although he was an inhabitant of the burgh of barony, within the bounds of the parish of Greenock.

Such are the proofs, as now collected, in regard to the birthplace of James Watt.

EDINBURGH : T. CONSTABLE, PRINTER TO HER MAJESTY.

D 18
/9